THE THINKING MACHINE

ALSO BY STEPHEN WITT

How Music Got Free: A Story of
Obsession and Invention

THE
THINKING
MACHINE

Jensen Huang, Nvidia,
and the World's Most
Coveted Microchip

Stephen Witt

BH

THE BODLEY HEAD
LONDON

1 3 5 7 9 10 8 6 4 2

The Bodley Head, an imprint of Vintage,
is part of the Penguin Random House group of companies

Vintage, Penguin Random House UK, One Embassy Gardens,
8 Viaduct Gardens, London SW11 7BW

penguin.co.uk/vintage
global.penguinrandomhouse.com

First published in Great Britain by The Bodley Head in 2025
First published in the United States of America by Viking in 2025

Copyright © Stephen Richard Witt 2025

The moral right of the author has been asserted

Brief portions of this work originally appeared,
in different form, in the *New Yorker* in 2023

Designed by Meighan Cavanaugh

Printed and bound in Great Britain by Clays Ltd, Elcograf S.p.A.

The authorised representative in the EEA is Penguin Random House Ireland,
Morrison Chambers, 32 Nassau Street, Dublin D02 YH68

A CIP catalogue record for this book is available from the British Library

HB ISBN 9781847928276
TPB ISBN 9781847928283

Penguin Random House is committed to a sustainable future
for our business, our readers and our planet. This book is made
from Forest Stewardship Council® certified paper.

For Jane

Practice even what seems impossible.

—Marcus Aurelius

CONTENTS

Introduction   *xv*

PART I

1. The Bridge   3

2. Large-Scale Integration   13

3. New Venture   26

4. Thirty Days   37

5. Going Parallel   45

6. Jellyfish   58

7. Deathmatch   67

8. The Compulsion Loop   81

9. CUDA   90

10. Resonance   106

11. AlexNet   118

PART II

12. O.I.A.L.O.   133

13. Superintelligence   144

14. The Good Year   156

15. The Transformer   170

16. Hyperscale   181

17. Money   189

18. Spaceships   197

19. Power   204

20. The Most Important Stock on Earth   210

21. Jensen   222

22. The Fear   230

23. The Thinking Machine   241

    Acknowledgments   247
    About the Author   249

INTRODUCTION

This is the story of how a niche vendor of video game hardware became the most valuable company in the world. It is the story of a stubborn entrepreneur who pushed his radical vision for computing for thirty years, in the process becoming one of the wealthiest men alive. It is the story of a revolution in silicon and the small group of renegade engineers who defied Wall Street to make it happen. And it is the story of the birth of an awesome and terrifying new category of artificial intelligence, whose long-term implications for the human species cannot be known.

At the center of this story is a propulsive, mercurial, brilliant, and extraordinarily dedicated man. His name is Jensen Huang, and his thirty-two-year tenure is the longest of any technology CEO in the S&P 500. Huang is a visionary inventor whose familiarity with the inner workings of electronic circuitry approaches a kind of intimacy. He reasons from first principles about what microchips can do today, then gambles with great conviction on what they will do tomorrow. He does not always win, but when he does, he wins big: his early, all-in bet on AI was one of the best investments in Silicon Valley history. Huang's company, Nvidia, is today worth more than $3 trillion, rivaling both Apple and Microsoft in value.

In person, Huang is charming, funny, self-deprecating, and frequently self-contradictory. He keeps up a semicomic deadpan patter at all times. We met in 2023 for breakfast at a Denny's diner, his favorite restaurant chain. Huang had developed the business plan for Nvidia at this same restaurant thirty years earlier; chatting with our waitress, he ordered seven items, including a Super Bird sandwich and a chicken-fried steak. "You know, I used to be a dishwasher here," he told her. "But I worked hard! Like, really hard. So I got to be a busboy."

Huang, born in Taiwan, immigrated to the United States when he was ten. Denny's was the crucible of his assimilation—working there as a teenager, he ate through the entire menu. Still, he told me, he maintains an outsider's perspective. "You're always an immigrant," he said. "I'm always Chinese." He cofounded Nvidia (pronounced IN-vidia, not NUH-vidia) in 1993 when he was thirty, first targeting the nascent market for high-end video game graphics. His products were popular; his customers liked to build their own PCs, sometimes buying transparent housing to showcase their Nvidia hardware.

In the late 1990s, seeking to better render the *Quake* series of games, Nvidia made a subtle change to the circuit architecture of its processors, allowing them to solve more than one problem at a time. This approach, known as "parallel computing," was a radical gamble. "The success rate of parallel computing was zero percent before we came along," Huang said, rattling off a list of forgotten start-ups. "Literally zero. Everyone who tried to make it into a business had failed." Huang ignored this dismal record, pursuing his unconventional vision in open defiance of Wall Street for more than a decade. He looked for customers besides gamers, ones who needed a lot of computing power—weather forecasters, radiologists, deep-water oil prospectors, that sort of thing. During this time, Nvidia's stock price floundered, and he had to fend off corporate raiders to retain his job.

Huang stuck with this bet, losing money on it for years, until in 2012 a group of dissident academics in Toronto purchased two consumer video game cards to train an exotic kind of artificial intelligence called a neural network. At the time, neural networks, which mimic the structure of biological brains, were deeply out of favor, and most researchers considered them obsolete toys. But when Huang saw how fast neural networks trained on his parallel-computing platform, he staked his entire company on the unexpected symbiosis. Huang now needed two underdog technologies to work—two technologies that had always failed the test of the marketplace in the past.

When this audacious corporate parlay hit, Nvidia increased in value several hundred times. In the past decade, the company has evolved from selling $200 gaming accessories to shipping multimillion-dollar supercomputing equipment that can fill the floor of a building. Working with pioneers like OpenAI, Nvidia has sped up deep-learning applications more than a thousand times in the last ten years. All major artificial-intelligence applications—Midjourney, ChatGPT, Copilot, all of it—were developed on Nvidia machines. It is this unprecedented increase in computing power that has made the modern AI boom possible.

With a near-monopoly on the hardware, Huang is arguably the most powerful person in AI. Certainly, he's made more money from it than anyone else. In the strike-it-rich tradition, he most closely resembles California's first millionaire, Samuel Brannan, the celebrated vendor of prospecting supplies who lived in San Francisco in 1849. Except rather than shovels, Huang sells $30,000 AI-training chips that contain one hundred billion transistors. The wait time to purchase his latest hardware is currently more than a year, and on the Chinese black market, his chips sell for double the price.

Huang doesn't think like a businessman. He thinks like an engineer, breaking down difficult concepts into simple principles, then leveraging those principles to great effect. "I do everything I can not to go out of business," he said at breakfast. "I do everything I can not to fail." Huang believes that with AI, the basic architecture of digital computing, little changed since it was introduced by IBM in the early 1960s, is being reconceptualized. "Deep learning is not an algorithm," he said. "Deep learning is a method. It's a new way of developing software."

This new software has incredible powers. It can speak like a human, write a college essay, solve a tricky math problem, provide an expert medical diagnosis, and cohost a podcast. It scales with the amount of computing power available to it and never seems to plateau. The evening before our breakfast, I'd watched a video in which a robot, running this new kind of software, stared at its hands in seeming recognition, then sorted a collection of colored blocks. The video had given me chills; the obsolescence of my species seemed near. Huang, rolling a pancake around a sausage with his fingers, dismissed my concerns. "I know how it works, so there's nothing there," he said. "It's no different than how microwaves work." I pressed Huang—an autonomous robot surely presents risks that a microwave oven does not. He responded that he has never worried about the technology, not once. "All it's doing is processing data," he said. "There are so many other things to worry about."

Where this will lead is anyone's guess; many technologists now worry that AI's capabilities pose a direct threat to the survival of the human species. (Among these "doomers" are the Toronto scientists who first implemented AI on Huang's platform.) Huang dismisses such pessimism. For him, AI is a pure force for progress, and he has declared that it is spurring a new industrial revolution. He doesn't permit much disagreement on this topic, and his force of personality can be intimidating. ("Interacting with Jensen is like sticking your finger in the electrical socket," one of his executives said.) Huang's employees worship him—I believe they would follow him out of the window of a skyscraper if he saw a market opportunity there.

In May 2023, hundreds of industry leaders endorsed a statement that equated the risk of runaway AI with that of nuclear war. Huang didn't sign it. Some economists have observed that the Industrial Revolution led to a relative decline in the global population of horses and have wondered if AI might do the same to humans. "Horses have limited career options," Huang said. "For example, horses can't type." As he finished eating, I expressed my concerns that, someday soon, I would feed my notes from our conversation into an intelligence engine, then watch as it produced structured, superior prose. Huang didn't dismiss this possibility, but he assured me that I had a few years before my John Henry moment. "It will come for the fiction writers first," he said. Then he tipped the waitress a thousand dollars and stood up from his many plates of half-eaten food.

I found Huang to be an elusive subject, in some ways the most difficult I've ever reported on. He hates talking about himself and once responded to one of my questions by physically running away. Before this book was commissioned, I had written a magazine profile of Huang for *The New Yorker*. Huang told me he hadn't read it, and had no intention of ever doing so. Informed that I was writing a biography of him, he responded, "I hope I die before it comes out."

Still, Huang offered me access to a great number of people to report this book. I spoke with almost two hundred people, including his employees, his cofounders, his rivals, and several of his oldest friends. The beloved and even somewhat goofy family man who emerged from these interviews bore little resemblance to the unapologetically carnivorous executive who made Nvidia succeed, but it is these same attachments that spur Huang's ambition: he spoke frankly with me of his insecurities, his fear of letting his employees down, his fear of bringing shame to the family name. Some executives speak of profit as "keeping score," but not Huang; for him, the money is only temporary insurance against some future calamity. There was something a little touching about hearing a man worth a hundred billion dollars talk in this way.

But if Huang is motivated by anxiety, he is also motivated by fascination with the seductive power his technology has unlocked. He had not set out to be an AI pioneer, not even when he'd turned his attention to parallel computing, but once it arrived, Huang became determined to push his maximalist agenda for machine intelligence as far and as fast as it could possibly go. Even the most optimistic visionaries in the field urge *some* degree of caution; the supposed mission of OpenAI, for example, is to ward off catastrophe. Huang, almost alone, believes that AI can lead only to good, and it is this belief that motivates him to work twelve to fourteen hours a day, seven days a week, even after three decades as CEO.

Of course, Huang would work hard anyway. It is in his nature. If there is a theme to his life, it is amplification; he has executed on the same simple precepts of diligence, courage, and mastery of fundamentals again and again and again, to greater and greater effect. I was surprised to learn how much of the man he later became was present in the immigrant child arriving unaccompanied by his parents in the United States in 1973 to an environment so unconducive to flourishing that it seems a miracle he survived it. To understand Huang fully, we begin not at Denny's restaurant, nor in the giant cathedrals of technology he later commissioned, but at this tiny rural school.

PART I

ONE

The Bridge

Sometime toward the end of 1973, ten-year-old Jensen Huang rose from bed in his dormitory and set off on the perilous journey to school. Huang, born in Taiwan and raised in Thailand, had recently arrived in rural Kentucky. His path led down a sloping hillside to a floodplain situated among forested hills, and across a rickety pedestrian footbridge, which was suspended by ropes and missing many planks, through which could be seen the frigid and rushing waters of the river below.

Huang, a bright and conscientious child, had skipped a year and was in the sixth grade. He was undersized even for his age and was often the smallest boy in class. He spoke imperfect English and was the only Asian student. His classmates at Oneida Elementary were the children of tobacco farmers and coal miners. Almost all of them were white, and many were impoverished. Some had no running water in their homes.

Huang had arrived with his older brother, Jeff, in the middle of the academic year, while their parents remained in Thailand. The two lived at the Oneida Baptist Institute, a nearby boarding school, but Jensen was too young to attend OBI and was sent to Oneida Elementary instead. On his first day, the principal had put his arm around the boy and told the class to welcome the new student, who was from a different part of the world but was also extremely intelligent. The bullying started at once. "He was a perfect target," said Ben Bays, Huang's classmate.

Before Huang's arrival, Bays had been the designated victim. Like Huang, Bays was small, and also like Huang, he was a good student. The bullies honored these qualities by sealing him inside the school's lockers, sometimes for hours. Following Huang's arrival, their focus shifted and acquired a racial element—many of Huang's Kentucky classmates had family members who had fought in Vietnam. "The way you described Chinese people back then was 'Chinks,'" Huang told me, fifty years later in a sterile conference room during our first conversation. His face showed no emotion. "We were called that every day."

The bullies targeted Huang in and out of class, at every opportunity. They shoved him in the hallways and chased him on the playground. The bridge was their favorite location. Huang had to cross it alone, a hazardous proposition in the best of conditions. Sometimes, when Huang was in the middle, the bullies would emerge from hiding on either side of the river, then grab the ropes and begin to swing, attempting to dislodge him into the river below. "Somehow it never seemed to affect him," Bays said. "Actually, it looked like he was having fun."

Bays and Huang were fast friends. Despite the language barrier, Huang excelled academically, supplanting Bays as the best student. He was a talented artist and had perfect penmanship, although he only wrote in capital letters. He also taught Bays how to fight. Whatever the local boys knew about Chinese culture came from the films of Bruce Lee. Huang initially ran a bluff, telling his classmates that he was a martial-arts expert. This was quickly disproven in the schoolyard, but what Huang lacked in technique, he made up for in determination. When challenged, he would always fight back, sometimes wrestling even larger boys to the ground. In Bays's recollection, at least, Huang was never pinned. ("That's not how I remember it," Huang said, laughing.) Nevertheless, Huang inspired Bays to fight back as well, and after a time the bullying subsided.

Bays's own family was desperately poor. He had five siblings, and his father, a preacher, was itinerantly employed. He lived at the mouth of a small, sheltered valley known as a "holler" in a dilapidated house with pit toilets in the back. Nothing in his experience had prepared him to meet anyone like Huang, and he could only wonder about the circumstances that had delivered this precocious, unsupervised child to the Appalachian backwoods of Clay County, Kentucky, one of the poorest counties in the nation.

HUANG, THE MIDDLE OF THREE BROTHERS, had been born in Taipei, Taiwan, in February 1963. His father was a chemical engineer, and his mother had taught primary school. Huang's parents were from the city of Tainan, on the southwestern coast. They spoke the Taiwanese dialect of Hokkien natively but had lived most of their lives under foreign rule. Taiwan had been a Japanese colony until 1945; in 1949 the Chinese general Chiang Kai-shek, having lost the mainland to Mao, fled to Taiwan with his army, and soon the island was placed under martial law.

When Huang was five, his father, Shing Tai, found work at a petroleum refinery in Thailand and relocated the family to Bangkok. Huang's memories of Southeast Asia are hazy. He recalled pouring lighter fluid on top of the pool at the family home and setting it ablaze. He recalled a pet monkey that belonged to a friend. In the late 1960s, Huang's father visited Manhattan on his way to train with the air-conditioning giant Carrier, which was transforming office life with precise climate control. He was astounded by New York City and returned determined to relocate his family to the United States.

In preparation for the move, Huang's mother, Chai Shiu, began to teach the boys English. She spoke no English herself, but this was only a minor hindrance. Drawing on her experiences as a schoolteacher, each night she had her sons memorize ten new words randomly selected from the dictionary, then drilled them on the words the following day. After a year or so of this, she enrolled the three boys in an international academy, and Huang began formal schooling in English, while continuing to speak Taiwanese with his parents.

The family's plans to relocate accelerated in 1973, when Thailand was beset by political unrest. In October of that year, half a million protestors took to the streets of Bangkok, demanding the dissolution of the country's military dictatorship. The government responded with force, and Huang recalled seeing tanks rolling through the streets. Fearing further unrest, Jensen's father sent him and Jeff to Tacoma, Washington, to live with an uncle. Jensen's parents and his younger brother stayed behind. The uncle decided the boys belonged at a boarding school and searched for an institution willing to house two unsupervised Taiwanese children, ten and twelve years old, living thousands of miles from their parents. He selected the Oneida Baptist Institute in Kentucky, perhaps mistaking it for a prestigious college-preparatory school.

In fact, OBI was a juvenile-reform academy located in a town of three hundred people. The institute had been founded in 1899 by James Anderson Burns, a Baptist preacher looking to put an end to a lethal and long-running family feud. (Burns came up with the idea for the school after he was clubbed in the head with a rifle and left in a ditch to die.) By the 1970s, despite hosting a few international students, OBI was mostly known as a last-chance institution.

Upon arrival, the brothers found the grounds of the campus littered with cigarette butts. "Every student smoked, and I think I was the only boy at the school without a pocket knife," Huang said. Jensen, ten, was placed with a seventeen-year-old roommate; on their first night together, the older boy lifted his shirt to show Jensen the numerous places where he'd been stabbed in a recent fight. Huang's roommate was illiterate; in exchange for teaching him to read, Huang said, "he taught me how to bench press. I ended up doing one hundred push-ups every night before bed." Huang would stick to a daily push-up routine the rest of his life.

The Huang brothers anglicized their names to fit in. Jen-Chieh became "Jeff," and Jen-Hsun became "Jensen." (Their younger brother, Jen-Che, would later become "Jim.") Jeff and Jensen kept in touch with their parents in Thailand by sending audiocassettes through the international post. With each cassette, they would first listen to their parents' message, then record over it with their own. Jensen recalled only occasional homesickness. To him, the whole thing played out like some grand adventure.

During the summer, students at OBI were expected to earn their keep through manual labor. Jeff was sent to a tobacco farm; Jensen was left behind to clean the dormitory toilets. "It wasn't a punishment," Huang said. "It was just my job." Another of Huang's chores was cutting brush on the school grounds with a scythe. Bays recalled passing him on the way to church. "We was driving by the field, and he was just running around in circles, wearing a baseball shirt, cutting those weeds," he said.

By the end of his year at Oneida Elementary, Huang had all but conquered the school. He was the best student in his class, for which he was given a silver dollar at a school assembly. He had stood up to the racists and the name-callers, including, in at least one instance, a teacher. After the final school bell rang, Huang would take charge, running ahead of his classmates into forests of hickory and oak. Chasing behind him, in a friendly way, were the "rowdy boys" of Clay County, the soft Appalachian mud under their feet.

HUANG SPENT THE SUMMER of 1974 living at the dormitory. He looked forward to watching the *ABC Sunday Night Movie* with the other holdovers each week. As fall approached, he ate fresh apples from the tree outside his window. He began seventh grade at OBI, while Bays continued on the public-school track. Huang, relying on his battle-scarred roommate for protection, had few problems adjusting. A year after that, Huang's father secured employment in the United States, and the brothers left Kentucky to reunite with their family in Oregon. Bays and Huang would not see each other again for forty-four years.

In the interim, Bays became a nursing-home administrator. Huang became one of the richest people in the world. Bays was unsurprised; he told me that even as a boy, he believed that Huang was destined for greatness.

The two were reunited in 2019, when Huang returned to OBI to donate a building to the school. "He'd never forgotten me," Bays said.

For many children, the two years in Kentucky would have been traumatic. At ten years old, Huang had been sent eight thousand miles from his parents to a foreign land where he barely spoke the language. He was bullied, isolated, made to share a room with a knife fighter, and tasked with cleaning the latrine. What did it say about him that he thrived in this environment? "Back then, there wasn't a counselor to talk to," Huang said. "Back then, you just had to toughen up and move on."

Time may have softened Huang's memories of OBI. When he donated the building, in 2019, he talked fondly of the (now gone) footbridge he had crossed every day on the way to school; he neglected to mention that the other students tried to shake him off of it. When I asked him about doing chores at the school, he told me they taught him the value of hard work. "Of course, if you'd asked me at the time, I probably would have given you a different answer," he said. In 2020, Huang was asked to deliver a remote commencement message to the students of OBI. In his speech, he said his time at the school was one of the best things ever to happen to him.

IN 1976 HUANG matriculated at Aloha High School in the suburbs of Portland, Oregon. He dressed in denim and velour and wore his hair in the shape of a motorcycle helmet. He continued to excel academically, and his English rapidly improved. Aloha was a welcoming place, and he soon formed a close-knit clique with a few of his fellow nerds. "There were three or four of us, and we were all in the same clubs: math club, science club, computer club," Huang said. "You know, the popular kids! I didn't have a girlfriend."

The computer club was of particular interest. In 1977 the school purchased an Apple II, one of the first mass-produced personal computers. Huang was enthralled by the machine, using it to shoot Klingons on a grid of text in the primitive game *Super Star Trek* and to code his own version of *Snake* in Basic.

His other extracurricular interest was table tennis. At OBI, Huang had dominated the rec-room ping-pong table but didn't take the sport seriously. In high school, he began to play competitively. His mentor was Lou Bochenski, the owner of the Paddle Palace, a table tennis club located in a converted Elks Lodge ballroom. Bochenski's daughter, Judy, had visited Beijing in 1971, one of the lucky invitees in the "ping-pong diplomacy" exchange. But Huang had never played in Asia, and he used a Western grip.

For an entire summer, Huang did little but practice. Bochenski was so impressed that he wrote a letter to *Sports Illustrated*, calling Huang "the most promising junior ever to play table tennis in the Northwest," even though he'd played competitively for only three months. Huang's signature shot was his arcing forehand loop, which he used to defeat many higher-rated players, sometimes diving under the table to return seemingly irretrievable shots. Within a year Huang was nationally ranked and playing in the finals of the under-sixteen doubles championships in Las Vegas. "He picked up the sport of table tennis faster than anyone I'd ever seen," said Joe Romanosky, a friend from the Paddle Palace.

Huang was athletic and had good reflexes, but his unique quality was his exceptional focus. When he set his mind to self-improvement, the rest of the world faded away. He outworked everyone; he didn't seem to get frustrated or stuck; he never hit a plateau. Instead, Huang watched, with measured satisfaction, as his patient dedication to the fundamentals slowly manifested itself as skill.

Huang spent almost all his time at the Paddle Palace. When he wasn't practicing, he worked there, scrubbing the floors at night to earn money for tournament fees. Bochenski gave him a key, and sometimes, rather than return home to his parents, Huang would sleep in the ballroom. The tables were set among opulent surroundings, with chandeliers above, hardwood floors below, and padded benches set into the walls. A photograph from this time shows Huang, maybe fifteen, wearing high-cut 1970s gym shorts and striped tube socks. He stands low to the table, a small guy with a bowl cut, striking the ball with an expression of competitive intensity. "He was a very aggressive player, on offense all the time," Romanosky said.

As graduation approached, Huang got a job at Denny's. The nationwide restaurant chain was known in that era for its burnt coffee, its reconstituted powdered eggs, its reheated sausage patties, and its round-the-clock operating hours. Huang loved the place. He began as a dishwasher and worked his way up to server. "I find that I think best when I'm under adversity. When the world is just falling apart, I actually think my heart rate goes down," he later said. "Maybe it's Denny's. As a waiter, you've got to deal with rush hour. Anyone who's dealt with rush hour in a restaurant knows what I'm talking about."

Denny's provided Huang with a crash course in American cuisine. There he had his first bacon cheeseburger, his first pigs-in-a-blanket, his first chicken-fried steak. He methodically ate his way through the menu; his favorite item was the "Super Bird," a grilled sourdough sandwich stuffed with turkey breast, bacon, tomatoes, and cheese. For an immigrant adapting to the culture of a new country, gorging on diner slop was as American as you could get.

HUANG RECEIVED OUTSTANDING GRADES and was inducted into the National Honor Society. The desire to achieve came from somewhere within; Huang told me that his parents were not "tiger parents" and that they had not put undue academic pressure on him. "Actually, both of my brothers were terrible students," he said, although he quickly added that they were both very bright. When I asked Huang why he, the middle child, was alone motivated to perform well in school, he shrugged. "I don't have an answer for you," he said. "I try not to analyze myself in that way."

By the time he graduated from high school, Huang had skipped a grade, was a nationally competitive athlete, and had a near-perfect GPA. Yet he opted out of the college-admissions scramble, choosing to enroll at nearby Oregon State University. There wasn't much thought behind the decision, Huang told me, and no pressure from his parents to go anywhere else. His high school buddy Dean Verheiden was a legacy Oregon State student, and Huang chose to go as well. "I just followed my best friend," he said.

Others had a different interpretation. Huang, then seventeen, had lived in three countries and attended at least five separate schools. At the time, OSU had an acceptance rate above 70 percent and wasn't the highest-ranked public school in Oregon, but the campus was a ninety-minute drive from his parents' house. "He could have gone anywhere—Ivy League, Stanford, East Coast, you name it," one longtime friend said. "He went to OSU because he wanted to stay close to home."

Huang matriculated in 1980. At the time, Oregon State didn't offer a dedicated computer science degree, so Huang majored in electrical engineering. His introductory sequence in this field determined much of the course of the rest of his life. He learned how to design circuits, which he spent the rest of his career doing. And he met his future wife.

Lori Mills was an earnest eighteen-year-old Oregon State freshman with glasses and curly brown hair. Her personality was friendly and easygoing, but she craved structure, and she lived her life according to a fixed timeline of responsibilities: career by twenty-two, marriage by twenty-five, kids by thirty. She was randomly assigned as Huang's lab partner during their first week of class. "There were, like, two hundred and fifty kids in electrical engineering, and maybe three girls," Huang said. "She was the best-looking." Competition broke out among the male undergraduates for Mills's attention, and Huang felt he was at a disadvantage. "I was the youngest kid in the class," he said. "I looked like I was about twelve."

Not liking his chances with conventional flirting, Huang took a different approach. "I tried to impress her—not with my looks, of course—but with my strong capability to complete homework," he said. Every weekend, Huang would call Mills and pester her to do homework with him. And he was good at homework, which he sometimes called his "superpower." Lori accepted, and the two became study partners.

In their laboratory studies, Jensen and Lori hunched over a rectangular plastic grid known as a "breadboard," wiring components to build amplifiers and adding machines. The work was delicate and painstaking and involved a fair degree of close-quarters contact. The flow of electricity began at a power source, made a loop through various components, then returned to the source where it started. Primitive circuits might power light bulbs or digital clocks. More advanced circuits took advantage of a special component called a "transistor," which could act like a digital switch. By combining transistors, you could create a "logic gate," and, by combining logic gates, you could perform rudimentary calculations: one plus zero, say, or one plus one. And by chaining these simple adding machines together, you could do serious mathematics. The final step was always closing the circuit, creating a loop for electricity to flow. After six months of breadboarding, Huang asked Mills out on a proper date. She said yes, and after that the two were seldom separated.

Huang completed his studies early and graduated with highest honors. His timing coincided with the silicon revolution of the 1980s. Students might use breadboards, but the preferred medium for commercial circuit logic was a treated silicon crystal known as a "semiconductor." Technicians "printed" logic circuits onto silicon discs using concentrated ultraviolet light, then diced them into tiny squares called "microchips." Because all the electrical components on a chip were fixed in place, microchips were also sometimes called "integrated circuits."

The personal-computer craze of the 1980s created tremendous demand for microchips. So, too, did the popularity of digital devices. Microchips were being placed in cars, CD players, children's toys, microwave ovens, and any other useful object one could think of. In time, they would move into power chargers, refrigerators, credit cards, and electric toothbrushes. This meant that skilled circuit designers were in limited supply. (They remain so today.) Nearing graduation, Jensen found employment in the world's microchip capital—Silicon Valley.

TWO

Large-Scale Integration

The dawn broke on a desolate stretch of mountain highway near the California-Oregon border just before Christmas, 1984. The trees cast westward shadows on the asphalt and across the sloping hood of the flashy vehicle that sped along the road. The Toyota Supra was a two-door sports car with angular styling and an inline six-cylinder engine. From the front, with the headlights popped, the car looked like some friendly breed of android. Jensen, behind the wheel, took a corner, then accelerated down the deserted road.

Surely, he must have felt confident. In the passenger seat sat his girlfriend—now fiancée—Lori Mills. Jensen had proposed to her the night before, at the magnificent office Christmas party thrown by Advanced Micro Devices, the microchip manufacturer where he worked. He'd started working at AMD at twenty, when he was not yet old enough to drink, and secured a starting salary of $28,700, a figure so impressive he could recite it from memory forty years later. Jensen lived frugally, and after a year he had saved up enough money to buy both the car and an engagement ring.

The AMD party was a natural place to propose. The holiday bash was one of Silicon Valley's most extravagant. AMD would rent out San Francisco's

Moscone Convention Center and treat the lucky employees to free drinks and music from well-known bands. That year, the rock group Chicago regaled the assembled engineers with danceable renditions of "Saturday in the Park" and "25 or 6 to 4." In 1984 the Bay Area tech scene remained a frontier outpost of the American economy; when Jensen joined AMD, the most valuable US firms were old-line industrial concerns like DuPont and General Electric. By the time his generation of entrepreneurs was finished, these industrial conglomerates would be gutted, and the stock market would be dominated by tech.

Lori accepted the proposal, of course. Even by the standards of the era, this was an early engagement. Jensen was just twenty-one. Lori, twenty-two, had not yet graduated from college. But both found comfort in domesticity, and their marriage would in time become the envy of their social set. After the proposal, Jensen suggested driving Lori home to tell her parents the happy news in person. He was close with the Mills family, particularly Lori's father, an affable all-American patriarch who resembled the actor Jimmy Stewart in both demeanor and appearance. The Mills family in turn adored Jensen and felt that their daughter, even at this young age, could not possibly have done better. Friends of the couple joked that Jensen was closer to Lori's parents than to his own.

But if Huang was dependable and preternaturally mature, he still occasionally entertained ideas that only a twenty-one-year-old would think sound, like embarking on a nine-hour drive in a sports car across snowy mountain roads in the middle of the night after a boozy office Christmas party. By the time the sun rose, Jensen and Lori had been on the road for over five hours. The country they traveled through was spare and depopulated, and some who lived there could trace their ancestry to that first wave of California fortune seekers who'd burrowed into the surrounding hills in search of gold. It was in the graveyard of these busted mines that Jensen hit the transparent layer of black ice that coated the freeway and sent the Supra into an unrecoverable glide. The tires spun without purpose, and the vehicle drifted onto the shoulder before rolling off the road.

Jensen and Lori were momentarily inverted. Then the car hit the ground with an awful crunch before banging along to a stop, shedding components of its upscale trimming along the way. The Supra was totaled, and the couple was trapped inside. Lori, wearing her new engagement ring, was mostly unharmed. Jensen was bleeding, and his neck was twisted bad. The sun was coming up, but the temperature was frigid, and it was the coldest moment of the day. When the first responders eventually arrived, they had to cut the couple out of the car. Jensen required stitches in multiple places and had to wear a neck brace for several months thereafter. When I asked him about the incident years later, he mostly expressed regret for the Supra. "Incredible car," he said.

HUANG EVENTUALLY RECOVERED, and the engagement was unaffected, or perhaps even strengthened, by the distress of the shared experience. As Lori finished school, Jensen returned to work. At AMD he sketched out microchip designs on paper. Each sheet represented a separate layer of the chip, with transistors at the bottom and various interconnects set above. When he was finished with a layer, he would bring it to the back of the office for fulfillment, where it would be transferred to a transparent sheet of colored cellophane. Those cellophane sheets were used to make stencils called "photomasks," then sent to a fabrication facility.

For some reason, all of AMD's photomask workers were Chinese women. They sat at workstations and arranged the colored stencils in precise patterns. The women didn't speak much English, and Huang, who'd grown up speaking the Taiwanese dialect of Hokkien at home, didn't speak Mandarin. The two languages are as different as German and English, but patiently, in conversations with the photomask crew, Huang began to learn Mandarin, the most commonly spoken form of Chinese. "Just phonetically, through regular conversations," he said. The women reminded him of his mother.

Huang spent two years at AMD, a time he recalled with fondness. He acquired some shares of AMD stock through an employee-purchase program and held on to these, with escalating irony, for the rest of his career.

But in 1985 a coworker convinced him to leave AMD for LSI Logic, an innovative Silicon Valley firm that developed the first software-design tools for chip architects. By the mid-1980s, engineers were putting hundreds of thousands of transistors on a single chip, surpassing the limits of paper draftsmanship. The closest analogy was covering a tennis court with a maze made from strands of human hair.

LSI's "large-scale integration" process automated low-level blocks of circuit design, freeing engineers to focus on higher-level architecture. Over time, these automated design tools evolved into the unfathomably complex "very large-scale integration," or VLSI, which remains the point of entry for most modern engineers. With VLSI you zoomed out so far that you forgot the individual transistor existed. As time went on, only Jensen and a few other graybeards would remember the artisanal microchip.

Lori graduated in 1985 and found employment at Silicon Graphics, a manufacturer of expensive 3D graphics workstations. SGI, as everyone called it, was the *other* place to work in Silicon Valley at the time, and at first Lori made more money than Jensen. Like AMD, SGI was located close to US 101, a narrow strip of highway that spanned the twenty-five miles from downtown San Jose to the Stanford campus in Palo Alto. Drive along this highway, and you would read exit signs directing you to the otherwise forgettable suburban municipalities of Cupertino, Santa Clara, Milpitas, and Mountain View—home, respectively, to Apple, Intel, Cisco, and Silicon Graphics. Talent here was clustered tightly, and no locale on Earth had ever generated so much wealth per square foot. Huang was bound to the place as if tethered, and he would spend the rest of his career working within a five-mile radius.

If the names of the towns were recognizable, the architecture for the most part was not. The Manhattan glamour that had bedazzled Huang's father was not to be found in Silicon Valley. There were no skyscraper canyons, no bustle of pedestrian energy in the street. Instead, there was a bland collection of modern, mid-rise boxes, surrounded by parking lots and strip malls and extended-stay business hotels, and crisscrossed by freeways in a geographic depression at the south end of the Bay. Behind the tinted glass one could find some of the finest minds in engineering, but from the outside the only signifier of activity was the traffic.

The buildings were just as boring on the inside. The climate-controlled office of the 1980s featured clunky cathode-ray monitors and drab carpeting and humming fluorescent lights and drop ceilings to hide the ductwork. The favored layout was the open-plan "action office," which featured reconfigurable arrangements of cubicles at varying heights. At LSI Logic, designers had opted for a low-slung cubicle grid that employees called "the pit." Huang arrived there in 1985. He wore large glasses and a tasteful watch and button-down shirts with slacks, but still kept his hair a little long. For him, the pit was heaven. There seemed no place in the world he'd rather be.

As he had in table tennis, Huang rapidly distinguished himself at LSI through his surreal work ethic. One of Huang's pit mates was Jens Horstmann, a fellow electrical engineer who had arrived at LSI from Germany as part of a six-month mentorship program and never left. Horstmann and Huang were both immigrants, they were around the same age, and they even had the same initials. They shared a readiness to sacrifice their personal lives and their sanity in service of solving an endless series of hard technical problems. "There was no notion of weekends," Horstmann said. "We'd come in at seven a.m.; then our girlfriends would call us at nine p.m. asking us when we were going to come home."

Over time, Horstmann became Huang's closest friend. Horstmann was charismatic, extroverted, funny, and in his personal life a little more reckless than Huang, with a broader range of interests and a wider social sphere. At work, though, Huang was the risk-taker. With characteristic dedication, Huang had mastered a software application known as the Simulation Program with Integrated Circuit Emphasis, or SPICE. Using a command line, Huang would input an ordered list of circuit components and would receive a text-only table of voltage data in return. The primitive SPICE software was often regarded as an academic teaching tool, but Huang used it to push the capabilities of the circuits further than anyone else thought possible.

When LSI's customers wanted new functions, most of the designers would simply respond, "There's no way." Huang would say, "Let me see what I can do."

Huang would spend hours fiddling with the simulator, attempting to arrange the list of components to enable what the customer wanted. This was painstaking work, conducted without the assistance of graphical user interfaces or even color monitors. His focus was admirable, but Horstmann knew many engineers who could become similarly absorbed in technical problems; what set Huang apart was his ability to avoid dead ends. "Similar people, they get lost, right?" Horstmann said. "They just get lost in these deep, deep ratholes. He doesn't. He has a great sense of seeing when a problem has reached a certain level of complexity, and he can't easily make further progress, and he has to go in a different direction."

LSI's most demanding customers were the computer-graphics designers, whose appetite for faster silicon knew no point of satiation. To serve them, Horstmann, with Huang's encouragement, began signing contracts to deliver products that, internally, the two had no idea if LSI could actually make. Older engineers advised the two to be more cautious. *Do you know what you're doing?* they'd say. *If this fails, it may be the end of your career.* "It was true, but that never troubled us," Horstmann said.

Almost everything Horstmann and Huang promised was eventually delivered. The rewards for solving these hard technical challenges were new, even harder technical challenges. Huang loved the difficulty curve; he relished leveling up in this way. "He had the ability to make $1 + 1 = 3$," Horstmann said. "By this, I mean we were not only doing work for our customers, but we were turning these orders into tools, and turning those tools into methodologies." Most engineers couldn't do this, Horstmann told me; most engineers couldn't even make $1 + 1 = 2$. "You're lucky to get one and a half," he said.

Among their friendship group, Jensen and Lori were the responsible ones. They were the first to get married and the first to buy a house. In 1988 they moved into a two-story, four-bedroom tract home on the east side of San Jose with a front-facing garage and a backyard patio where Jensen could work the barbecue. They worked stable, well-compensated jobs at respected employers and diligently maximized their contributions to their tax-deferred retirement accounts. They adopted a dog named Sushi and smothered it with unconditional affection. Sushi returned the sentiment, knocking aside objects with his enthusiastic tail wagging.

Horstmann admired Jensen's relationship and the orderly life he lived. He also admired Lori, who was a gifted engineer. Horstmann recalled talking with her about a technical problem he was working on: a customer's microchip, embedded in an orbital satellite, was malfunctioning because of interference from cosmic rays. Lori had worked on a similar problem, which required not just a working knowledge of electrical engineering but also particle physics. "It was just amazing, how deep and how structured her thinking was," Horstmann said.

The downside of this structured approach was that the Huangs were—well, they were kinda square. They worked constantly, traveled rarely, and barely socialized outside the semiconductor industry. Horstmann recalled introducing Huang to a friend who ran a craft microbrewery, an unusual profession in the 1980s. "Jensen was just, like, 'How do you know this person? How is this possible?'" Horstmann said. Huang didn't seem to have a single friend who didn't work in tech.

HUANG WAS REPEATEDLY promoted within LSI. He also began taking night classes at Stanford in pursuit of a master's degree in electrical engineering, but he was so busy at work that it took him eight years to finish. Now driving a sensible commuter car, Huang oscillated between school in the west of the Valley, his home in the east, and his job in the middle, traveling up and down and up and down the 101 for years. By the time he was finally awarded the degree, in 1992, much of what he'd learned in his introductory sequence was obsolete.

It was through his work at LSI that Huang came to know Chris Malachowsky and Curtis Priem, chip designers who worked for Sun Microsystems. Sun, like SGI, made high-end workstation computers for power users, and Priem and Malachowsky were tough customers who asked for functionality that average salespeople couldn't provide or even really understand. "LSI reached deep into the bowels of the company to find the most outward-looking technical person that they could assign to us," Malachowsky told me. "That was Jensen."

Malachowsky, Priem, and Huang made a good team. Priem was the architect who could think in circuits, charting the path of electricity through adding machines in his mind. Malachowsky was the mechanic, fond of cars and small-engine planes, who could build anything Priem could dream up. Huang was the logistician, in charge of tooling production at LSI to mass-produce their designs.

Of the three, Priem was the strangest. The pairing of his braniac face with his brilliant mind was a physiognomist's delight. Priem's forehead was enormous, almost elongated; his eyebrows were arched; and his narrow, squinting eyes wandered around the room as he talked. He spoke in a continuous technical monologue, like a tour guide, walking the listener through circuit architecture and pausing, here and there, to zoom in on important features. Often, the conceptual map of what Priem was describing existed only in his head, but he rarely seemed to notice, or care, whether his audience could follow what he was saying.

Priem had arrived in engineering through an indirect path. He had grown up in the suburbs of Cleveland, Ohio, where his mother's dream was that he would play the cello in a professional symphony. Priem had pursued this ambition until high school, when, on a visit to a music camp in North Carolina, he was seated in the last chair in the second orchestra. "I realized I was looking at a future as a high school music teacher," Priem said. He gave up the cello and got into computers, graduating from Rensselaer Polytechnic Institute in upstate New York before ending up in Silicon Valley, where his eccentricities were deemed within the acceptable range of tolerance—for a time, at least.

Malachowsky was a more practical fellow; of the three Nvidia cofounders, he was the one you'd trust to swing a hammer. He was burly, with broad shoulders, big hands, and a wide, friendly face. Growing up in New

Jersey, Malachowsky had been a self-described "long-hair" who'd enjoyed drinking beer and goofing off with his buddies. Although he got a respectable haircut at the end of the seventies, he retained a gruff, irreverent attitude and was quick to laugh. For Malachowsky, computers were not lofty abstractions, but tangible machines grounded in physical reality. Priem built his own flight simulator; Malachowsky flew his own plane.

Huang, a few years younger and technically an outside vendor, acted more like the two men's manager, working with the LSI fabrication plant to ensure the timely delivery of a high-quality product. All three men recalled how perfectly they were able to operate within their preferred domain of responsibility. "We just never stepped on each other's toes," Malachowsky said. This unusual arrangement was possible only because Priem and Malachowsky trusted Huang—indeed, they trusted him more than they trusted their actual bosses. "There was politics at Sun like you wouldn't believe," Priem said.

Huang eschewed drama and led by example, driving himself hard, refraining from gossip, and carefully apportioning credit for good work. If a product was going to be late or if LSI couldn't deliver on some promised function, Huang would immediately provide a detailed description of what had gone wrong, who was responsible, and what he was doing to fix it. "When he said he was going to do something, there was a reasonable likelihood that he would actually _do_ it, y'know?" Malachowsky said. Malachowsky struggled to think of other Silicon Valley product managers who fit that description.

If Huang had a flaw, it was that he embraced candor in the extreme, sometimes crossing into the territory of insult. The bluntness was part of his charm, of course, but it could leave people's feelings hurt. He didn't have much patience for people who disagreed with him, and he also seemed genuinely surprised that there were people working in his industry who didn't want to spend fourteen hours a day fiddling with the circuit simulator. Of course, for quarrelsome workaholics like Priem and Malachowsky, these traits were only further evidence of Jensen's managerial fitness.

The fruitful collaboration of Priem, Malachowsky, and Huang resulted in the 1989 debut of the Sun GX, a line of three-dimensional graphics processors that powered workstations for scientists, animators, and computer-aided-design modelers. The chip took as its input a wire-frame skeleton of points in space, then "painted" on textures, one pixel at a time, to create rotatable objects constructed of blocky polyhedra. To any modern observer, the GX's output would look clumsy, but if you squinted at its sixteen-color output on a cathode-ray tube monitor in 1989, you could maybe see the future of computer graphics.

Huang's success with the Sun GX caught the attention of Wilf Corrigan, the founder of LSI Logic. After its release, Corrigan promoted Huang to run a "system-on-a-chip" design platform that allowed customers to condense multiple functions—3D graphics, video, game controllers—onto a single piece of silicon. The platform was popular with customers, and Malachowsky, watching from outside, believed that Corrigan was grooming Huang to one day replace him as CEO. "They let this young, twentysomething-year-old kid start a whole division!" he said. "I mean, they saw something in him."

But Priem and Malachowsky saw something in Huang, too. Despite the success of the GX chip, when the two proposed making a cheaper version for PC video games, management at Sun turned them down. (A haughty executive informed them that Sun supplied scientists, not gamers.) Frustrated, Malachowsky and Priem wanted to build this consumer video game chip on their own, but neither felt comfortable managing a business—so in 1992 the two men approached Huang and asked him to run their start-up.

Huang had a tough decision to make. He respected Priem and Malachowsky, but he was in charge of his own division, with a secure job on the management track at an innovative corporation. The new company that Malachowsky and Priem were proposing didn't have a business plan, or even a name—just a rough sketch for a product that Sun had decided wasn't profitable enough to build. Also, although the two men insisted they were the perfect team, to coworkers their relationship seemed dysfunctional.

Malachowsky and Priem fought with each other all the time. "Chris and I would just have these yelling matches," Priem told me. These fights sometimes ended with one man storming across the workroom floor to slam the door to his office. "The people on our team would always ask, 'Are we disbanding?'" Priem said. "But this was just our way of interacting." Both men were also fairly stubborn. Priem spoke of Malachowsky's "impedance function," an engineering term used to describe opposition to the flow of electricity through a circuit. When I shared this with Malachowsky, he responded, "Yeah, well, I don't know how long you've talked with Curtis, but his user interface isn't terribly well-designed."

Working with Priem and Malachowsky meant committing to a lifetime of door slamming and engineering jokes. Worse, Huang's personal finances were stretched. In 1990, the Huangs' son, Spencer, was born, followed by their daughter, Madison, in 1991. (Sushi the dog responded to the new arrivals by trying to steal the children's pacifiers from their mouths.) The master plan called for both Jensen and Lori to continue their jobs while paying down their mortgage, but the family hadn't been able to find reliable child care, and Lori eventually left her job at Silicon Graphics to raise their kids.

Jens Horstmann was named godfather to both of the Huangs' children. His own wife had left the engineering workforce to raise children, as had Chris Malachowsky's wife, Tina. Horstmann told me that all three women were superior engineers. "For my own family, I feel, sometimes, a bit guilty of having taken the liberty to work so hard and to pour myself so into this," he said. "I mean, we tried nannies, we tried things—but maybe we should have tried a little harder." When I asked Huang about this, decades after the birth of his children, I could see the discomfort in his face as he recalled first asking his brilliant wife to suspend her career, then, with only six months of savings in his bank account, asking her permission to leave his job for a start-up. But Lori told him to go for it. "She always believed in me," Huang said.

IN LATER YEARS, Huang would describe his rapid rise from draftsman to CEO as a confluence of coincidences. "I was a technical staffer with a state-school education, and I wasn't particularly ambitious," he said in his 2020 commencement address for OBI. "If you were looking for someone to run a company someday, I don't think you would have picked me."

Huang handled his later career success with admirable humility—but sometimes that humility was itself exaggerated. Everyone I spoke with who knew him at this time in his life agreed that Huang was fibbing in his address. Malachowsky recalled him as a superbly competent striver with a master's degree from Stanford and an abundance of unconcealed ambition. "He wanted to run something by the age of thirty," Malachowsky said. "I distinctly remember we had dinner at his house, and he told us that."

Hans Mosesmann, a veteran industry analyst who would later help manage Nvidia's IPO, recalled talking with one of Huang's former managers at LSI who'd been tasked with giving Huang an employee evaluation. The evaluation form resembled a report card, but the manager left the grades blank. At the bottom, the manager wrote, "Jensen is an excellent employee. I look forward to working for him some day."

Horstmann remembered the friction Huang caused at LSI, where in his twenties he was in charge of a division with $250 million in annual revenue and with many older and more experienced employees answering to him. Seeking to mediate, Corrigan hired a senior director from Intel to comanage the product line. Huang was incensed—using the most profane word in the engineer's dictionary, he considered the hiring *political*. "He had built that division up from nothing, and now it was taken away from him," Horstmann said. Perhaps it was this final indignity that led Huang to defect. If Malachowsky and Priem could be obnoxious, they were also brilliant, and Huang was their first and only choice to run their graphics start-up—they just didn't trust anyone else.

But Huang did not commit at once. He knew that start-ups were difficult, hardware start-ups were more difficult, and consumer-hardware start-ups were the most difficult of all. Most did not make it past the prototype stage, and many didn't even make it that far. Decision-making, for Huang, was a clinical process with little room for useless emotions like hope. To him, business was just another engineering problem.

Engineers looked to break down complex problems into simple governing principles, which could then be leveraged to powerful effect. To launch a start-up, then, Huang needed first to understand those principles. He had to research the market, the supply chain, the competition, the technology, and the product fit. He had to arrange exploratory phone calls with customers, game developers, and computer-graphics experts. He had to pore through years of dull state-of-the-industry reports, paging through bar charts and sales figures and customer surveys in search of a glimmer of an upward trend. In other words, he had to do his homework. And there was only one place to do that.

THREE

New Venture

The Denny's of legend was situated adjacent to a freeway in San Jose, its pole sign shining like a beacon amid a downscale landscape of gas stations and money-transfer storefronts. The carpeted floors of the restaurant were patterned in mauve and burgundy, and, in 1993, you could still find ashtrays on some of the tables. A long diner counter with stools faced the kitchen; around back was a quiet area where patrons could enjoy endless refills of coffee for hours at a time. A poster on the front window advertised the Grand Slam breakfast, which consisted of eggs, sausage, bacon, and pancakes for the price of $3.99. The restaurant never closed.

Huang had suggested the meeting spot. It was close to his house, and he sometimes took his children there to eat. The quiet area in the back was usually populated by police officers drinking coffee and filling out reports. In 1993 California was suffering through the worst crime wave in its history, with more than four thousand people murdered in the state in a single year. Despite its adjacency to wealthy Silicon Valley, the city of San Jose was not spared.

Huang sat at a table surrounded by cops, with his laptop and his research papers scattered around him. Chris Malachowsky and Curtis Priem sat with him. Not especially enthusiastic about the cuisine, the two mostly abused the coffee-refill promotion. Huang atoned for this transgression by chatting with the waitstaff, ordering plate after plate of food, and leaving extravagant tips.

Sun Microsystems had declined to pursue the consumer marketplace for PC video game hardware. So had Lori's former employer Silicon Graphics, the industry leader in three-dimensional graphics. (Employees there were busy animating the CGI dinosaurs for *Jurassic Park*.) The failure of the major players to invest in PC gaming created a vacuum in the marketplace, which a brigade of start-up businesses were now scrambling to fill.

The concept was to take the hardware used to paint the wire-frame skeletons of model airplanes and dinosaurs and repurpose it to create controllable animated figures in three-dimensional games. Execution required the mass production of cheap, efficient circuits as well as a thin layer of software that "ran on top of the metal" so that game programmers could access the computing structures beneath. The finished device would be a peripheral circuit board with a graphics chip at its core. To install the board, home computer users would unscrew the computer's exterior metal housing and click the circuit board into a designated slot on the motherboard.

The product was known as a "graphics accelerator," and at least thirty-five competitors were trying to build one. Huang worried there was no space for a thirty-sixth. The leading expert in computer graphics was Jon Peddie, who had written several textbooks on the topic. Huang had reached out to Peddie to get a sense of the market, and the two soon became friends, with Huang calling incessantly, asking questions late into the night. Peddie advised Huang that the space was too crowded and that many of the best engineers were already working for other start-ups. "I told him not to do it," Peddie said. "That was the best advice he never took."

At Denny's, Priem and Malachowsky mostly spectated. "I was there for the pie," Priem recalled, "and really, just to watch him." Huang's magic number was $50 million, which he had determined was the minimum revenue his start-up would have to produce each year to make it worth the effort. He had a spreadsheet running on his laptop, containing revenue projections for the next few years. Huang would tinker with a variable in a cell, and the projections would drop below $50 million. Then he would tinker with a variable in another cell, and the projections would jump above.

After a few such sessions, Huang had talked himself into it. Soon after, the still-unnamed firm of Priem, Malachowsky, and Huang walked into the office of Palo Alto lawyer Jim Gaither, seeking incorporation. Gaither, who had once attended 129 separate board meetings in a single calendar year, was one of the Valley's most sought-after advisers. He was impressed by the men, especially Huang, who struck him as a natural leader. "I made a quick decision that there was no way they were going to leave our offices without deciding to stay with me," Gaither said.

Gaither discussed corporate structure with the founders, then drew up the paperwork. The start-up didn't have a name, so for a placeholder, Gaither wrote "NV": new venture. This was a striking coincidence, as Priem and Malachowsky were already calling their prototype graphics chip the NV1, joking that it would, like the Sun GX, make competitors "green with envy." Priem drew up a list of words that riffed on the "NV" concept, using dictionaries from a variety of different languages, including Latin. From this list, the three settled on "Nvision"—until a records search revealed that this name had already been taken by an environmentally friendly manufacturer of recycled toilet paper. The next selection from the list was "Nvidia," from the Latin word *invidia*, for "envy."

The men returned to Denny's to finalize the details of the agreement. Huang would be the chief executive officer of Nvidia, Priem the chief technical officer, and Malachowsky the vice president of engineering. Each man would retain an equal share in the company. As Priem and Jensen discussed details, Malachowsky wandered over to a sheet-glass window facing a wide arterial road. He gazed out upon a Taco Bell and a decaying gas station lit by lamps of sodium vapor. It was a squalid, anonymous view without much to recommend it, and his gaze drifted upward until he realized with a jolt that the top of the window he was looking through was pitted with bullet holes.

Malachowsky hurried back to his cofounders. "Take a good look at that window," he said in a controlled whisper. "It's full of bullet holes! I think people are going up to that overpass to shoot at the cops!" Priem and Huang looked up from their paperwork to survey the evidence. They settled their bill, left a giant gratuity, and fled the restaurant for the relative safety of Priem's condominium. It would be years before any one of them returned.

Thus, the story that Nvidia was founded inside of a bullet-pocked Denny's was not strictly true—the founders actually signed the paperwork inside of Curtis Priem's San Jose townhouse. Still, as corporate mythmaking went, it was good enough, and the dining section where the men met for coffee is now graced with a handsome plaque. (The address is 2484 Berryessa Road in San Jose, if you'd like to see it. Management says it has been years since anyone shot at the restaurant.)

The final step for Nvidia was capitalization, a formality that could be done with an arbitrary amount of money. Upon their bringing the signed paperwork back to Gaither's office, Gaither suggested that Jensen simply give him all the cash in his wallet, which turned out to be about $200. In exchange, Jensen was formally awarded a third of Nvidia's shares, which over time would prove to be a decent investment. He collected his cofounders' share of the money the next time he saw them, and the firm came into being. Jensen turned thirty in February 1993; Nvidia's certificate of incorporation was filed in April, about six weeks later. "He just missed his deadline," Malachowsky said.

THE CLASSIC SILICON VALLEY company begins in a garage. Nvidia inverted the cliché by moving Priem's furniture *into* the garage and working out of the two upstairs bedrooms of his condominium instead. (Priem kept a third bedroom for himself.) Although it would be several months before the company received seed funding, the GX chip had been so impressive that several Sun employees left their jobs to work for Nvidia without immediate compensation, assuming that their salaries would be backfilled once Huang raised some money. "*We* thought we were special, but it was nice to see that some other people thought so, too," Malachowsky said.

Not everyone believed in Nvidia. Horstmann recalled drinking beer with Huang at his house and Huang getting a phone call from his mother. Horstmann couldn't follow the conversation, which was conducted in Taiwanese, but remembered it growing heated. After Huang hung up, he returned, exasperated. "Can you believe it?" he said. "My mom just told me to quit Nvidia and go back to work for a large company."

At the condo, one of the bedrooms was taken by the hardware group, designing circuitry on high-end Sun workstations. The other bedroom was taken by the software group designing the protocols that video game developers would need to communicate with the chip. The office of the CEO was located on the first floor at a small circular table adjacent to the kitchen. By design or happenstance, Jensen had placed himself at the center of the natural flow of foot traffic—employees going to the refrigerator for drinks or snacks had to pass him. No matter how powerful he grew, he would seek to remain in the center of traffic for the rest of his career.

Jurassic Park arrived in theaters two months after Nvidia's founding. For the first time, a film convincingly integrated computer-generated imagery into live-action footage. Doing so required preposterous computing power: one three-second shot of a Tyrannosaurus bursting through a log had taken animators ten months to render. The output from Nvidia's NV1 chip would be comparably primitive, although the difference was one of degree rather than type. "Even today, interactive video games and special effects in movies are essentially still just blocks sliding around hitting each other," Peddie said.

The most important objective for Nvidia was to somehow differentiate the NV1 from the dozens of other products coming to market. To do so, Priem, the architect, loaded both the chip and the software with esoteric features. To paint the wire-frame skeletons, the NV1 used a method called "quadratic texture mapping," which was intended to add depth and realism to the process. For the software, Priem used an "object-oriented" approach, which allowed programmers to design reusable blocks of code. The first time I asked Priem about the architecture of the NV1, he spoke uninterrupted for twenty-seven minutes. "I wanted to build an architecture that would last for one hundred years," he said.

As Priem led development of the NV1, Huang raised money. With Gaither's assistance, Nvidia secured audiences with Sequoia Capital and Sutter Hill Ventures, two of Silicon Valley's largest venture-capital firms. The night before his presentation to Sequoia, Huang struggled to come up with a business plan for his company. "I spent all night on it, but at the end I didn't have anything," he said. "I still don't."

What he did have was the support of LSI's founder, Wilf Corrigan. The following day, Huang and Priem traveled to Sequoia's offices to pitch Don Valentine, the firm's famously blunt founder. (Valentine's favorite question for start-ups was "Who cares?") The pitch went badly, with Huang fumbling over his presentation and Priem interrupting with irrelevant technical asides. After this uninspiring performance, Valentine took Huang aside. "Well, that wasn't very good," he said. "But Wilf Corrigan says I have to fund you, so you're in business."

Sequoia and Sutter Hill each wrote checks for several million dollars. In return, the investors were given board seats. Sequoia's seat was taken by Mark Stevens, an affable and extroverted thirty-three-year-old who had an MBA from Harvard. Sutter Hill's seat was taken by Tench Coxe, an affable and extroverted thirty-six-year-old who also had an MBA from Harvard. Both men wore a lot of Patagonia, and it could be a little difficult to tell them apart.

Coxe and Stevens agreed that it was Huang, specifically, rather than Nvidia's proposal that attracted their attention. "The reason we backed these dudes is because they were world-class computer scientists," Coxe said. "The average CEO will try to listen to the customer, but in computing, that's a big mistake, because customers just don't know what's possible. They just don't know what can be done!" Coxe observed that Intel and Microsoft had later struggled under more conventional management: "Jensen, from the beginning, was a world-class engineer who could see what was possible."

BY 1994, Nvidia had secured office space in a Sunnyvale strip mall and begun work on the NV1. The office was dingy, with frayed carpet, a water-stained drop ceiling, and linoleum floors in the break room. The smells from an adjacent Chinese takeout restaurant often filtered into the ventilation, and the bathroom was shared with another company. Facing the office was a Wells Fargo bank that was a target for local stick-up crews. "While we rented that space, that bank was robbed twice!" Malachowsky said. "You could watch the robberies from our front window."

The back of the office was converted into a recreation center. Lunch took place around a ping-pong table, where Huang would occasionally take his employees to school. In another room was the computer laboratory, where dismantled equipment sat alongside a small portable television attached to a Sega gaming system. Sega, the only console manufacturer to use the quadratic-texture-mapping approach, was Priem's favored platform. He held the high scores in most of the games and often played in the middle of the workday, leaning back with his foot atop his knee and steering a motorcycle on a nine-inch screen.

Adjacent to the laboratory was the conference room, where Huang set up his command center. There, in his immaculate all-caps handwriting, Huang had drawn whiteboard descriptions of the business strategy and approaching deadlines for the NV1. Using dry-erase markers, he had also drawn precise diagrams of the chip's architecture in green and red and orange. Running out of whiteboard space, Huang proceeded to draw on the conference room walls. Huang had no artistic background and had not studied calligraphy, but everything was crisp and color-coordinated—he just liked things neat.

Standing inside Huang's office was like standing inside his brain. Board members were impressed to see his master plan for Nvidia wrapping around the room where they convened. "His handwriting is unbelievably good," Coxe said. An important early milestone was "tape-out," when the blueprint for the first prototype chip would be sent to the fabrication plant. Huang was holding a board meeting as the tape-out date approached when he heard a cheer from his employees outside. He rushed out of the room to the laboratory, hoping to see a finished schematic for his first product. Instead, he found his workers clustered around a gaming console, where Priem had set a record time in *Road Rash*. Furious, Huang confiscated the console and gave it to his kids. "Jensen was always the adult in the room," one early employee said. "Even when he was the youngest guy in the room, he was the adult."

NVIDIA FOLLOWED A "MERCHANT CHIP" business model—it outsourced the fabrication of the chips to a factory in Europe, and it outsourced assembly, distribution, and retail sales of the finished circuit board to the US vendor Diamond. The only thing Nvidia handled was design and quality control of the microchip. As production dates approached, employees worked late into the night. Soon the laboratory was cluttered with empty food-delivery containers and boxes of bulk candy.

One of Nvidia's earliest hires was Jeff Fisher, who is still with the company. He used a VHS camcorder to document the day that the NV1 prototypes were delivered. In the grainy video, a motley crew of gamers gathers with excitement around a protective hard case. All are men. A buzz runs through the assembled crowd as the case is opened, revealing an array of fifteen chips encased in protective black shells. Priem, holding pliers, pries one case open to reveal a printed sheet of silicon the size of a fingernail. As the men appraise this tiny marvel, they are once again boys, their body language fidgety and energetic.

The Nvidia employees in the video wear splendid nineties button-down shirts with loud patterns printed onto thick fabric. Many of them have tucked their shirts into the waistbands of their beltless jeans. Huang, away with his family, missed the unboxing of the prototype, but a photograph taken around this time shows him wearing thick round glasses and a red-and-white striped button-down shirt under a jaunty vest. Fisher recalled the excessive starch Huang used in his laundry. "He was very, very, very well-pressed," Fisher said.

Nvidia now had to "validate" these prototypes for flaws. Running this effort was Dwight Diercks, another early Nvidia hire who is still with the company. Diercks had been born into a distinguished family of Minnesota pig farmers and still looked the part. He was a large, fleshy man who lumbered—honestly, lumbered—around Nvidia's headquarters with his oversized plaid shirt tucked into his drooping denim. He had blond hair, blue eyes, and a no-nonsense Midwestern affect. Several people at the company told me not to underestimate him.

Diercks ran a series of graphics clips known as an "art demo" through the prototype, then inspected each frame for errors. It was painstaking work, akin to editing a movie one frame at a time. Once validation was finished, Nvidia sent an error-corrected blueprint back to the European fabricator, which put the chip into mass production. Even with the launch date for the NV1 approaching, Huang was looking ahead to the NV2 and had signed a deal with Sega to develop the graphics accelerator for the forthcoming Dreamcast console. As part of the deal, Nvidia also outfitted its NV1 boards with a sound chip and a joystick controller, allowing Sega to port its games to the PC. The biggest draw was *Virtua Fighter*, which rendered martial artists in blocky quadrilaterals. Advertisements for the game showed a man made of rectangles being tossed through a television screen.

The chip could not come out fast enough. By 1995, the market for 3D graphics had surpassed Huang's most optimistic predictions, thanks to two blockbuster games. *Myst*, released in September 1993, was an elegant brain tickler set on a mysterious island and rapidly became the bestselling title in PC gaming history. *Doom*, released three months later, was a sci-fi/horror mash-up in which the player traveled around Mars spraying demons with buckshot. *Myst* and *Doom* represented opposing conceptual poles of what video gaming could be—but each sold millions of copies, and each sent gamers rushing to stores to purchase graphics accelerators.

The NV1 launched into a crowded marketplace in the fall of 1995. Customers walking into electronics retailers that Christmas season found dozens of chipmakers competing for attention. In addition to Nvidia, there were Matrox, S3, 3dfx, Cirrus Logic, and ATI. The confusing situation was not improved by Nvidia's circuit-board partners, which sold Nvidia chipsets under the trade name "Diamond Edge" while simultaneously selling competing 3dfx chipsets under the trade name "Diamond Monster."

The packaging for this equipment was ugly, and the retail display shelf for computer peripherals, previously home to a somber assortment of modem and printer components, was reduced to a psychedelic mess. The products were also expensive; a Diamond Edge card with the NV1 chipset cost $249, which was more than a Super Nintendo. Open the ugly box, and you'd find an even uglier circuit board, a sheet of green plastic studded with capacitors and molded epoxy housing. The thing looked flimsy and disposable, as indeed it was—graphics accelerators went obsolete quickly and required replacement every couple of years. The most important variable in Huang's spreadsheet was the number of customers willing to commit to this expensive upgrade ladder.

The answer turned out to be more than anyone expected. Game developers, inspired by *Myst* and *Doom*, were embracing the PC, which liberated them from the controlled hardware ecosystems of Sega and Nintendo. Classic titles like *Civilization II* and *Command & Conquer* appeared around this time, hypnotizing gamers with endless replayability and interminable streams of small decisions to be made. PC gaming was not always "fun," exactly, but it was utterly addictive, and players would lose hours or even days to the experience. A player who'd invested in a quality graphics card could witness the rise and fall of an empire before turning to the clock in the wee hours of the morning and pressing his palms into the sockets of his bleary eyes.

By the end of the year, Nvidia had sold more than one hundred thousand NV1 chips, driven by demand for *Virtua Fighter*, which came bundled with the cards. Confident in his product, Huang went on a hiring spree, and Nvidia grew to more than a hundred employees. "Suddenly, it seemed like we were a real company, right?" Diercks said. "The Christmas party that year was really over the top." It was not until the first quarter of 1996 that the problems surfaced. After the charms of *Virtua Fighter* were exhausted, customers found that the NV1 had trouble rendering other games. Most programmers preferred to build 3D objects using triangles, not quadratic mapping. "It didn't have a depth buffer, and it only rendered curved surfaces," Tim Little, a game developer who worked with the NV1, said. "As a result, you couldn't really determine how to sort the objects in the scene." This led to the serious "clipping" errors, where game characters would sink into sidewalks or teleport through walls. In the worst cases, the NV1 ceased communicating with the Windows operating system entirely, producing the notorious Blue Screen of Death. "It was catastrophic," Little said.

With few supported titles, NV1 sales tapered off, and dissatisfied customers took advantage of the generous return policies of the big-box retailers to take the cards back to stores. A few months after the launch, Diercks went shopping at Fry's Electronics, where he saw dozens of garish Diamond Edge boxes on the shelves, opened and marked down in price. Just as Nvidia had ramped up its payroll, demand for its only product vanished.

Meanwhile, game developers were moving away from Priem's experimental approach. In 1995, tired of watching graphics peripherals crash their operating system, Microsoft announced that it was launching its own DirectX standard for game developers. The standard supported triangles only, leaving the NV line stranded. Despite its promising start, the NV1 was a dud.

Decades later, Priem was still defending the product, but the other two founders spoke of the NV1 with the kind of bemused, shake-of-the-head bitterness reserved for recollections of failed relationships or tax audits. (Specifically, Huang called the NV1 a "disaster," and Malachowsky called it a "piece of shit.") But it was even worse than that because Nvidia had built its entire supply chain around future iterations of this same device. Huang's master plan called not just for the rollout of Sega's NV2 but also for the NV3, which was based on the same architecture. Now his perfect handwriting and his intricate diagrams would have to be erased, with the smears of ink on the whiteboard serving as a taunting reminder of his best-laid schemes. "We missed everything," Huang said, of those early days. "Every single decision we made was wrong."

FOUR

Thirty Days

When David Kirk arrived at Nvidia's offices for the first time, in 1996, he could see at once that the company was doomed. Kirk was a graphics expert who consulted throughout the Valley, which was like being a connoisseur of failure. He had watched a great many start-ups falter, including his own, and Nvidia exhibited all of the symptoms of a company hurtling toward insolvency. The employees looked haggard and demoralized, the quirky product didn't fit with the market, and the supposedly chummy founders were now deadlocked in a "technical discussion" that was obviously more than just a discussion and obviously about more than just technology. Kirk was skeptical of Nvidia—as a condition of his employment, he had insisted on receiving a hand-delivered paper check at the end of each workweek. He wasn't sure the company would stay in business longer than that.

The vibe at Nvidia was atrocious. Shortly before Kirk's arrival, Huang had briefed his assembled staff on the fallout from the NV1 debacle. The company was running out of money, and the original NV1 architecture would have to be abandoned, Huang said. Nvidia's best hope for survival was to abandon Sega and slither into bed with Microsoft; the company would then try to beat the rest of the manufacturers to market with an affordable knockoff chip. Unfortunately, this "pivot" meant that most employees were being let go. The remaining staff would work overtime as Jensen looked for corners to cut in order to design, manufacture, and ship a generic graphics accelerator in record-breaking time.

Following the announcement, Huang reduced the head count from more than a hundred general staff to a skeleton roster of thirty-five engineers. Joining in the aftermath, Kirk walked into an eerie, half-abandoned office. Fluorescent lights hung over blocks of low-slung cubicles, most of them empty. At the back of the office sat a "hardware emulator," a strange and ugly contraption that Huang had used the last of the company's funds to purchase. Nvidia's survival relied on the performance of this mysterious eyesore. The hardware emulator allowed you to build fake microchips and test them. But this explanation understates things a bit—essentially, the emulator *was* a fake microchip, only crafted in code rather than silicon. The machine was cumbersome, and slow, and appeared half-finished, with circuitry exposed and visible tangles of cable snaking out onto the floor. It was too large to fit in the computer lab, so employees had shoved aside the ping-pong table to make space for it in the break room.

Huang's plan was to use this emulator to skip the costly prototyping step and go straight to mass production with nothing more than a digital napkin sketch. In the history of the semiconductor industry, no firm had ever skipped prototyping before—but it had to work. Huang assigned double shifts on the emulator, with Diercks working the machine during the day and Kirk taking over at night.

After a few weeks programming the emulator, Kirk realized he had a second, tacit role at Nvidia: curbing the technical ambitions of cofounder Curtis Priem. Kirk had invented the quadratic-mapping technique used in the NV1, but when he arrived at Nvidia, he advised the company to abandon it. "It was just an idea I had," Kirk said. "I have lots of ideas." But this only made Priem promote quadratic mapping more aggressively. Priem was a purist who dismissed technical compromises as spineless concessions to the money guys. "The way Curtis thinks is for the end point," Malachowsky said. "But he doesn't really have it in his makeup to, like, stay in business."

Kirk soon realized that the abstruse question of whether or not to use quadratic mapping was a proxy for the more interesting question of who was actually in charge at Nvidia. Priem, the CTO, wanted total autonomy to set the company's technical road map. Huang, the CEO, wanted customers to stop returning his product to stores. Malachowsky, the mediator, seemed to have lost control of the discussion—by the time Kirk arrived, what had begun as a closed-door argument about circuit architecture had escalated into public shouting in full view of the small number of dismayed employees who remained.

Many people found Priem difficult to work with. "Curtis and I did not get along super well," Kirk said, echoing a sentiment that others expressed in a less polite way. "He was an absolutely brilliant technical person, but he was not a people person." Priem was certainly weird, and he often engineered idiosyncratic solutions to straightforward problems. One example was his approach to the issue of email spam. Most people used a spam filter or just lived with it. Priem's solution was to create thousands of different email addresses, one for every correspondent.

But as stubborn as Priem could be, he was not a match for Huang. When Jensen explained his point of view for the first time, he would do so in a measured voice, moving from premises to arguments to conclusions. At this point the fuse was lit, and the interlocutor had two options: agree with his line of thinking or risk detonation. Those who contradicted him were often shocked when he exploded in fury, berating them furiously in front of an audience of colleagues. This was the Wrath of Huang.

THE ORIGINS AND CAUSES of Huang's anger were not clear, even to those who knew him well. Jens Horstmann, his closest friend, told me that when Huang worked at LSI Logic, he was not known for temperamental outbursts;

it was only when he moved into the CEO role that he regularly began to blow his stack. "I will never forget the first time I saw him erupt," one Nvidia employee told me. "I'd been working there for a couple of months, and Jensen was always so charming and self-deprecating. Suddenly he's screaming at the top of his voice in front of a hundred people."

Spectators were important to Huang—when he dressed down an employee, he usually did so in public so that others could learn from the experience. ("Failure must be shared," Huang said.) If a project was delayed, Huang would command the person responsible to stand up and explain to the audience, in detail, every single thing that had gone wrong. Huang would then deliver a withering analysis of their performance. Such corporate struggle sessions were not for everyone. "You can kind of see right away who is going to last here, and who is not," Diercks said. "If someone starts getting defensive, you just know that person won't be long at Nvidia."

Diercks believed there was a method to it. "He would never just yell at somebody," he said. "He would wait for a meeting, with a bunch of people around, so he could make it an educational opportunity for everyone." But Huang's criticisms weren't always constructive—sometimes they were just verbal abuse. One former employee recalled a time when he bungled a minor assignment. Huang confronted him in front of three dozen executives, asking him how long he'd been with the company and what his salary was. The employee sheepishly provided the numbers; in his head, Huang then calculated the employee's career compensation and asked for all of it to be refunded. The exercise didn't feel like a joke. "He was kind of serious," the employee said. "I practically didn't sleep for three weeks."

It was almost as hard to watch one of Huang's tirades as it was to be its recipient. Several Nvidia employees described squirming in discomfort as Huang dissected one of their colleagues. Kirk told me Huang yelled at him only once, when he tried to intervene on someone else's behalf. "Jensen's up there torturing this guy, and I just couldn't stand it anymore, so I stepped in. Suddenly, I'm the target!" Kirk said. "It's kind of like on a battlefield, where the gun is shooting at something and you stand up and say, 'Hey, stop shooting!' Well, then the gun turns and starts shooting at you."

. . .

PRIEM HAD AN EQUAL stake in Nvidia, and the papers of incorporation had
been signed in his house. He had *invited* Huang to run his company; he
could have invited someone else. As Malachowsky observed, the implicit
agreement in their working relationship had always been that the founders
didn't step on one another's toes—in other words, that Huang stuck to business and Priem stuck to tech. So perhaps it was understandable that when
Huang violated that arrangement, Priem reacted as if betrayed.

But Priem had no leverage. Despite holding around a tenth of Nvidia's
shares, Priem had neither sought nor been offered a seat on the company's
board. Malachowsky didn't have a board seat either. Huang had convinced
both men that as the CEO, only *he* should be on the board—and Malachowsky and Priem, who disliked business and sales calls and board meetings so much that they hired someone else to be their boss, peaceably if
somewhat naively went along with this arrangement. With the board supporting the Microsoft strategy, Huang finally just overrode Priem unilater-
ally. What was Priem going to do?

There was one more painful conversation to be had. Sega had agreed to
pay Nvidia $1 million upon receipt of working prototypes of the NV2. In
the middle of 1996, Huang delivered these prototypes, the only chips of their
kind ever made. With great deference, Huang then informed Sega that
Nvidia would not help build the Dreamcast because the company was surrendering to Microsoft, but given that the delivery of the prototypes technically fulfilled the terms of the contract, he was hoping Sega would pay him
anyway, or Nvidia would go bankrupt. "They took it pretty well, considering," he said.

Once the Sega check cleared, Huang used it to buy the emulator. This
was the last of Nvidia's money. Already the triage had begun, with the company's bills organized in the order in which payment could be delayed. First,
vendors would get stiffed, then utilities, then finally employees. Whatever
else happened, Huang was determined to make payroll until the day the
lights were turned off.

Emulation was a wild gamble. If the transistors on the forthcoming NV3 chip were arranged in error, the busted real-world production run would ruin his company. But Huang was opening himself up to new frontiers of risk. For most of his life—in academics, in athletics, on the corporate ladder—Huang had been vying for first place. Now he could enjoy the blessings of coming in last. Staring at the long queue of competitors in front of him, Huang realized that being in last place was kind of fun—better than being in the middle, actually. A last-place firm could do whatever it wanted. It could take the shortcut no one else dared take.

Of course, for those tasked with working the emulator, last place was less exciting. Video games of the time rendered around thirty frames per second to generate the illusion of motion. The emulator inverted this ratio, rendering about one frame every thirty seconds, breaking the illusion and making game play impossible. Under the leadership of Diercks, engineers reviewed the demo reel in agonizing ultra-slow motion. The mind-numbing auditing process took weeks, but slowly the emulator relinquished its secrets. "We shrank what was typically a twelve-month development cycle into about three months," Diercks said.

When Diercks finished for the day, Kirk took over in the evening. He was often the last worker in the office, and late at night he vented tension with a plastic gun, beating Priem's high scores at the Sega shooter *Virtua Cop*. "Once you figure out the mechanics of a game, you can figure out how to beat it," Kirk said. "Annoying Curtis was just a bonus." As the emulation neared completion, tensions between Huang and Priem flared up once again. Priem recalled one argument in a hallway over technical concerns. "I told Jensen what he *should* do, and he started yelling at me about all the stuff he *had* to do," Priem said. "That's when I realized he was all alone."

ANOTHER NICE THING about coming in last was that you could move after everyone else had acted. To scare up publicity, Nvidia's competitors were sending preview cards to hardware reviewers at magazines and websites. Kirk finessed his contacts in the media to see what capabilities these competitors had managed to implement. Because Nvidia planned to skip both the prototype stage and the sneak previews, there was just enough time to clone these capabilities in the NV3.

The NV3 reached the tape-out stage in early 1997. When the blueprints were sent to Europe for production, Nvidia's three dozen employees celebrated with beers at a cheesesteak franchise in a nearby strip mall. At the restaurant, Jensen led a toast, but he later admitted he had no idea if the NV3 would actually work. "It was fifty-fifty," he told me, "but we were going out of business anyway." While the chips were being fabricated, Jensen approached Kirk with a permanent job offer and borderline-stupid equity compensation. Although it meant working for Curtis Priem, Kirk felt the offer was not one he could in due conscience decline. Huang gave him the title of chief scientist.

The finished NV3 chips arrived in late spring. The survival of the company depended on whether every one of the 3.5 million transistors in each case perfectly accorded with the emulation. Diercks mounted the cases into a circuit tester and played back the demo reel. It ran smoothly, flawlessly, creating the illusion of motion at thirty frames per second for the first time.

The NV3 was mostly a copycat chip, but it had a couple of innovations. First, it could transport 128 bits at a time from memory to processing, double the industry standard. Second, it had Swiss Army multifunctionality: it could accelerate video games, it could resize a spreadsheet, and it could play a DVD. To emphasize this breadth of capabilities, the NV3 was rebranded as the Real-Time Interactive Video and Animation accelerator, or Riva 128.

The chip was distributed to Nvidia's downstream vendors, which mounted it in circuit boards and sold it at Best Buy. By the time the boards arrived in stores, in August 1997, Nvidia was running on fumes. "Vapors," said Huang. "We had nothing left." Nvidia, having shipped no previews to the gaming press, now had to beg for media coverage. Fortunately, reviewers liked the product. "Rendering up to five million triangles per second, this is the best accelerator money can buy," one wrote. Nvidia sold a million Riva cards in the first four months.

Following the Riva's launch, Huang invested in emulators and gave up on physical prototypes. "To this day, we are the largest user of emulators in the world," Huang said. The bias in the semiconductor industry in favor of hard prototypes had seemed reasonable—imagine trying to sell a car that had never undergone a real-world crash test. Prototyping seemed like the practical approach that the "adult in the room" would take. But Jensen, who worked all hours and confiscated his employees' gaming systems, was learning that the adults in the room weren't taking enough risks. The NV1, a revolutionary design that followed best practices for industry workflow, had been a flop. The NV3, a wannabe product slapped together in a berserk, improvisational rush, had been a success. Sometimes, you had to gamble.

The experience was liberating for Huang. Desperation, not inspiration, was the mother of victory. Huang encouraged his employees to preserve the mindset they'd adopted during the Riva crunch, asking them to constantly behave as if the company was teetering on the verge of bankruptcy even when it was making massive profits. For years to come, Jensen opened staff presentations with the words "Our company is thirty days from going out of business." Even today at Nvidia, this sentence remains the corporate mantra.

FIVE

Going Parallel

The final argument between Jensen Huang and Curtis Priem lasted for the better part of a day in 1998. No one could remember its precipitating topic, only the long battle in the conference room with each man shouting at the other, then calming down and regaining his composure, only to rise in anger once again. As the hours dragged on, both men grew hoarse, and although Nvidia staff were by now inured to this dysfunction, employees sensed that the situation had reached a crisis and that divorce was imminent. In the end, Priem broke first, walking stiffly and quickly to his office and slamming its door, remaining there to sulk. When he came out, he refused to speak to Huang at all.

Priem exhausted all goodwill with his intransigence. With the NV1, he had been given a blank sheet of paper to design exactly what he wanted—but when he saw his remaindered product piling up on retail shelves, his ego never really recovered. Earlier that year, Huang had promoted David Kirk to codevelop Nvidia's technical architecture, making Priem's former subordinate his peer. Shortly thereafter, in what appeared like a childish attempt to retain influence, Priem had locked a number of employees out of the production database, preventing them from submitting their work.

Chris Malachowsky, who'd adjudicated such disputes in the past, finally gave up. At the advice of the board, Nvidia hired a mediator. "The mediator had previously worked with John Sculley and Steve Jobs at Apple, which ended up with Jobs getting fired," Priem told me. "She said Jensen and I were significantly worse." Nvidia management had by this point developed a saying: "Never let Curtis talk to investors, and never let Curtis talk to customers." As Priem later admitted, "Both of those things were true."

Following mediation, Priem was demoted twice more. He briefly became Kirk's technical adviser but found this role unsuitable. "He didn't want to work for me or any of the other people that he had previously had as direct reports," Kirk said. Eventually, Priem was reassigned to managing Nvidia's patent portfolio, a job that kept him out of the flow of daily decision-making. Kirk would go on to oversee close to a thousand people at Nvidia. Priem would never again manage more than four.

Despite the humiliation, Priem retained his Nvidia shares. Both Huang and Malachowsky still considered him a friend, and when Priem got married in 1999, a year after his second demotion in three years, Malachowsky served as his best man. Priem had seen the potential in the video game market, he had given the company its name, and he had sheltered the fledgling start-up in the bedrooms of his home. But from 1998 onward, he had little to do with Nvidia's success.

DAVID KIRK BECAME Huang's consigliere. Kirk had an academic background and didn't enjoy the high-pressure work culture of Silicon Valley; the first time I spoke with him, he called me from Hawaii, where he was wearing a shirt that read "Procrastination University" and drinking a glass of wine. He seemed like a popular professor whose course had a wait list, not an entrepreneur. But Kirk's gentle manner cloaked a pitiless attitude toward the competition—his absent father was an alcoholic, and he'd been a sickly child whose physical development had been limited by chronic bouts with strep throat. Perhaps these experiences had given him an edge. "Those people who say that winning doesn't matter?" Kirk asked, his voice rising with a delicate, unthreatening lilt. "They've never won anything."

Kirk and Huang each combined a commanding breadth of technical expertise with a talent for low cunning. As Nvidia succeeded, many of the other graphics start-ups failed. Huang, sensing opportunity, created a master list of competitors on the whiteboard in his office. Then, in consultation with Kirk, he identified the two or three best engineers at each company and began strategizing on how to poach them.

Kirk recalled showing off the Riva 128 to a competitor at a trade show. When the engineer saw what it could do, he gave up on the spot. "I hired him within a few days—and that killed that company, right?" Kirk said. "Because, you know, I removed its brain." Kirk, mild and professorial, had a predator's instincts. "We had all the geniuses from all the other start-ups, and as we were successful in overtaking more and more of these little companies, the remaining companies had a harder and harder time staying alive."

At Denny's in 1993, Huang had envisioned sharing a large market with many competitors. By 1998, he wanted the cake to himself. "There are still forty companies in this space," Huang told Kirk. "In five years, there will be three: a big one in charge, a laggard playing catch-up, and a small one trying to disrupt the other two." Huang intended to be the one in charge.

Although he seemed perfect for the role, Huang had not been a natural entrepreneur at the beginning. "Initially, there was a great deal he didn't understand," recalled Tench Coxe. But he could learn—he really liked to learn. Huang educated himself by reading every business book he could find. "If you go into his office today, it's totally abandoned; he never uses it," one employee told me. "But it's filled with stacks and stacks of business books."

From a literary perspective, or even a mass-market perspective, Huang would not be considered well-read. Popular books among the Silicon Valley set included Ayn Rand's *The Fountainhead*, Isaac Asimov's *Foundation* series, and Douglas Adams's *The Hitchhiker's Guide to the Galaxy*. Huang hadn't read any of them—in fact, Huang told me that he had never read a single work of science fiction at all and that the only novelist he could recall enjoying was Paulo Coelho.

But Huang's knowledge of business books was encyclopedic. Dwight Diercks recalled Huang arguing with another executive about how much Nvidia's products should cost. "The guy had an MBA, but he'd never read a book about pricing," Diercks said. "Jensen had read probably ten or fifteen." As the argument progressed, Huang halted the discussion and asked the MBA to name his three favorite books on pricing. The guy fumbled around for a bit, unable to name a single title. Huang listed out his three favorites, then told the executive he'd resume the discussion once he'd finished them.

Huang's best-loved business book was *The Innovator's Dilemma*, by the Harvard Business School professor Clayton Christensen. First published in 1997, the book popularized the term *disruptive innovation* to describe how incumbent firms lose out to start-up competitors. Although the word *disruption* has since grown meaningless through overuse, the source material is worth revisiting. In Christensen's model, small firms can chisel away at large ones by serving niche, marginally profitable customers that the market leaders have dismissed.

Christensen's disruptive innovators weren't necessarily high-tech—they included scrap-metal recyclers and manufacturers of hydraulic shovels. His canonical disruptor was Honda, which had initially had success in the early 1960s selling the off-road Honda Super Cub motorcycle to American teenagers. (The Beach Boys wrote a song about it.) The dirt-bike market was ignored by larger firms like General Motors because, setting all else equal, you'd rather sell a Cadillac to a businessman than a Super Cub to Brian Wilson. But in scorning the bikes, GM gave Honda the opportunity to thrive. With time, Honda leveraged its expertise to make a compact car and raided the US automotive industry from below.

Christensen's insight was that it was easier to go up the escalator of profitability than down. Going down meant voluntarily shrinking profit margins by deliberately making inferior goods, which tended to upset investors and made executives feel like they were jogging in place. This led Christensen to his most enduring and most counterintuitive recommendation:

"There are times when it is right *not* to listen to customers, right to invest in lower-performing products that result in *lower* margins, and right to pursue small, rather than substantial, markets." It was a point that the buzzword discussion of "disruption" in the popular press usually missed.

Huang became obsessed with Christensen, a towering but exceedingly kind Mormon bishop who'd played basketball at university. He read all of Christensen's books, assigned *The Innovator's Dilemma* to his executive staff, and later contracted Christensen as a consultant. It was Christensen who explained, really for the first time, why the big players like Sun and Silicon Graphics had declined to invest in PC video game hardware—not because they hated gamers but because the margins sucked compared to workstations and because, succeed or fail, gamers would not initially make a substantial difference in their bottom line.

But in ceding the PC gaming market to Nvidia, the workstation companies had made a fatal mistake, just as GM had by ignoring Honda decades earlier. Nvidia, like Honda, was today selling low-margin products to teenage boys, but if the analogy held, tomorrow they might overtake the business workstations of Sun Microsystems and SGI. Sometimes Jensen would even speak to his clustered executive staff about the possibility of disrupting Intel, then one of the most valuable firms on Earth.

In the meantime, Nvidia would survive in Intel's territory through a strategy of continuous tactical retreat. "To this day, we don't compete with Intel," Huang said in 2023, describing their Tom-and-Jerry relationship. "Whenever they come near us, I pick up my chips and run." The gospel of Christensen counseled Nvidia to sell offbeat products that Intel would not conceive of making to customers it would never want to serve. "Jensen would tell us, even back then, that Nvidia could someday be bigger than Intel," Kirk recalled. "It was just a question of strategy."

DEMAND FOR NVIDIA'S RIVA cards outpaced what its European vendor could produce, so Huang began to look for other suppliers. The world's best independent chip manufacturer, by unanimous consensus, was the Taiwan

Semiconductor Manufacturing Corporation, whose massive complex in Tainan fabricated a significant portion of the world's silicon. TSMC didn't design its own chips; it simply manufactured chips for merchants like Nvidia.

The rise of such independent "foundry" services was responsible for a surge in computing innovation, permitting upstarts to experiment with radical designs. TSMC filled orders with incomparable precision and efficiency, the product of an extraordinarily demanding work culture. Workers there described the hierarchical corporate structure as "militarized," and they followed a "996" shift schedule, working from nine a.m. to nine p.m. six days a week.

Huang had repeatedly failed to get TSMC's attention. After leaving a series of voicemails, he'd written a personal letter to Morris Chang, the company's CEO, and put it in the mail, not expecting to hear back. A short time later, Huang got a phone call. It was toward the end of the workday, and many of his employees had started gaming. "There was quite a bit of ruckus in the office, and I pick up the phone, and people are laughing and yelling outside," Huang said. "And I say, 'Hey, guys, hold it down, it's Morris!'" ("Actually, what he said was 'Everybody shut the fuck up—I've got Morris Chang on the phone,'" according to one veteran engineer.)

Chang had spent his life in silicon. Born in China in 1931, he had arrived in the United States from mainland China as a teenager. He had been a successful executive at Texas Instruments for many years, but in the 1970s he'd been passed over for the top spot—a snub that some observers attributed to anti-Asian racism. Chang then moved to Taiwan and took control of TSMC, which, under his leadership, grew to become the largest tech company in Asia.

Chang took an immediate liking to Huang. "They were a very small company—in fact, almost facing bankruptcy," Chang said. "And I was an older person running a much bigger company. But he was so open and forthcoming and candid in our conversation! Just completely at ease." Soon, the two had a contract in place.

Chang and Huang had much in common. Both were Chinese immigrants working in a technology sector that, at the time, was almost entirely managed by white men. Relative to their proportion of the American population, Asian employees were overrepresented at Silicon Valley tech firms—but they were suspiciously underrepresented in positions of senior management. (In 2010, Asian Americans accounted for only 0.3 percent of corporate management positions, despite making up more than 5 percent of the skilled US labor force. Management consultant Jane Hyun has termed this phenomenon the "bamboo ceiling.") When I asked Huang about the bamboo ceiling, he seemed dismissive—I got the sense that identity politics were not his thing. "I'm the only Chinese CEO of the time," he said, "but it never occurred to me. And it doesn't occur to me today."

TSMC was key to Nvidia's long-term success, but the relationship got off to a difficult start. In early 1998, TSMC misapplied a chemical process at the end of the manufacturing process, introducing short circuits onto many of the chips. The mistake nearly ruined Nvidia, which had invested most of its working capital in the production run. More than half the chips needed to be discarded—Nvidia managed to save itself only by selling equity to some of its circuit-board partners. "We were close to bankruptcy that time, too," Diercks said. "It's not just a saying."

But over time, Nvidia's relationship with TSMC proved to be of great mutual benefit to both companies, especially as Nvidia's chips grew increasingly complex. For Huang, there was also a personal benefit—the arrangement gave him a reason to go back to Taiwan, which he hadn't visited since he was a child. Huang's first visit to a TSMC factory in the late 1990s brought him inside one of the most sterile environments on the planet. Clad in booties, gloves, and head covering, he entered an air shower, where he stood on a sticky mat and raised his arms, his coveralls flapping in the wind as an overhead fan blew lint, hair, dust, skin, dirt, grime, and other assorted detritus away. From the shower he passed through an airlock to the manufacturing center, where a gentler, continuous blower provided ceaseless vertical airflow from the ceiling through the grated floor.

Here were the sacred light-printing machines etching identical patterns across mirrored silicon plates in slow, invisible cycles. No one dared lay a finger upon one—so delicate was the printing process that a single footstep might upset it. After weeks of layering, the wafers were diced into individual chips by a diamond-crusted wire saw, then sent downstream for packaging. In a good year, TSMC's factories might produce tens of millions of chips.

Leaving the facilities, Huang returned to the country's famous night markets to gorge on the Taiwanese food he'd enjoyed as a child. He spoke the language and could almost pass as a local, but he remembered little about the place—save for one painful instance he would never forget. When Huang had been about four, he'd gotten too close to a vendor at one of the stalls, and the vendor, who'd been cleaning a knife, accidentally caught Huang on the cheek, drawing blood. Now Huang had returned, still bearing the scar from his accident years before.

No matter how wealthy or famous he became, Huang never missed an opportunity to return to the night markets. He often treated himself to a simmering bowl of beef noodle soup, the country's national dish. It was a meal best enjoyed while sitting on a plastic stool on the side of a busy street. Picking through braised short rib and mustard greens with a pair of disposable chopsticks, Huang was already conceptualizing a transpacific marriage between his scrappy American team and the great maiden of Taiwan.

JOHN CARMACK ALWAYS FELT let down by the hardware designers. The lead programmer on *Doom* and *Quake* was a code surgeon who liked to sift around in the guts of the graphics chips that rendered his bestselling games. To light up a corridor in a space station, most programmers would rely on pre-supplied algorithms. Carmack's team, by hacking the address structure of the underlying variable, had built its own approach, one that required Carmack to conceptualize the flow of information at the level of individual zeroes and ones. One commenter called it "the most beautiful piece of code you've ever read."

Carmack was blond, thin, and not possessed of any unusual amount of social grace. His voice was nasal, his delivery was rapid, and he punctuated his technical comments with an occasional "mmmmm." When coding, he would shut out the world for weeks, retreating to darkened bedrooms and working for fourteen hours a day. He usually emerged with something unforgettable. *Quake*, his masterpiece, was the first bestselling three-dimensional shooter. The game used graphics acceleration to render polygonal monsters that the player could shoot with a nail gun. (Trent Reznor had provided the game's sound effects.) *Quake II*, the splatterfest follow-up, sent gamers to a distant planet to fight zombified cyborgs constructed from dismembered human body parts. (The game came out during my first year of college. It set me back years.)

Both games featured a "deathmatch" mode that allowed for multiplayer combat. Carmack's custom tinkering meant the *Quake* games ran more smoothly than anything else on the market, but simultaneously rendering dozens of participants in the same combat arena remained a challenge. "We wanted a faster-responding *Quake* so that our customers could reach out and frag somebody," Carmack told me. "Most of these hardware accelerators couldn't deliver that."

Huang saw an opportunity. At the Nvidia offices in Sunnyvale, the Sega consoles sat unused. *Quake* had conquered all, and the staff were so addicted that Huang had issued a ban on daytime deathmatch. PC manufacturers like Dell were bundling Nvidia's graphics accelerators directly into new computers, skipping the retail peripheral channel. "It was becoming clear that whoever rendered this specific game the best was going to win the graphics wars," Kirk said. Huang tasked his team with building a new chip just for Carmack—a custom Stratocaster for programming's Jimi Hendrix.

One thing Carmack wanted was multiple "pixel shaders." These were the algorithms that assigned colors to individual pixels in a three-dimensional scene. By running more than one shading algorithm at a time, one could first decorate the wall with a light source, then subsequently decorate it with blood spatter.

But twin shaders meant twice as much computation. 3dfx, the leader in the graphics-accelerator market, had solved the problem by putting two graphics chips on the same card. Kirk and his team had a more radical solution in mind. What if you split the pixel-shading into two datasets, then ran the same instruction set on each pipeline at the same time, all on a single chip? The method was suitable for graphics rendering, which tended to run the same types of calculations over and over and over again.

Huang was skeptical at first. This approach, known as "parallel computing," had been tried before by vendors of expensive supercomputers. "Silicon Valley, it's littered with corpses of previous parallel-computing platform companies," he said. "Not one parallel-computing company has ever been created with the exception of us—not one, zero." But then Huang began to reason from first principles. Carmack wouldn't stop at two separate pixel pipelines, he surmised. As the shooting games grew in complexity, he'd always want more. Imagine a scene with many sources of illumination: an arena full of lights, with multiple guns firing and a spaceship crashing in the distance, on a world lit by twin suns. By dedicating a chip to each light source, 3dfx would eventually run out of real estate on the circuit board. The only way to meet Carmack's *future* needs was to multiply pipelines on a single silicon square.

Before committing, though, Huang had to do his homework. He had to understand why the approach had failed so many times. Seymour Cray's powerful parallel supercomputers were floundering, with customers complaining about their high costs and complexity. Larry Ellison, the founder of Oracle, had invested millions in the parallel start-up nCube; by the late 1990s, it was failing too. The issue was that programming in parallel was difficult—acting on two or more data streams at once required swapping between multiple memory banks, and the learning curve was steep. This left the parallel-computing companies vulnerable to Intel.

Intel's chips used the standard serial approach, doing one calculation at a time. But their power grew exponentially, doubling every eighteen months or so, following a prediction first made in 1965 by former Intel CEO Gordon Moore—a prediction that had been validated so many times it was known as "Moore's Law." Outside of specialized technical domains like weather prediction and high-energy physics, Moore's Law guaranteed that one processor—the all-consuming CPU—was enough to meet the needs of even the most demanding users. "If you had a piece of software and you needed it to run faster, you had a choice," parallel-computing specialist Bill Dally told me. "You could move it to a parallel computer and rewrite a million lines of software. Or you could just wait for the CPU to get twice as fast in two years."

Moore's Law had already consumed the peripheral circuit-board market segment in which Nvidia originally operated. As first conceived, in 1993, the 3D graphics accelerator would be one of many slot-in add-on cards, alongside sound cards, networking cards, printer cards, et cetera. But by the late 1990s, Intel had folded sound, networking, and printing functionality into the motherboard.

Only the 3D graphics cards remained, the lone survivors of a decimated ecosystem. They held out by being hungry; they absorbed all available computing capacity and asked for more. The other functions of the multimedia PC were bounded—once you were processing audio at equivalent quality to a compact disc, you didn't need more computing power. With 3D graphics, however, demand never stopped. With 3D graphics, you weren't finished until you were living inside the Matrix. "That was something Intel missed, just how much further the graphics firms had to run," Hans Mosesmann said. "Demand for processing power in that space was basically infinite." The CPU would not catch up to 3D rendering, not now, not ever. Twice as fast was nowhere good enough.

THE RIVA TNT LAUNCHED in June 1998. The "TNT" stood for "twin texels," dual pixel-rendering pipelines governed by a sophisticated switching mechanism. The delighted Carmack embraced his Stratocaster—he called it "the perfect card." He tailored *Quake III: Arena* specifically for the twin-pipeline architecture and advised his legion of admirers that *Quake* games were best played on Nvidia hardware. Carmack also saw what Huang had prophesied: that gaming would give Nvidia a base to disrupt the more profitable workstation market. "The TNT was really better, in many cases, than a $10,000 computer," Carmack said.

He was not the only programmer to notice. Kirk, in addition to skimming the best employees from the failing start-ups, was now poaching employees from Silicon Graphics. One of them was Dan Vivoli, a former engineer who'd switched roles into marketing. Vivoli used the TNT to establish Nvidia as a brand. Following Carmack's endorsement, customers began to fetishize Nvidia products, attracting Jensen's attention. The pile of reading material in his office soon contained numerous textbooks on marketing.

Nvidia never directly advertised the TNT's parallel capabilities to customers—why confuse them? Instead, it leveraged the dream of somehow living *inside* the computer. This fantasy had a strange and powerful allure. The concept of the "Matrix"—a shared-computing hallucination— had originated not with the 1999 movie but with William Gibson's 1984 novel *Neuromancer*. In a 2011 interview with *The Paris Review*, Gibson recalled his inspiration:

> I remember walking past a video arcade, which was a new sort of business at that time, and seeing kids playing those old-fashioned console-style plywood video games. The games had a very primitive graphic representation of space and perspective. Some of them didn't even have perspective but were yearning toward perspective and dimensionality. Even in this very primitive form, the kids who were playing them were so physically involved, it seemed to me that what they wanted was to be inside the games.

Nvidia didn't have a mission statement (Huang didn't believe in them), but Gibson's observation might have served as one. The goal was immersion, total immersion, in digital worlds rendered with such pointillist detail that they made reality fall away. What Gibson had intuited from body language, Huang was rediscovering from deductive reasoning. Nvidia's work wasn't finished until the gamers lived inside the game.

But in pursuing this goal, Nvidia engineers were playing a far more dangerous game than even they realized—for inside the TNT was a secret, a lurking, demonic secret buried so deep in the architecture of the silicon that neither Huang nor Kirk nor Carmack nor Vivoli nor anyone else in the world suspected that it was there. If you popped the cover off that TNT chip and inspected the naked circuitry with a microscope, you would find a change not just in the arrangement of transistors but a change to all computers, and perhaps to all of humanity, forever. Inside that tiny chip was a secret that would change the world.

SIX

Jellyfish

The proposition gamblers gathered around the backgammon board in the elegant hotel room at the Bristol Suites in Dallas, Texas, in 1997. The match before them was unlike any other they had seen. Representing humanity were Nack Ballard and Mike Senkiewicz, two of the best players alive. Acting as an agent for the machines was Malcolm Davis, betting heavily against the human race and playing moves dictated by the computer at his side.

A few months earlier, Garry Kasparov had lost to the IBM chess computer Deep Blue, in a match that drew interest from around the world. ("Swift and Slashing, Computer Topples Kasparov," read the headline in *The New York Times*, accompanied by a photograph of the great Russian grand master with his face buried in his hands.) The equivalent backgammon competition in Dallas drew no such attention, save for the gamblers wandering in and out of the room. These men spent their lives indulging their obsessions with abstract games of strategy. They played Go, and poker, and Scrabble, and contract bridge, and chess, often at an elite level. They laughed and chattered and exchanged wads of cash after nearly every throw of the dice. The men were not always well-dressed or generally very physically fit, and outside of specialist circles their names were hardly known. But it was this unheralded competition in Dallas, not Kasparov's defeat in New York City, that marked the dawn of the new machine age.

Ballard was the best of them. He was a jolly, portly man with a wide face and sideburns who studied backgammon for six hours a day and had been ranked number one in the world several times. With a muted clatter, he shook the dice in the leather cup, then tossed them onto the board. Kasparov had been visibly unsettled by Deep Blue, but Ballard had a Zen-like focus on the position at hand. He pondered his move in silence, then moved two checkers on the board.

When he was finished, Davis rolled his own dice, then consulted the computer on the updated position. Davis was also a backgammon master, but by 1997 he was certain that software was surpassing humans at the game. He'd backed this assertion by offering to play as the computer's agent against any takers for $200 a point. Backgammon was a streaky affair, and if Davis's assessment of the computer's abilities were incorrect, it might cost him $100,000 or more. But he had confidence in his machine, which ran a radically different kind of artificial-intelligence software than any that had come before.

The program was called "Jellyfish." What made Jellyfish special was that it was a "neural net" whose structure was inspired by the biological brain. Rather than executing code written by human programmers, Jellyfish made decisions by passing information to a grid of artificial neurons whose synapses were represented in the computer as an enormous matrix of numbers, or "weights." The grid evaluated the position and passed an answer back through this synthetic nervous system.

A clunky dialogue box popped up with Jellyfish's recommendation. Davis moved the checkers on the board. Occasionally, the program recommended a controversial move, sparking disagreement among the spectators and prompting a flurry of side bets. As the chatter continued, Ballard rolled the dice again and resumed his reverie over the board.

. . .

THE DALLAS BACKGAMMON match drew no more interest from the AI community than it did from the press. In 1997 mainstream computer scientists regarded neural nets as little more than toys. They were first conceived of as "nervous nets" in the 1940s, when early experimenters physically recreated the neurons and synapses of the brain using complex electromechanical hardware. These giant contraptions absorbed lots of power and money while producing little of use until, in 1969, the influential MIT researcher Marvin Minsky demonstrated that a single layer of neurons was unable to perform even one of the simplest logic operations. Funding evaporated, and most of the machines were dismantled.

AI suffered many false starts in the years that followed and developed a reputation as a career graveyard. Early progress with "symbolic" AI sputtered out in the first AI winter, in 1974. In the 1980s, revived interest in "expert systems" AI created a brief stock market bubble that popped following the 1987 crash. The governments of Japan, the United Kingdom, and the United States all launched ambitious AI initiatives, spending billions in taxpayer funds on grand strategies for research. In each case, independent analysts concluded that the money was mostly squandered.

Meanwhile, throughout the 1970s and 1980s a coterie of renegade computer scientists continued to pursue research on neural nets, believing that the rickety machinery of yore might be re-created with software and that multiple layers of neurons might overcome limitations that a single layer could not. Most AI researchers regarded these mavericks as misguided, or possibly insane, but in 1986 cognitive psychologist David Rumelhart, working with computer scientists Geoffrey Hinton and Ronald Williams at UC–San Diego, published an elegant mathematical procedure for training multilayer neural nets called "backpropagation."* The method allowed re-

---

*Backpropagation uses multivariable calculus and linear algebra to attribute new findings across a stack of layered grids. Backpropagation accomplishes this by first determining the degree to which the output of the existing neural net is in error. This error value is then used

searchers to fine-tune the computer's artificial neurons in response to new information, in the same way that the human brain formed new synaptic connections when a task was learned.

Backpropagation revived the dormant neural-net community, allowing computers to function in an entirely new way. Backpropagation allowed for computer software that didn't need to be explicitly programmed. Backpropagation allowed computer systems to make their own rules. Backpropagation allowed computer systems to *evolve*.

In the late 1980s, the researcher Gerald Tesauro, also working at IBM, opted out of the company's popular chess research group to conquer the lowly game of backgammon. Lacking the cachet of chess or the mystique of poker, the game was essentially a race in which players tried to hit one another's checkers while moving in opposite directions around a twenty-four-point board, subject to the rolls of two six-sided dice. The unpredictability made the game attractive to gamblers, but for Tesauro, backgammon had a different appeal. By simulating dice rolls, he could rapidly generate hundreds of thousands of artificial backgammon games—and this was training data from which a neural net might learn.

Tesauro worked on this niche project almost entirely by himself; as with neural nets, few AI researchers took backgammon seriously. He first trained his neural nets to mimic the best human players, but this approach produced little of value. Around 1990, Tesauro decided to try a different approach. He

---

to compute a collection of partial derivatives known as the "gradient," essentially attempting to determine which neurons have it most "wrong." Once the gradient is determined, backpropagation tweaks the neurons in the opposite direction. The entire process is then repeated any number of times.

The backpropagation technique was first discovered in 1970 by the Finnish mathematician Seppo Linnainmaa, although Linnainmaa did not explicitly apply it to neural networks. In 1974 American computer scientist Paul Werbos independently rediscovered backpropagation and presented the technique to Marvin Minsky at MIT as a work-around for the problems outlined in Minsky's book *Perceptrons*. But Minsky, according to Werbos's account, all but threw him out of his office and discouraged him from using the technique. (Werbos later theorized that Minsky was upset he hadn't discovered backpropagation himself.) In 1986 Rumelhart, Williams, and Hinton reintroduced backpropagation as a method for neural-network training, bringing the technique to widespread attention.

stripped all strategic advice about the game of backgammon out of the neural net, leaving only the rules and an initial set of randomly weighted neurons. Then he had the computer play hundreds of thousands of games *against itself*.

The technique was known as "reinforcement learning," and Tesauro was the first person ever to get it to work. At first the program was hopeless and moved the checkers around aimlessly. After a few thousand games, though, the neural net had learned that leaving one checker alone was bad but that stacking two checkers together was good—this brought it to the level of a competent beginner. After tens of thousands of games, the neural net was employing more advanced concepts, like using multiple stacks of checkers to build a wall. After two hundred thousand games, the neural net, which Tesauro called TD-Gammon, was playing at a strong intermediate level. Over the next few years, Tesauro exposed TD-Gammon to millions of simulated games, and by 1995, TD-Gammon was employing strategies never before seen by humans. The neural net was no longer just learning. It was innovating.

Unencumbered by received wisdom, TD-Gammon discovered a new approach to backgammon. It determined that human players were risking too much to establish an advantage up front and that conservative openings were better. At the same time, it would often forgo a guaranteed win in the endgame in a greedy attempt to double its score, a strategy most human players considered reckless. In the middlegame, TD-Gammon made a variety of more subtle moves that human experts understood only after deep introspection. In 1995 backgammon instructor Kit Woolsey wrote to Tesauro with praise after playing against his creation. He noted that chess computers excelled in tactical positions where a precise sequence of moves could be calculated, but struggled with more abstract, strategic positions. For TD-Gammon, it was just the opposite: it seemed to have developed an "intuition" about how to play. "Instead of a dumb machine which can calculate things much faster than humans such as the chess playing computers, you have built a smart machine which learns from experience pretty much the same way humans do," Woolsey wrote.*

But IBM failed to commercialize Tesauro's project—why would a vendor of business servers sell commercial backgammon software to a few hundred customers? Why, indeed.

This adorable nook in the marketplace was filled in 1994 by the Norwegian researcher Fredrik Dahl. Dahl was an unusual man who enjoyed backgammon, chess, simulated tank battles, jiu-jitsu, and foraging in the woods for edible fungi. He worked for Norway's defense establishment, where he simulated outcomes from a hypothetical Soviet invasion. His work drew inspiration from the 1983 movie *WarGames*, starring Matthew Broderick. In that movie, an AI attempts to start a nuclear war.

Dahl assured me that this was not his own ambition, but he did show a keen interest in military affairs—after the Soviet Union collapsed, funding for Dahl's research was eliminated. "It was a terrible time," he said. (He was kidding, I think.) For his doctoral thesis, Dahl had built a neural net that modeled combat outcomes by having the computer fight millions of simulated battles against itself. This framework was easily ported to backgammon, and Dahl soon surpassed Tesauro's results.

In 1994 Dahl unveiled Jellyfish, the first neural net ever sold to the public. Jellyfish had trained on many millions of backgammon games, but despite this intensive computational process, the finished product was small enough to fit on a 3.5-inch floppy disk, which Dahl sold via his primitive website. In this way an early distinction was established between the cumbersome training stage of AI, which was how the computer learned, and the inference stage, which was how the computer deployed its knowledge. The latter was far less expensive—a parallel might be drawn between the three-pound human brain, which handles inference, and the hundreds of millions of years of evolutionary conditioning that provided its training.

---

* quotations taken from an excerpt of a letter from Woolsey to Tesauro, published in the March 1995 edition of *Communications of the ACM*.

Dahl was attuned to these biological analogies. He had selected the name "Jellyfish" as an homage to the ancient aquatic cnidarian whose "nerve net" controlled its systems of stimulus and response. His program "had only about a hundred brain cells, which I figured was about on par with the jellyfish," he said. That was the power of neural structures: all it took to conquer backgammon, or survive for half a billion years in a dangerous marine ecosystem, or maybe even fend off the Soviets, was a hundred little cells.

TO PROVIDE A PROPER statistical sample, Ballard and Senkiewicz had each agreed to play three hundred games apiece against Jellyfish. Ballard, who'd once played for eighty-four hours in a row, was used to such backgammon marathons and managed to maintain his focus. He beat the computer by fifty-eight games, pocketing $11,600. But Senkiewicz lost a nearly equivalent amount, Davis broke even, and the competition was declared a tie. Ballard was happy with his individual win—but later analysis showed he'd gotten lucky with his dice rolls, and he knew his time had come. Never again would a human be so foolhardy as to challenge a backgammon program for money.

News of the Jellyfish match spread rapidly throughout the clannish backgammon community. Deep Blue was an expensive supercomputer whose brute-force approach was not replicable by humans, and thus it did not fundamentally change the expert approach to chess. (In fact, Deep Blue was dismantled after its 1997 victory.) Jellyfish, by contrast, was affordable software that could run on any Windows machine, and it revolutionized the game. Consulting Jellyfish on his home computer, the instructor Kit Woolsey published *New Ideas in Backgammon*, a collection of positions where the neural net's opinion diverged sharply from human intuition. It soon became clear the computer was always right. In time, analysts learned to evaluate the skill of a human player not by how many games he won or lost but simply by how much his play differed from this ideal computer result.

Jellyfish was the first neural net to surpass humans at any game. Dahl next turned his attention to poker. Using reinforcement learning techniques, he soon built—or perhaps the better word is *evolved*—a neural net capable of beating anyone in the world at the two-player, "heads-up," limit Texas Hold'em variant. Dahl licensed this neural net to a slot-machine manufacturer that installed the poker bot at casinos on the Vegas strip, offering to play all takers for real money. Once again, no one could get the better of the machine.

But the revolution stopped there. Although he made a fair amount of money from the slots operation, when Dahl attempted to build them a similar program for *no*-limit hold'em, he ran into problems. One could bet any amount at no-limit, and the synthetic dataset was larger than the closed universes he'd constructed for limit poker and backgammon. Dahl's no-limit neural net struggled to learn from this overwhelming amount of data. "It made reasonable plays, but it would never quite do what I was hoping," he said.

Dahl worked on this problem for many years. The obstacle was that he had almost no idea how his poker bot actually worked. The structure of its neural net was no easier to interpret than the nervous system of an invertebrate, and trying to tease out game-playing strategies by examining the individual weights of the grid was like trying to unravel consciousness by looking at brain cells through a microscope.

This was the criticism of neural nets and the thing that so biased the academic community against them. Once a neural net hit a training plateau—and they almost always did—there was rarely an obvious way to make it better. Classical programming was orderly and logical, but tinkering with neural nets required a different cast of mind. Dahl compared it to running a biology experiment: outcomes were unpredictable, and altering seemingly minor variables could have all manner of unanticipated results. Dahl tried everything he could think of to improve his no-limit poker bot. He fiddled with its evaluation function, he futzed with his computer's memory, he replaced the activation trigger for the neurons, he even synthesized a simpler data universe for the bot to explore—but he never got it to play at an expert level.

Eventually, Dahl, like so many neural-net researchers before him, gave up. He put the poker bot to the side and got a job analyzing medical data with conventional techniques. Many critics of neural nets were similarly disillusioned apostates who'd enjoyed early success with the technology before spending years posting subpar results. Dahl never quite joined the ranks of disbelievers, but his faith was sorely tested. "I dismissed it," said the man who sold the public its first neural net. "I dismissed it because I just didn't have the data." He saw no solution, and he tried everything. He just could not imagine what might make neural nets succeed.

SEVEN

Deathmatch

Johnathan Wendel aimed his weapon at the pile of ammunition and waited. Playing under the screen name "fatal1ty," Wendel was one of the first professional gamers, and by 1999 he was looking to be the best. He had a long string of tournament wins in *Quake III: Arena* and would often score flawless victories—his strength was his ability to get inside his opponents' heads. He'd noticed that this opponent seemed a little too fond of ammunition, and he was preparing to spring a trap.

Most pro gamers were skinny nerds, but Wendel was a muscular athlete who played ice hockey, tennis, and golf. With pale blue eyes, sandy-blond hair, and a broad, masculine face, he looked like a fraternity jock from an eighties comedy. Wendel had discovered his talent for competitive *Quake* when he was fifteen, beating a hundred college kids in a tournament in Wichita, Kansas, in 1996. He then dropped out of college to play video games as a job. "The thing is, if you win just one tournament, you'll be forgotten, right?" Wendel said, referencing his hero Tiger Woods. "These people will *forget* me if I don't win more."

Wendel focused on *Quake* with the demented competitiveness of a professional athlete. He conducted deathmatch sparring sessions eight to twelve hours per day and broke up with his girlfriend so he could practice more. He won dozens of tournaments and was the number-one earner in competitive gaming for seven straight years. Once, after winning a tournament in Texas, he stripped off his headphones, pumped his fist, and let off a triumphant whoop, as his bespectacled opponent shrank back into his zippered hoodie. Wendel, much larger and wearing an NFL windbreaker and cargo pants, looked like he might give the guy a wedgie.

Wendel used drills to hone his twitch-shot instinct. He would sit in front of his screen with his finger on a mouse; then, when the screen turned green, he clicked the mouse as fast as he could. With practice, he was able to get his response time down to 140 milliseconds. In between training sessions on the computer, Wendel would run for miles, which he believed helped his reflexes. Fond of sports metaphors, he compared himself to a Formula One driver slamming on the accelerator at the start of the race.

Through his headphones, Wendel heard his opponent's footsteps approaching the ammunition pile. Wendel's training kicked in, and he set his finger lightly on the button of the mouse. The trick was to start shooting just *before* the opponent appeared. At the critical moment, Wendel pressed the button, and time slowed down.

Wendel used an Nvidia TNT2 to render the game. Commodity processors might render *Quake III* at twenty to thirty frames per second. Nvidia's parallel-processing technology could push that to sixty to seventy frames. This critical improvement doubled from five to ten the number of frames in Wendel's 140-millisecond reaction window. That was the edge he needed.

Wendel began firing a frame or two before he could see the guy. Thirty milliseconds—three one-hundredths of a second—ticked by. Then the enemy stepped into Wendel's line of fire. The Nvidia processor updated. One frame of damage, and the processor updated again. Another frame of damage, and another, and with each frame the processor ran about two hundred million individual calculations. Through his headphones, Wendel heard satisfying grunts of pain until the final frame, when the opponent collapsed in a pulp—and with that, "fatal1ty" had tallied another kill.

Wendel compared his relationship with Nvidia to Michael Jordan's relationship with Nike. The company supplied him with free hardware, and in return he advertised their capabilities whenever he could. Wendel knew little about the parallel-processing technology that made the cards run; when I asked him in 2024 about the technology, he responded with a shrug. All he knew was that nothing rendered deathmatch like the TNT2. "The frame rate on that thing was insane," Wendel said. He upgraded his card with every cycle, and soon every pro gamer was doing the same.

WALL STREET LOVED IT. Nvidia shipped new cards on a six-month cycle, twice as fast as any other manufacturer. The company introduced a new product line for the back-to-school cycle each fall, then updated that product in the spring. Demand accelerated when flat-screen monitors arrived, and within a few years graphics accelerators were standard on most PCs. In early 1999, fewer than six years after its founding, Nvidia went public with a $600 million valuation. Sequoia, which had initially valued Nvidia at $6 million, tallied a hundred-bagger, subsidizing the losses from countless other speculative investments. The stock, priced at $12 on the NASDAQ under the ticker symbol NVDA, immediately doubled; by the end of the year, it had hit $60. Corporate filings showed that Priem, Malachowsky, and Huang each owned more than three million shares.

Huang was now a centimillionaire, but his newfound wealth did not distract from his objective of crushing and absorbing the competition until only his firm remained. Dwight Diercks recalled no parties, no champagne, no sense of relief, not even congratulations from the boss. He shared with me an email he had saved from Huang. "The TNT2 team needs to do whatever it takes to get over the finish line," Huang had written. The email continued in a tone of panicked desperation, with Huang complaining about missed deadlines and fretting over ascendant competitors. Huang's life would be transformed by the influx of wealth from Nvidia's new shareholders, but he evinced no sense of victory or pride—none whatsoever. "Get it done," Huang ended tersely.

Diercks shook his head in amazement. "He wrote that the day after the IPO," he said.

COMPETITORS ATI AND S3 were mentioned in the email, but Nvidia's nemesis was 3dfx. Its Voodoo cards had been the leading graphics accelerators for the past two years. In late 1999, Huang debuted the Voodoo killer. It was called the GeForce, short for "Geometry Force." Powered by the NV10, it could render ten million triangles per second and alter the colors of pixels in the 3D scene to match the placement of movable light sources. Unifying "transformation and lighting" in a single platform was a long-sought achievement, and Nvidia wanted to crow about it. "Basically, they could now do for $2 what a workstation could do for $2,000," Jon Peddie said.

Huang turned to Dan Vivoli, the marketer he'd conscripted from Silicon Graphics. Vivoli was a clever guy who viewed a limited budget as an opportunity. He had noticed that in making purchasing decisions, gamers relied on a half-dozen independent hardware reviewers. Vivoli reached out to the reviewers, informing them that the GeForce was the world's first "graphics-processing unit," or "GPU." Vivoli had, in fact, made this term up, but the reviewers began grouping products in the category. Soon, graphics accelerators were universally known as GPUs. "We invented the category so we could be the leader in it," Vivoli said.

Engineers at 3dfx bristled at Nvidia's gamesmanship. "There were situations where Nvidia played a few tricks in benchmarking," Peddie said. "So yeah, they out-marketed them. But they also out-engineered them! They just ran their company better." The GeForce could juggle four rendering pipelines on a single chip. A prototype for 3dfx's more expensive Voodoo 4 employed four chips and still couldn't do the same work. Nvidia's frenzied six-month shipping cycle left the perfectionists at 3dfx at a disadvantage. At one point, one of 3dfx's founders publicly speculated about declaring a truce between the two companies so that technical standards could be established before the next generation of products shipped. "That's when I knew we had him," Kirk said. "We were in a death struggle with 3dfx, and one of us had to die."

Kirk's brain-extraction experiments were another source of continuing discord. As engineers defected to Nvidia, they often brought with them proprietary ideas. This created legal problems—between 1996 and 1999, S3, Silicon Graphics, and 3dfx all filed patent-infringement lawsuits against Nvidia, and a fourth competitor, Matrox, filed a suit alleging that Nvidia had encouraged its employees to violate confidentiality agreements. The other three lawsuits were settled out of court, but 3dfx did not go to arbitration—the failing company instead staked its survival on victory at trial. In August 2000, during a disastrous earnings call, 3dfx CEO Alex Leupp told investors that 3dfx was on pace to lose more than $100 million in a single quarter. An hour later, Nvidia announced it was countersuing 3dfx, making rather questionable patent-infringement claims of its own. Many found the timing of the lawsuit cruel; some speculated that Huang had deliberately filed a nuisance lawsuit that he knew he would not win, just to run up cash-poor 3dfx's legal bills.

A month later, the judge in the case issued a preliminary ruling in 3dfx's favor while rejecting Nvidia's countersuit completely. 3dfx scrambled to collect, but Nvidia, through shrewd legal maneuvering, was able to stall the payout. Desperate, Leupp tried to sell 3dfx to Intel, offering the favorable ruling against Nvidia as the only thing of value that it owned. But Intel wanted no portion of this petty squabble, and neither did anyone else. With the money running out and its product floundering, 3dfx was forced to admit defeat and offer itself to Nvidia.

Huang had won. His reward was an incoming brigade of new employees who hated him. Court filings later revealed that, inside 3dfx, Huang was referred to as "Darth Vader." ("Actually, they called him worse than that," Peddie said. "I can tell you, some of the other things they called him were not very polite.") The rumors about Huang by this point were almost mythologically sinister: he poached employees; he lifted ideas; he spun the reviewers; he kicked his fallen competitors in the teeth. Mostly, though, they hated Huang because he had whipped their collective corporate ass. "Nvidia made enemies all along the way as they rose to power, including with partners and suppliers," Peddie said. "Jensen, you could say he's a personal friend of mine—but he was ruthless."

PROGRAMMER BEN GARLICK got his notice on a Friday afternoon in December, along with the rest of the 3dfx Austin office. The workstations locked everyone out, and security escorted the employees out of the building, pausing to inspect backpacks and purses. The staffers loitered around the parking lot until a human resources manager summoned them to attention and directed them to reconvene in the warehouse across the street. Office complexes in Texas were not designed with pedestrians in mind, and so began an undignified procession of business-casual hostages who first marched into a drainage ditch, then continued in a disorderly scramble across an unmarked frontage road, and finally arrived at a warehouse full of unsold and, indeed, unsellable graphics hardware. Here the employees were informed that, effective immediately, 3dfx was laying them all off. "That was a fun day," Garlick said.

There was consolation for the lucky ones, however. Nvidia had declined to purchase the entirety of 3dfx but had offered to buy specific assets for $70 million. Leupp had accepted, and the lawsuit was dropped. Internal documents later revealed that Huang valued 3dfx's best engineers at $1 million per head. This estimate reflected both their worth to Nvidia—and the value of keeping them away from Nvidia's rivals. At the warehouse, the laid-off employees were told to go home for the weekend and wait by the phone for a potential job offer from Huang.

Out of about five hundred or so candidates, Huang, in consultation with Kirk, had drawn up a list of 120 3dfx employees whom Nvidia wanted to keep. These employees were distrustful of Huang. Over the weekend, whispers circulated that Nvidia was a sweatshop and that Huang was a tyrant who screamed at employees at the top of his voice.

Some contended that there was no price at which they would work for such a man. Garlick was more realistic. Christmas was coming, and he needed a job.

He was among the first to receive an offer. Garlick was a skilled programmer, though a modest one. (I asked him if his contributions were worth $1 million. "Something like that," he said.) He returned to the warehouse the following Monday, and Huang, in person, presented him with a 20 percent raise, benefits, and stock options. Garlick took the job and remained at Nvidia for the next seventeen years. "My theory is that Jensen is a good person at heart who had to be ruthless," Garlick said. "As opposed to some other CEOs, who were ruthless at heart and trying to pretend to be good people." Such were Huang's charms that, out of the 120 employees he recruited, 106 joined the dark side.

Garlick was given access to Nvidia's code base. He was appalled at what he saw. "Basically, it was cancer," he said. "Y'know, cancer cells aren't efficient. They just mutate, grow, and expand." At 3dfx, Garlick had taken pride in the elegance of his programming, developing orderly systems with lucid commenting, allowing other programmers to easily maintain and improve his work. "In the time we spent making it clean, we went out of business," he said. Nvidia's approach was slapdash, with blocks of code written during some delirious midnight crunch serving as the foundation for critical systems. "What a shit show! The code was crap, the tool-chain was a mess, and the thing was, they didn't give a shit!" Garlick said. "They didn't give a shit about anything but the next tape-out."

In this manner, Nvidia had accrued a great deal of "tech debt," repeatedly taking shortcuts that led over time to less maintainable code and creating problems for programmers later on. But as Garlick acclimated to these shortcuts, he came to see the value of the Nvidia approach. "There was a bizarre brilliance to it all: just iterate, iterate, iterate, execute, execute, execute," he said. "The way I see it now, tech debt is the battle scar of the survivor."

. . .

WITH THE NEW HIRES, Nvidia had more than six hundred employees, up from just thirty-five four years earlier. The company relocated to a new headquarters down the road in Santa Clara, leasing a complex of curved, multistory, glass-and-steel buildings joined by skyways, festooned with sculpture, surrounded by parking, adjacent to the expressway, and spread across eleven acres of land. The new offices didn't smell like takeout food. They didn't smell like anything. Modernist respectability, with its boring and predictable implications, had arrived.

The trappings of the suburban office park—the cubicle farms, the endless lines of cars, the dreadful chain restaurants—were memorably satirized in Mike Judge's 1999 movie *Office Space*. Judge had based the movie on his time working at one of Nvidia's competitors, a graphics-card start-up located just a couple miles down the road. Judge had hated this work environment, but the Nvidians I talked to never mentioned boredom or a sense of missed opportunity. They'd made the decision to spend much of their life in the cubicles, and the corporate world suited them just fine. Huang did his part by relentlessly hunting for bureaucratic idiocies to eliminate. The main character in *Office Space* is reminded by multiple bosses to use the correct cover sheet for his TPS reports. Real-world software engineers often did file such "test procedure specification" paperwork, but if Huang were ever to discover that one of his managers was wasting precious engineering time with concerns about cover sheets, I suspect he would have dragged him to the center of the cubicle pit and crucified him.

Many new hires at Nvidia, used to working for gaming companies, showed up expecting a looser culture. "At 3dfx, the motto was 'Work hard, play hard,'" one former employee said. "At Nvidia, it was more just 'Work hard.'" Long hours were the default, and the six-month release cycle created relentless pressure. "The end result was almost nonstop deadlines and a perpetual sense of being behind schedule," another employee recalled.

Others appreciated Nvidia's professionalism. "At least you knew the place was going to stay in business," one veteran said. Gaming companies rarely had a dress code, and some coders indulged in performative slobbishness. Karen Huaulme, another 3dfx hire, recalled getting lost in a suburban Dallas office complex looking for the headquarters of iD Software, the maker of *Quake*. She resolved her problem by following the worst-dressed person she could find, a pasty young man with long stringy hair in flip-flops and a tattered T-shirt. He led her straight to iD's front door.

No one ever wore flip-flops to the office at Nvidia. Huaulme also told me that at past firms her male colleagues would sometimes aggressively question her credentials; at other times, they would assume a kind of handsy overfamiliarity. There were few female employees in Nvidia, especially in those days, but Huaulme found it a place of relative safety. "I felt protected from that sort of thing at Nvidia," she said.

Kirk ran many of the hiring interviews. Years earlier, at his own start-up, he'd been forced to lay off a hundred engineers, an experience so painful that days later he himself had quit. Resolved never to repeat this experience, Kirk determined that the best way to avoid layoffs was to be selective about who he hired. The initial interview format at Nvidia consisted of several rounds of interviews, followed by a consensus hiring decision. But the technical staff, reluctant to make people squirm, stuck to standard interview bullshit: "Recall a time you overcame adversity," "What's your greatest weakness?," "Why are manhole covers round?"

Kirk, frustrated, felt that his staff were wasting time. He knew how Jensen would respond: by gathering the technical staff in a conference room and screaming at them. Like Diercks, Kirk believed that Huang's outbursts were purposeful. "Yelling at people was part of this motivational strategy," Kirk said. "You might think he's just mad, but I think it was premeditated. And it works! It annoys people, but it does work." The audience, Kirk believed, was crucial: "He wants everybody to benefit. He would never just yell at some guy in the hall. When he's torturing people, he's forcing them to learn a lesson—and they certainly would never forget it."

Realizing that his employees didn't know how to hire their own replacements, Kirk opted for the Jensen Huang Instructional Method. Deliberately, and with great intentionality, Kirk gathered his engineers together in a conference room. Then Kirk—gentle Kirk, who eschewed conflict and rarely raised his voice—began to yell. "What the fuck are you doing?!" Kirk screamed at his staff. "You just interviewed a guy who you're going to be counting on to do half of your work, and you didn't even bother to find out if he can do it! Now *you're* gonna have to do twice as much work, and he's gonna get half your salary!" Kirk, with satisfaction, regarded the stunned silence of his employees. "We're gonna bring him in again, and I'm going to ask him questions now, because none of you know how," he said.

The unfortunate job seeker returned to find himself in a theater of interrogation. With his staff in attendance, Kirk opened the interview with a softball: "Are you familiar with how to draw a triangle?" Once the candidate answered that question, Kirk gently increased the difficulty. "OK, how do you draw the edges of a triangle?" With that answered, Kirk kept going: "What if one of the coordinates of the triangle is zero? You can't divide by zero, so what do you do?" Kirk pushed into more difficult territory until he felt he'd reached the limit of the candidate's understanding. Then came the final question, a demanding technical challenge that Kirk was certain the candidate didn't know how to answer.

The offer of a job hinged on what came next. Often, candidates would lie or try to make something up. That was an automatic fail. Others would admit blankly that they didn't know. That was usually a fail, too. The engineers who passed the test were those who realized they were participating not in a job interview but a Socratic dialogue. These engineers could walk back through the series of questions that had led up to this point, then advance their knowledge *in the interview*, using the previous answers to figure out the new one. In fifteen minutes, Kirk learned more about the candidate's capabilities than his staff had in eight hours of structured interviews— and his staff learned how to ask the right questions.

NO ONE WAS MORE SELECTIVE in whom he hired than Huang. As Nvidia succeeded, Huang's family pressured him to distribute the spoils.

"His parents pushed and said, 'Look, you've got to give your brothers jobs,'" Jens Horstmann said. Huang refused, leading to tense conversations. "Basically, he said, 'I can't justify that. I don't think they fit our culture,'" Horstmann recalled. Despite the family encouragement, Huang never hired his brothers.

Jensen's older brother, Jeff, held a variety of engineering jobs during his career. Horstmann recalled a time when the three of them were building a deck in Jensen's backyard. Horstmann and Jensen did the construction; Jeff supervised. "He couldn't even hold a nail gun," Horstmann said. Jensen's younger brother, Jim, had followed Jensen to OSU, earning the same electrical engineering degree. While Jensen was managing Nvidia out of Priem's townhouse, Jim had played it safe, going to work for Intel. He remained there for the next thirty years, building and maintaining software tools. "He was a hardworking, solid engineer," Horstmann said. "But this sort of entrepreneurial risk-taking—you know, being willing to accept failure, and be punished for it—I didn't see that in him."

Rather than giving his brothers jobs, Huang gave them real estate. In the early 2000s he liquidated some of his Nvidia shares and used the proceeds to buy a sizable plot of land in Los Altos Hills, an affluent community overlooking Silicon Valley that is currently the third-wealthiest zip code in the United States. There, with Lori's oversight, he commissioned a six-thousand-square-foot mansion with five bedrooms, seven bathrooms, a swimming pool, and an oversized garage. He bought two Ferraris (his and hers) and started collecting expensive whiskey. He donated his old house, with the deck, to Jeff.

But not even a custom dream house could meet Jensen's standards. As his wealth increased, he developed the persnickety "just so" attitude of the very-high-net-worth client. Returning home from work one day, he noticed that the glass doors to the garden of his mansion did not perfectly align with the view to the pool house out back. The lack of symmetry annoyed him, so he ordered the pool house uprooted and, at considerable expense, had it moved eighteen feet to the side.

. . .

THE GEFORCE line established Nvidia as the market leader. Simultaneously, Nvidia launched Quadro, a line of professional GPUs for advanced computer modeling and digital animation. As foretold, Nvidia was coming for Silicon Graphics—and, as foretold, some of Jensen's former managers were coming to work for him. In 2000 Huang hired Tommy Lee, who had been his first boss at LSI.

The growth in the 3D accelerator sector coincided with a frothy time in the stock market. Nvidia wasn't some vaporous dot-com: it shipped an actual product, it had real revenues, and it posted real profits. Still, it was a technology company operating in a technology bubble. In early 2000, Nvidia announced an agreement to develop a chip for Microsoft's as-yet-unnamed home-gaming console, and Nvidia's stock price popped above $100 a share. The price triggered the fulfillment of a number of corporate dares made over drinks at some boozy corporate offsite a few months before. Malachowsky got his ear pierced. Priem shaved all the hair off his head, except for a square patch at the top, which was dyed green and sculpted into the Nvidia logo. Huang got the logo tattooed on his upper arm, then complained about the pain for many years after.

By 2001, Nvidia was selling a billion dollars' worth of GPUs per year. The only firm able to match Nvidia's pace of innovation was ATI, based in suburban Toronto. ATI's flagship product line was the Radeon. The Radeon, like the GeForce, was a fan-cooled accelerator with parallel pixel pipelines. Its chips were manufactured in the same TSMC facility as the GeForce, and Kwok Yuen Ho, the company's cofounder and CEO, was, like Huang, an immigrant with a fiercely competitive streak whose company had skirted bankruptcy several times before succeeding. With the introduction of the Radeon line, the GPU market settled into a static duopoly, and over the next two decades, GeForce and Radeon would battle for supremacy, with each product line spending time at the top. (Today, GeForce has pulled well ahead.)

Despite the success, Huang remained wary. In 1996, the leading graphics accelerator firm was S3 Graphics. By 1999, it was gone. In 1998, the leading firm was 3dfx. By 2000, it was gone, too. There was no guarantee the same wouldn't happen to Nvidia. One of the business books stacked in Huang's office, written by Intel CEO Andy Grove, was titled *Only the Paranoid Survive.*

Competitive threats were inherent in any capitalist enterprise, but in the microchip sector those threats were of a different order. For a business like Coca-Cola, once you established a winning formula, the product sold itself—your job was not to tamper with success. The microchip industry was more like the fashion business—if your product today resembled your product from yesterday, you had made a terrible mistake. In semiconductors, everything was reinvented from scratch every few years. This was true of the software tools used to design the chips; it was true of the ultraviolet photolithography machines used to print them; it was true of the architecture of the chips themselves. The first Nvidia chip contained a million transistors. By 2000, Nvidia's chips contained twenty times that number, cooled by high-speed fans and packed into half the space. "All that is solid melts into air," one early observer of capitalism wrote, or, as Andy Grove declared a while later, "We all need to expose ourselves to the winds of change."

Jensen was not the only gambler in the sector. Every executive had to be one. The ever-increasing precision of transistor manufacturing raised the cost to participate with each new product cycle, and as such, the industry resembled a high-stakes poker tournament in which the stakes were constantly increased. Stand pat in the tournament, and your stack would dwindle away. Your only chance to survive was to find a promising hand and shove in all your chips—then do it again.

One expensive gamble Huang took was to add programmable shaders to the GPUs. Graphics technology at the time often rendered scenes with a "plastic" or "rubbery" appearance. Kirk wanted to give programmers better lighting tools, but adding the shaders meant sacrificing profits to build infrastructure that not many game developers would use, at least not at first.

"If you do this, it's gonna cost a little bit more for a while," he told Huang. "But then everybody's gonna want it, and it'll make everybody try to catch us."

As with the parallel pipelines, Huang was initially skeptical. He became convinced only when he started to consider the cost of *not* implementing the shaders. The lone guarantee in his industry was that more transistors were coming. As that happened, graphics would get cheaper and easier to render. Huang had managed to stay ahead of his competitors so far, but his asset-light "merchant" business was essentially just a collection of engineers sitting around a Silicon Valley office park. If those engineers weren't constantly developing new, difficult-to-replicate technology, manufacturers in Asia would start knocking off his chips, and Nvidia would cease to exist. "If we don't reinvent computer graphics, if we don't reinvent ourselves, and we don't open the canvas for the things that we can do on this processor, we will be commoditized out of existence," Huang later said. Not to gamble was the biggest risk of all.

The first GeForce models to feature programmable shaders debuted in June 2001. The Xbox, Microsoft's gaming console, launched in November 2001, accompanied by its signature game, *Halo*. The game was a shooter in the tradition of *Quake* and *Doom*, except instead of taking place in Hell, it took place in a ring-shaped artificial world with beautiful, naturalistic lighting, rendered by Nvidia's hardware. The success of *Halo* pushed Nvidia's total market value above $20 billion. Two weeks later, Nvidia was added to the S&P 500 stock market index. It replaced Enron.

At thirty-eight, Huang was one of the youngest CEOs in the index. In eight years he'd gone from brainstorming product ideas in a diner booth to running one of the five hundred most valuable companies in America. He had outcompeted and assimilated all but one of his competitors, and in the weeks after the index selection, Huang even briefly became a paper billionaire. But the stock market was a fickle arbiter of value, and Huang's glory was short-lived. It would be fourteen years before he saw that much money again.

EIGHT

The Compulsion Loop

J ensen drove the ball across the table with a satisfying *thwock*, generating terrific spin. He was practicing his forehand loop, which had been his kill shot in his competitive days. He reset his body as the next ball came, coiling and exploding, twisting his hips, and swinging his paddle up and across, sending the ball in a curving trajectory over the net. *Thwock.* He repeated this action, striking and resetting, striking and resetting, his body turning around his pivot foot like a mechanical piston.

Things were not going well at work. *Thwock.* The stock market was crashing as the dot-com bubble deflated. *Thwock.* The latest GeForce product had shipped with a defective fan that made it sound like a leaf blower. *Thwock.* The Xbox deal was collapsing. *Thwock.* Nvidia was being investigated for accounting fraud. *Thwock, thwock, thwock, thwock.* Jensen put down the paddle, covered in sweat.

Huang had returned to the tables in 2002 after contacting Joe Romanosky, his old friend and table tennis partner. Romanosky was surprised by the call; he hadn't talked to Huang in nearly twenty years. The two talked cordially for a while, catching up on old times. Romanosky recalled the time in college when Huang had participated in a table tennis tournament at a state penitentiary. Winning easily in front of an audience of prisoners, Huang couldn't resist showing off. "He had a bunch of trick shots, but he'd been able to mask it like it was part of the match," Romanosky said. "You know, like the Harlem Globetrotters."

On the call, Huang mentioned that he'd started a company that made equipment for video games. "He seemed very excited about it," Romanosky said. Huang sent a GPU to Romanosky's son, who built a computer around it. Romanosky, returning the favor, ordered Huang his favorite make of table tennis paddle. Soon, Huang was practicing again and hired a former Olympian to train him.

Romanosky, who worked in San Diego as an engineer for Boeing, began flying to the Bay Area with his wife to spend time with Jensen and Lori. In the garden next to his relocated pool house, Huang had installed a large Japanese teppan grill, where he was practicing the tricks of a Benihana chef. He tossed fried rice, threw food in the air, and was experimenting with an onion-ring volcano. He never quite mastered the art of catching a grilled shrimp in his hat, however, and many ended up on the floor.

At the backyard dinners, Huang talked about his family, his kids, his interests—anything but business. Romanosky was careful not to ask; he could read the headlines. Huang treated Romanosky to his expanding whiskey collection, the two men's wives became friends, and Romanosky invited Huang to go camping in the Sierras. (Huang declined.) "He is very warm, very engaging," Romanosky said. "He's not at all a superstar executive when he and I sit down. I feel like he's very authentic."

Romanosky's impressions of Huang bore little resemblance to the obsessive tycoon his colleagues and competitors described. Romanosky saw only a high-spirited, high-energy, fun-loving mischief-maker—the same Jensen he had always known. Somehow, it seemed, Huang was able to compartmentalize his business persona from his home life. I wondered whether Romanosky had ever seen a glimpse of Darth Vader. "If that's there, he's turned that side of himself off," Romanosky said. "Just a very warm, down-home kind of guy—that's the Jensen I know."

. . .

BETWEEN THE SUMMER OF 2001 and the fall of 2002, Nvidia's stock price declined more than 90 percent. Huang's wealth plummeted with it. The problems started in January 2002, when the Securities and Exchange Commission opened an investigation into Nvidia's accounting. Similar investigations had revealed schemes to inflate earnings at Worldcom and Enron, leading to widespread suspicion of corporate shenanigans. In July, Nvidia was forced to restate three years of earnings, and shortly thereafter, CFO Christine Hoberg was let go.* Tench Coxe told me that her firing was unfortunate and that the board never lost confidence in Huang. "The SEC was on a fishing expedition," he said. He had a point; the restated earnings showed that Nvidia was more profitable than previously reported.

The accounting scandal occurred during one of the worst bear markets in history. Suffering under the simultaneous bursting of the dot-com bubble, the 9/11 attacks, and the Enron bankruptcy, the S&P 500 lost nearly half its value. Coincident with these misfortunes, Nvidia started squabbling with Microsoft. The dispute was attributed to pricing and intellectual-property issues, but Nvidia's growing sense of entitlement played a role.

Nvidia employees were unabashedly elitist. They considered themselves the best—and they were—but their pride could sometimes sound like narcissism. In the weeks before the Xbox's launch, Microsoft had hosted a celebration banquet to launch the console, with Bill Gates giving a congratulatory speech. The Nvidia technicians were seated near the back, sharing their table with the manufacturers of the rubber stabilizers that kept the Xbox from sliding off ledges. Talking with me decades later, Kirk recalled this seating arrangement with the wounded indignity of a bridesmaid slotted at the rejects' table. "Yeah, you know, we're an important partner on this project— right up there with the guys who make the little rubber feet," he said.

---

*The SEC later charged Hoberg with fraud, accusing her of hiding $3 million of unrecorded expenses from corporate auditors. Hoberg paid a $600,000 fine, but she admitted no wrongdoing.

Kirk stressed that he was joking, but as with Huang, Kirk's jokes were often delivery mechanisms for barbed, unpleasant truths. Perhaps it was an oversight by an event planner, but to Kirk, being sequestered with the rubber-injection and molding specialists felt like a deliberate signal that Microsoft was not to be held captive by a lowly hardware supplier. The slight was not soon forgotten, and shortly thereafter the business relationship soured. Microsoft started asking Nvidia for large shipment volumes and reductions on price, Nvidia claimed that its contract did not obligate it to meet such demands, and the argument was sent to arbitration. For the next generation of the Xbox, Microsoft switched to ATI.

Yet, of all these woes, the worst for Nvidia was the slow adoption of the programmable shaders. For the gamble to work, the company had to convince developers to adopt a new coding language. To do so, Nvidia marketed its shaders via "Dawn," an inadequately clothed CGI pixie with butterfly wings, antennae, and large breasts. Dawn graced the cover of Nvidia's programming textbook, *The Cg Tutorial*, whose less titillating contents consisted of ten chapters' worth of vertex transformations, pixel pipelines, and sample computer code—and, of course, homework exercises. Uptake was slow.

HUANG'S ANGER, invisible to Romanosky, found increasing room to express itself at work. In early 2003, Nvidia shipped the infamous GeForce FX, prone to slow rendering speeds and known to gamers as "the dustbuster" for its faulty, overactive fan. The device was panned by reviewers and customers, including Huang's thirteen-year-old son, Spencer. Jensen arrived home one evening to find a gaming magazine featuring a harsh review of the device waiting for him with a Post-it note attached. "Dad," the note read, "I think you need to kick it up a notch."

Huang arranged a meeting in which the product managers presented, to a few hundred people, every decision they had made that led to the fiasco. Huang then screamed at them, near the top of his voice, for nearly an hour. "'Terrifying but cathartic' is how I would describe it," said Sharon Clay, one of the engineers responsible for quality control. Huang's tirades inspired as much guilt as fear, and he often described, in detail, how in letting their customers down, Nvidia employees had let one another's families down as well. ("I think I'm driven as much by guilt as anything else," Huang told me.)

Nvidia conducted regular performance reviews of employees, and following the GeForce FX debacle, Clay feared that her next one would read RI: "Requires Improvement." This, at Nvidia, was like being handed the Black Spot. For the GeForce FX, Clay had run four or five quality-control tests. For its successor, she expanded to one hundred, and ultimately to thousands. "When we started the whole process, I could not have imagined the solution that we ended up coming up with when properly, uh, *pushed* to think," she said.

So demotion never came, not for Clay or for anyone else on the quality-control team. Instead, Nvidia's marketing team shot a satirical video starring the product managers, in which the card was repurposed as a leaf blower. This was distributed to the press, and the updated GeForce shipped to acclaim six weeks later. Many people at Nvidia told me that Huang's anger enforced a kind of discipline within the company, in the manner of a military general or a pro football coach. "I'm not sure he yells more than any other Fortune 500 CEO," one employee said. "Look, it's not really his job to be your friend. It's his job to push you beyond where you think you could ever go."

Even those who disliked such managerial tactics often had positive things to say about Huang personally. Former employee Tim Little recalled receiving an email with the subject heading "Drag Your Sorry Ass Across The Finish Line." Little had been traveling for weeks, away from his family, working late nights at the circuit simulator; feeling he had nothing more to give, he responded to the email by submitting his resignation. A few nights later, at around two in the morning, as Little was finishing one of his last shifts, Huang arrived and sat down at the simulator beside him. The glow from the monitor illuminating his exhausted face, Huang recalled his own career, the sacrifices he'd made, the many late nights he'd spent away from his family, often working the circuit simulator himself. He expressed, frankly, that he wasn't sure it was all worth it. He offered Little his job back if he wanted it; when Little declined, Huang thanked him for his service to the company and left. "That was absolutely the high point of my employment there," Little said.

Of more than a hundred former and current Nvidia employees I spoke with for this book, almost all had a tender story about Huang to relate. One employee—the same one whom Huang had humiliated in front of dozens of people, asking for a full refund of his salary—told me that when he was later diagnosed with a serious medical issue, Huang offered to pay in full, out of pocket, for his treatment. When Ben Garlick decided to leave Nvidia for a start-up, he was startled to receive an impassioned, personal plea from Huang to stay. "We're sitting together at this conference table, and he's gotten so close to me we're almost bumping knees, and he's, like, begging!" Garlick said. Garlick was a frontline manager in charge of ten people at a company of thousands. "I didn't even think Jensen knew my name," he said. Huang's combination of love, fear, and guilt was a seductive and powerful motivator. "You felt like you couldn't let him down," Clay said. "You just *couldn't*."

AROUND THIS TIME, Curtis Priem finally tapped out. His responsibilities had been limited for years, and eventually he stopped coming into the office. ("He had a conflict with another executive staff person, and I think he decided he was fired," Kirk said.) Priem began liquidating his Nvidia stock to make a large series of donations, mostly to his alma mater, the Rensselaer Polytechnic Institute in upstate New York. Priem was named to the school's board of trustees, and the money was used to build a $200 million performing arts center and, later, to buy a quantum computer.

Priem retreated to a splendid $6 million ranch in the Diablo range east of Oakland. His perch on the ridge gave him a commanding view of the Bay—gazing out toward the setting sun over his fenced-in herd of cattle, he could, on a clear day, make out all five of the major bridges that spanned the glittering water. He purchased a Gulfstream jet to shuttle from California to RPI and back; to offset his carbon footprint, he invested in experimental green technology and moved his ranch off the grid. He suffered through a messy and unpleasant divorce, then began to look for a formula that might, in his words, "repair the earth."

In a series of chunk transactions between 2004 and 2006, Priem sold all his Nvidia shares. "That's why the stock flatlined," he said. "We basically sold into strength whenever it started going up." Had he held those shares and done nothing but play cowboy for twenty years, Priem would today be worth more than $100 billion, making him one of the wealthiest people alive—but he told me he didn't regret his decision. Doing so would have required him to have 99.9 percent of his net worth invested in the volatile stock of a risky tech company he no longer worked for, which didn't seem like a good idea.

Channeling George Bailey, Priem asked me to consider where his vanished windfall profits had gone. "The shares went out there, but it's not like they disappeared. It's in pension plans. It's in people's houses. It's sort of like I contributed $100 billion to our economy," he said. "I'm on track to give away half a billion in my lifetime, and that has taken most of my time and effort. In the back of my mind, I'm trying to figure out what I would do with a $100 billion foundation, and it is not easy. I wouldn't even know how to give that away."

NVIDIA WAS RESCUED by the gamers in the end. Even with its stock in the toilet, the company was shipping some of the most complex silicon ever manufactured. These chips, combined with the arrival of home broadband Internet and the maturation of the multimedia home computer, inaugurated what some critics later called the Golden Age of PC gaming. Developers leveraged the new hardware to deliver classic titles like *Call of Duty*, *Half-Life 2*, *The Sims*, and *World of Warcraft*. "PC gaming peaked somewhere between 2000 and 2005," one nostalgic commenter opined.

Was this the best use of such technology? The subculture of PC gaming was toxic—from it grew 4chan and later the Gamergate harassment campaign. PC gamers termed console gamers "peasants" and referred to themselves as the "PC master race." Graphics pioneers were frustrated by the arrested aesthetic development evident in the leading titles, which reflected —or maybe produced—the stunted maturity of the customers. Nvidia had gifted the developers an extraordinary tool. The developers had used that tool to render monsters, gunfights, car chases, and gore. "It's astounding when you think about all the work that goes on and the triviality of some of the results," Jon Peddie said.

But it made good business sense. The PC gamers were the best kind of customers: addicts. By design, video games offered rewards on a randomized schedule. Casinos used similar tactics to keep slot-machine junkies pasted to their chairs. In 2001 John Hopson, a researcher who worked for the studio that made *Halo*, described gaming's "compulsion loop": upgrade the player's character, send them off to complete a quest, reward them with loot, then repeat. Some players found the loop hard to escape. Researchers noted that hardcore gamers exhibited behaviors associated with substance abuse. They binged. They suffered withdrawal. They lied to friends and family members about how much time they spent gaming. They deleted their games one day, then downloaded them again the next. In 2013, the American Psychiatric Association's diagnostic manual added an entry for "internet gaming disorder," noting that young men were especially susceptible. Symptoms added "poor performance at school, work or household responsibilities," and "a decline in personal hygiene."

For others, though, the games offered spellbinding alternative worlds pregnant with meaning, challenge, and opportunity. *World of Warcraft* might be addictive, but through it gamers befriended compatriots all over the world. About a quarter of gamers played two hours a day or more. Nvidia called them "enthusiasts," and they were the best customers. Many had started on Nintendo as children, then graduated to the PC scene in adulthood. In absolute terms, the PC market had fewer customers than the console market, but those customers spent far more on their systems. In between gaming sessions, some even managed to secure jobs.

With Nvidia's encouragement, the gaming PC became to the neckbeards what the muscle car was to gearheads. Custom-built gaming computers termed "rigs" could be tricked out with thousands of dollars' worth of aftermarket equipment. Vendors sold transparent computer casing with colored interior lighting to showcase the hardware. Just as automobile fanatics popped the hoods of their cars to advertise their engines, the enthusiasts posted photos of their rigs to online forums, bragging about their overclocked motherboards and the rendering speed of their GPUs.

As the gaming market matured, Nvidia's stock price recovered. In fact, even when the stock was cratering, Nvidia had never stopped growing. By the start of 2004, the company had more than a thousand employees and was reporting record earnings. And so began the chronic struggle among Wall Street analysts to figure out what Nvidia was even approximately worth. Few companies created greater headaches for money managers: analyzing prior years' figures was of little use, because any money that Nvidia earned Huang immediately reinvested in speculative technologies that would either revolutionize computing or flop trying. By the mid-2000s, his track record looked a little worse than breakeven: he'd succeeded with the GPU and parallel processing but whiffed on a number of other initiatives, resulting in a corporation that was successful on paper but whose stock chronically underperformed. What mattered at Nvidia wasn't profits or revenues. What mattered was the obsessive chief executive and his crazy long-shot bets. Either you believed in him or you didn't. And if you didn't, you were certainly in for a tough ride, for Huang was about to make his craziest bet yet.

NINE

CUDA

Gamers like Johnathan Wendel lowered their screen resolution to maximize the frame rate in deathmatch. Ian Buck took things to the opposite extreme—he wanted to blow up the action as big as it could go. Buck, a graduate student in computer graphics at Stanford, realized that with a little technical expertise he could distribute the rendering requirements for a single game across multiple Nvidia cards. In 2000 he chained thirty-two GeForce units together to render *Quake III* across eight projectors. "It was the first gaming rig in 8K resolution, and it took up an entire wall," Buck said. "It was beautiful."

Poking around in the circuits, Buck began to wonder if his GPU daisy chain might be useful for tasks other than shooting grenades at his friends. If you wanted to hand-render thirty frames of *Quake III* in 8K using pencil and paper, and you were willing to work twenty-four hours a day to do so, the arithmetic would take about sixteen thousand years to complete. Buck's GeForce array was doing that every second. Plus, the whole rig cost only about $20,000 to assemble—a pittance by the standards of high-performance computing. To play *Quake* on the wall, Buck had inadvertently built a low-budget supercomputer.

Buck figured this affordable horsepower would be useful to science and industry, but the code Nvidia had packaged with the cards only spoke the language of triangles. If Buck wanted to use his GPU array for some other purpose, he was going to have to hack it. He immersed himself in Nvidia's shading textbook—the one with the pixie on the cover—becoming one of the first programmers to master it. Ironically, in doing so, he lost interest in computer graphics. He'd been sucked, à la *Tron*, into the technological substrate below.

Buck was intense, and balding, and he radiated intelligence. The closer he got to the circuits, the more obsessive he became about their capabilities. Like a veteran astronomer setting aside his telescope to contemplate the vastness of the universe, Buck remained perpetually astonished at how much arithmetic the computer could do. Sixty gigaflops—sixty billion operations—every single second, and that was just one card. No matter how much low-level circuit hacking Buck did, the sense of awe never left him.

With a grant from DARPA, the Department of Defense's research arm, Buck assembled a group of researchers. In 2003 Buck and his team released an open-source programming language called "Brook." Using Brook, scientists could smuggle demanding mathematical payloads—say, simulating the formation of a galaxy or modeling the ignition process of a nuclear bomb—into hardware built to render carjackings and disembowelments. The graphical output of a Brook program was a meaningless series of triangles, but in rendering these images, the GPU coincidentally executed important scientific calculations at speed. "You really had to understand computer graphics to be able to hack those triangles," Buck said.

Brook made parallel computing accessible. Academics began bulk-purchasing GeForce cards and chaining them together, developing applications in financial modeling, weather simulation, high-energy physics, and medical imaging. The gaming cards were more than just gaming cards now; they were jerry-rigged scientific tools. The emergence of this new kind of customer did not escape Huang's notice. "I got a bunch of papers published, and everyone was very supportive," Buck said. "And then, around 2004, Jensen asked me to come to Nvidia and do it for real."

. . .

BUCK'S EXPERIENCE MIRRORED that of many researchers who went to work for Nvidia. In 2005, Silicon Graphics, unable to compete with Nvidia's Quadro line, was delisted from the New York Stock Exchange. (Its head-quarters became the Googleplex.) As it had with 3dfx, Nvidia absorbed many SGI asylum seekers, doubling its staff to 2,000 people. Of those, 1,200—60 percent of the company—were classified as working in research and development. To outsiders, Nvidia still looked like a slightly ridiculous manufacturer of gaming hardware, but to insiders, it was beginning to feel like a scientific laboratory.

Bill Dally, the chair of Stanford's computer science department and a longtime parallel-computing evangelist, had observed with excitement the growing "arithmetic intensity" of Nvidia's chips, which he thought might act as the backbone for a new kind of computer entirely. He wrote several papers praising the company's innovations, and in 2003 Huang dropped by his university office to offer him a consulting job. Dally had spent years pitching parallel-computing concepts to indifferent executives; now Huang was coming to him. "He technically understands things at an extremely deep level, and he always asks the right questions," Dally said. "Sometimes he's even a step ahead of you, and it's something you think you're an expert on."

But Dally was also skeptical of Huang. He had heard stories of his emotional volatility and of Nvidia's unforgiving work environment. Huang, perhaps anticipating these objections, produced at their first meeting a signed paper check made out in Dally's name. Dally, one of the world's leading academics, agreed to consult.

Buck, Dally, and dozens of other talented engineers were being recruited for a secret Nvidia project called Compute Unified Domain Architecture, or CUDA. (The name was purposefully imprecise.) The concept behind CUDA was to take the parallel-computing circuits used for video games and repurpose them for scientists. No more hacking at triangles to get to those precious gigaflops—the architecture was being opened up. "Basically, the way to think about CUDA is you have a video game card on one side, but it has a switch on it," Dwight Diercks said. "So you flick that switch, and turn the card over, and suddenly the card becomes a supercomputer."

THE INVENTOR OF CUDA was John Nickolls, an Nvidia engineer who had previously cofounded one of the parallel-computing start-ups whose corpses littered the road. Nickolls was an expert downhill skier and model-train enthusiast whose office was decorated with framed pictures of microchips. He was passionate about making computers run faster: at his "massively parallel" MasPar Corporation, he had attempted to implement TSMC's 996 work schedule, asking employees to work twelve-hour shifts six days a week. Even after his company tanked, Nickolls never gave up on parallelism, believing that it would eventually triumph as a consequence of the laws of physics.

For decades, an engineering principle called "Dennard scaling" had governed the miniaturization of electronics. Dennard scaling dictated that transistors would continue to efficiently process electricity as they got smaller—basically, it was the reason computers got faster every year.* But Nickolls had calculated that sometime around 2005, the Dennard scaling relationship would collapse. The coming generation of light-printing machines would craft transistors a mere one hundred atoms in width. This was six thousand times thinner than a human hair and seven hundred times thinner than a red blood cell. At this fine scale, the transistors' conductive properties would be compromised, and they would leak electricity into the surrounding circuitry. Once that happened, computers would slow down.

Nickolls could see that the industry was in denial about this problem—especially Intel, which was confidently predicting linear gains from shrinking transistors down to components a single atom in width. Nickolls believed

---

*Technically speaking, Dennard scaling states that as transistors get smaller, their power density remains constant. It was first proposed in 1974 by Robert Dennard and his colleagues at IBM.

this was impossible, and in early 2003 he sent an unsolicited letter to Huang outlining his heretical thoughts. Nickolls didn't panic or exaggerate. Rather, with a precise but measured sense of urgency, he explained, using principles of electricity, why Intel's long domination of the semiconductor industry was about to expire. "We had all seen it coming for a while, but it was Nickolls who convinced me that Moore's Law was truly dead," Huang said. "He deserves so much credit for what this company has become."

Huang hired Nickolls and put him in charge of a pilot project developing scientific applications for the GeForce. Even at Nvidia, Nickolls was considered intense. Two weeks after his first day of work, he was diagnosed with malignant melanoma. He continued working seventy-two hours a week while receiving cancer treatment, concealing from both family and colleagues the discomfort he was experiencing. Soon, Nickolls's melanoma was in remission, and the earliest versions of the CUDA platform were live.

Nickolls had no interest in video games at all. He didn't even care about computer graphics; he cared only about making microchips go faster. In every other way, though, Nickolls was the model Nvidia employee. "My dad was always one to yell," his son, Alec, told me. "I remember overhearing my dad take meetings on the phone and yelling at people. Not in a toxic way but just, like, make sure you know what you're doing. Make sure you're being productive."

Nickolls drove as hard in his personal life as he did at work. He tricked his son into skiing black diamonds with him, and at the model-train club he preferred to lay track rather than socialize. When Alec was young, he had struggled with a classic Boy Scout survival drill that required him to use his pants as a life preserver. Nickolls wouldn't let his son out of the pool until his pants were filled with air.

Nickolls was obsessed with getting the CUDA platform to work. Friends sometimes asked him why he was working for a video game company when he didn't play video games. Nickolls informed them he wasn't working on video games; he was working on one of the most important technologies of all time. He was building a platform so fast it would make every other computer look like a calculator watch. "Few inventions will have the impact on the world that CUDA will ultimately have," he would say.

This was more of a statement of faith than anything else. By the late 2000s, computers were fast enough for most consumer purposes, and there were not obvious customers for what Nickolls was building. Bundling CUDA with a retail circuit board was like attaching a minivan to a rocket sled and trying to sell it to suburban commuters. Nickolls was undeterred. He did not want merely to get around Moore's Law; he wanted to smash it forever.

To do so, Nickolls had to ratchet up the arithmetic intensity of the circuits. Microchips kept time with a furious internal metronome that got faster every year. By the mid-2000s, that metronome was pulsing hundreds of millions of times per second, and the delicate wiring could not keep up with the beat. Parallel computing solved this problem not by speeding things up but by getting more transistors to respond to each pulse. An Intel CPU fired only a few transistors at a time. An Nvidia gaming GPU fired thousands.

Nvidia struggled to find users who actually needed such power. "Initially, our only customers were two breast cancer researchers," Diercks recalled. The researchers, working at Massachusetts General Hospital, had written to Nvidia with a proposal to upgrade their mammogram scanners. Huang enlisted the hospital to alpha-test CUDA, investing several million dollars in a pilot project that would ultimately sell exactly two graphics cards. "But Jensen loved that, right?" Diercks said.

Mammogram imaging was the first example of what Huang would later call the "zero-billion-dollar" market. Huang had long sought a way to differentiate Nvidia from its competitors. Hardware innovations wouldn't get him there; they were too easily cloned. Online, silicon fetishists swapped "die shots" of Nvidia's microchips obtained by ripping the chip out of a retail board, dissolving the case in boiling sulfuric acid, then scanning the circuitry with a metallurgical microscope. The enthusiasm of the hobbyists paralleled professional espionage efforts by reverse-engineering teams at chipmaker laboratories. The denuded silicon was technically patented, but the 3dfx experience had shown the futility of lawsuits. "Everyone takes a look at their competitors' hardware and how it works," Diercks said. "It's not even black ops. We just do it."

To distinguish himself, Huang had to pursue a strategy that so defied conventional business logic that ATI wouldn't follow. He had to build an exploratory product, like a $300 entry-level scientific supercomputer that not only didn't have competitors but also didn't even have obvious customers. The zero-billion-dollar market, by definition, was one that only he would participate in—one that only he would even *see*. Huang was going to build a baseball diamond in a cornfield and wait for the players to arrive.

PARALLEL COMPUTING DIVIDES A BIG problem into smaller pieces, then solves them all at once. The complexity of its inner workings would require a textbook to accurately explain, but some of what happens is accessible through analogy.

First, let's consider the action of the circuits. Imagine that the microchip has been blown up to the size of a dance floor. The floor is packed with partiers waving glow sticks, who represent the transistors. The lights are flashing, and the beat is raging, but most of the dancers are frozen—they can move only when it is their turn. One dancer moves on the first beat of the first measure, another on the fourth beat of the second measure, and so on. You can see glow sticks waving here and there, but most of the dancers aren't dancing. They're waiting to act.

The serial DJ has been trying to get the crowd moving by speeding up the beat, but this has diminishing returns. Then the parallel DJ takes the stage. Rather than speeding up the beat, the parallel DJ choreographs far more complicated movements among the dancers. This works: the activity grows frenzied, the floor begins to shake, and the place is suddenly much hotter—some dancers are so active they might overheat. Now thousands of glow sticks shake with every beat.

Reworking the circuits in this way is a bottom-up change that alters everything above it. This is the challenge of parallel computing—harnessing the complex choreography is logistically difficult, and requires programmers to think about problems in an entirely new way. It is easy to feed instructions to Intel's CPUs, which work like a delivery van, dropping off one package at a time. The truck is slow, sure, but it requires little from the programmer. Have a package to be delivered? Throw it in the back of the van!

Nvidia's parallel GPU acts more like a fleet of motorcycles spreading out across a city. The drivers deliver every package at roughly the same time, and the entire process can be completed in half an hour. But this rapid parallel solution is far more difficult to execute; it requires more drivers, more machines, and more logistics. Here, with motorcyclists constantly circulating in and out of the warehouse, every package has to be assigned to the correct vehicle and precisely routed to its destination.

For decades, programmers had preferred the van—but as Nickolls had predicted, now the van was running into the traffic jam of electromagnetic physics. Once that happened, he believed, programmers would finally take the time to learn how to manage the fleet of motorcycles. In fact, they'd be *forced* to learn this. They'd have no choice.

Still, it was not really the programmers that Nvidia was targeting; they were intermediaries. The true customers, if they ever arrived, would be doctors, astronomers, geologists, and other scientists—highly educated academic specialists who were skilled in specific domains but who maybe didn't know how to code at all. It was these end users who would ultimately direct money toward CUDA, and for them an even gentler metaphor was required.

For scientists, the best way to think of the difference between serial and parallel computing is to think of Intel's serial CPU as a high-end stainless-steel Wüsthof kitchen knife. The knife is a beautiful multipurpose tool that can make any kind of cut. It can julienne, batonnet, chop, slice, dice, or hack. With a little skill, a chef can build a whole meal with just this one implement—but the knife can only ever chop one vegetable at a time.

By comparison, Nvidia's parallel GPU acts more like a Cuisinart. It is a specialty tool that is loud, indelicate, and power-intensive. It cannot chiffonade tarragon or score a crosshatch on a tube of calamari. But to mince a bunch of vegetables quickly, the GPU is the tool.

Now, just as you would struggle to cook a meal with only a Cuisinart and no kitchen knives, you cannot run a computer on a GPU alone. The architecture of the device is too specialized for that; a CPU is always necessary. In this sense, the CPU is always the primary tool, while the GPU is an expensive add-on. And, like a lot of kitchen gadgets, it's one that was initially sneered at by purists.

But imagine that a chef arrives to work one day to find that a semitruck full of fresh vegetables has pulled up to the loading dock. The chef no longer has time to chiffonade; she must mince these hundreds of pounds of vegetables before they spoil. *This* chef might find the Cuisinart useful. In fact, she might want dozens or even hundreds of Cuisinarts running at the same time.

The truckload of vegetables in this analogy represents Big Data. In the mid-2000s, the scientific loading dock was piling up with datasets that were exponentially larger than anything that had come before: astronomical data, geo-engineering data, medical data, government data, financial data, and the sprawling, ever-expanding human-generated dataset of the World Wide Web. In the past, a scientist might count herself lucky with one crate of vegetables every couple of weeks. By the mid-2000s, a scientist could expect delivery of several shipping containers' worth of vegetables every day.

Intel's timeless kitchen knives just weren't up to the challenge—you needed a machine-driven spinning blade. OK, so the cuts weren't always so beautiful. So what? Another truck was coming in a few minutes anyhow. The GPU was data's Cuisinart. It was the machine that processed data into rough-hewn cubes.

UNDER NICKOLLS'S DIRECTION, Nvidia's designers began segmenting their microchips into "CUDA cores," which were arrays of circuitry that could simultaneously execute the same instruction in parallel across multiple groupings of data. Arjun Prabhu, Nvidia's director of hardware engineering, compared designing the new microchip to urban planning, with different zones of the chip dedicated to different tasks. As Tetris players do with falling blocks, Prabhu would sometimes see transistors in his sleep. "The best ideas happen on a Friday night, when I'm literally dreaming about it," Prabhu said.

The decision to ship dual-purpose chips was controversial within Nvidia because it raised the GeForce's cost of production above that of the Radeon, a cost that was internally referred to as the "CUDA tax." Huang was gambling that his gaming customers, entranced by *Half-Life 2*, wouldn't notice that they were subsidizing a risky and possibly pointless side quest into the arcane realm of high-performance computing. "Many of the ideas employed in CUDA cores had been used long before in supercomputers and specialty processors, but they were too expensive for the small, specialty markets they served," Brett Coon, one of the first CUDA engineers, recalled. "In my opinion, the 'genius' of CUDA is getting gamers to pay for the massive chip development costs."

Several layers of software had to run on top of Prabhu's circuits. The first was the machine code layer, which broke down complex mathematical formulae into simple arithmetic. Much of Ian Buck's work took place here, building ideas from the circuit board up. This was the catacombs of computing, the lowest-level code you could write, whispering directly to the metal. Many programmers found this layer mind-numbing, but Buck loved it—he was later granted patents on several assembly-level techniques. "It's where the rubber meets the road," he said.

Buck hired a team of numerics specialists, many of them graduates of Moscow State University. ("You know, a lot of Pyotrs, a lot of Borises," Buck said.) Working with the Russians, Buck took the complicated mathematical structures that scientists liked—differential equations and higher-dimensional matrices and such—and rewrote them as primitive equations consisting of only plus, minus, times, and divide. Running these elementary operations in parallel across many datasets at once required an unusual talent for holistic reasoning. "Human beings think linearly," Buck said. "You give instructions to someone on how to get from here to Starbucks, and you give them individual steps. You don't give them instructions on how to get to any Starbucks location from anywhere. It's just hard to think that way, in parallel."

Sitting above Buck's layer was the "compiler," which translated programming languages like C++ and Python into machine code. Bas Aarts, the Dutch developer who wrote the first CUDA compiler, was similarly obsessive. He could retreat into his mind for weeks at a time, forsaking friends, relationships, and hobbies to conceptualize how a computer might interpret information. "Certain people in my life think that I'm pretty one-dimensional," he said. "But it's—it's elegant! It's complicated. It's challenging. And if I don't get challenged, I get bored."

Business strategy for CUDA took a long-term view. Huang encouraged Nickolls to embrace the scientific customers—to embrace them very tightly and not let go. The performance gains from CUDA had to be so great, and so obvious, that customers would voluntarily build whole new academic disciplines around the platform. "After that, you will never want to leave," Aarts said. "It's vendor lock. There is no out."

In this way Nvidia built what software developers called "the CUDA stack." At the bottom were the circuits, above this was the machine code that pushed the electrons around, above this was the compiler that translated from machine to human, and at the top was the software that faced the scientists. The stack turned ideas into electricity and turned electricity into results.

CUDA PUBLICLY LAUNCHED in late 2006. The software package was free, although it worked only on Nvidia hardware. In 2007 it was downloaded an underwhelming thirteen thousand times—in that first full year, not one hundredth of one percent of the hundreds of millions of GeForce owners out there bothered to flick the switch on their video game hardware to transform it into a supercomputer. Skeptical investors wondered who this technology was for. "Not only did Wall Street not think CUDA was valuable; they thought it had *negative* value," one employee close to the situation said.

Many programmers found CUDA difficult to use. To maximize the power of the GPU, programmers had to break apart large tasks into hundreds of smaller subtasks called "threads." Then they had to carefully—very carefully—feed these threads into the CUDA cores. This was a tricky bit of business with many hidden pitfalls. Programmers had to manage multiple memory banks without getting confused; they also had to avoid timing mismatches that could produce incorrect results. The learning curve for parallelism was steep, and it built on advanced concepts in computer science. Academics who'd trained in other fields, like physics or medicine, rarely possessed the programming chops needed to make CUDA work.

Kirk, looking to repeat the success he'd had with the shaders, tried marketing the technology with a textbook, *Programming Massively Parallel Processors*, which he cowrote with computer scientist Wen-Mei Hwu. In the introduction the authors observed that computer architecture had not evolved since the Hungarian genius John von Neumann had laid out its basic schematics in 1945. "Computer users have also become accustomed to the expectation that these programs run faster with each new generation of microprocessors," they wrote. "Such expectation is no longer valid from this day onward." Few professors incorporated the textbook into their classes. There was heresy, there was blasphemy, and then there was questioning John von Neumann.

In industry, Nvidia sought a range of customers, including stock traders, oil prospectors, and molecular biologists. At one point, the company signed a deal with General Mills to simulate the thermal physics of cooking frozen Totino's pizza. But most of these deals fizzled out after a couple of quarters—pizza chefs needed only so much computing power.

The high cost of R&D for CUDA was a drag on Nvidia's financial returns, but CUDA was expensive in subtle ways as well. The project caused internal dissension within Nvidia—Nickolls had to fight for resources, sometimes forcefully. "It was a lot easier to convince the hardware designers why it was important to improve performance on *Unreal* or *Doom* than on, say, matrix multiplications or Fast Fourier Transforms," Coon recalled. Meanwhile, the still-cancerous code base swelled in complexity: the complete Ge-

Force software package would soon surpass one hundred million lines of code, making it more complex than some Windows operating systems.

Perhaps the biggest hidden cost was that CUDA distracted Huang from serving his core customer. Rumors of manufacturing problems at Nvidia first surfaced in late 2006, with gamers complaining about GPUs in notebook computers that stopped functioning after a few weeks of use. By the time the problem was acknowledged, the gaming forums had grown conspiratorial, with posters accusing Nvidia of incorrectly attaching their chips to the soldering "bumps" on the circuit board beneath. "Bumpgate" had begun: gamers defected to competitors, and Nvidia stock once again plummeted, losing close to 90 percent of its value for the second time in six years. Board members consulting the stock chart on a Bloomberg terminal compared it to an EKG of a heart attack.

Delighted Radeon loyalists—haters, all—piled on, accusing Huang of orchestrating a cover-up. "Nvidia is tanking, we told you so," one wrote. In early 2009, Dell dropped Nvidia as a preferred supplier for its popular line of gaming laptops. "For a long time, we have wondered when Nvidia's abject stupidity would have a price," wrote one caustic tech columnist. "The answer, at least at Dell, is now."

Huang, seeking to get ahead of Bumpgate, set aside $200 million for customer refunds. The reserve wiped out Nvidia's profits for the year, and for the first time since going public, Nvidia lost money. Huang arranged a Q&A with the press to explain the situation. He arrived in spectacles, black jeans, and a loose-fitting gray athletic T-shirt that revealed the surprising definition of his upper body—the result of his diligent, lifelong push-up routine. "I just don't want the consumers to fight the process," he said in a relaxed and patient voice. "It's a little bit messy because the competition wants to stir it up, but it's not really that complicated." Only seasoned observers of Jensen could intuit the anger coiled beneath the patter.

Nvidia held regular offsites to discuss corporate strategy. Looking to save money in the wake of Bumpgate, the 2008 offsite was relocated to the company cafeteria. "That was the most I ever heard him yell," said Sameer Halepete, one of Huang's top hardware engineers. The target of Jensen's wrath was an extraordinarily skilled and dedicated chip architect with many years of service to the company. The architect stood in one corner of the cafeteria; Huang stood in the opposite. Lining the walls were some 150 senior executives of the company mutely observing the excruciating scene. "I still vividly remember Jensen just nonstop berating him for a good hour and a half," Halepete said. "Honestly, maybe it was two hours—he was just *livid*."

Yet the architect kept his job. "Very rarely does Jensen make significant changes as a result of execution issues," Halepete said. "He's very conscious of having an even slightly chilling effect on people's willingness to take risks and innovate. As a result, his level of forgiveness for even the largest screw-ups is extremely high." Halepete surmised that the tirades were what Jensen did *instead* of showing you the door. "He will berate you, he will yell at you, he will insult you—whatever," Halepete said. "He's never going to fire you."

TO RESTORE CONFIDENCE, Huang turned to Deb Shoquist, who managed Nvidia's worldwide network of suppliers. Shoquist's portfolio took her from Guadalajara to Hanoi to Bangalore; it was her job to make sure that the company's components arrived on time and in sufficient quantity. The job required a fair amount of screaming on the telephone, and Shoquist, voluble and expressive, was not one to back down from a confrontation. Shortly after arriving at Nvidia in 2007, Huang had asked her to shorten the lead time on deliveries from a Taiwanese packaging vendor downstream from TSMC. Shoquist regarded this as an impossibility; Taiwan was famous for its efficiency, and she doubted that there was any gristle to trim from the process. The two began to argue about the difference between lead times and cycle times, until Shoquist directly contradicted Huang. "You don't understand how this works," she said.

The argument took place around a conference table, where executives sat with their laptops open. The moment Shoquist told Huang he didn't understand, her inbox lit up with messages from her colleagues. "Stop!" one read. "Stop, don't go there. Try to listen to him." But it was too late. Huang erupted at Shoquist, screaming at her that she didn't know how to do her job. "I thought you were an ops person. You're not an ops person!" he shouted. "You don't know ops!"

Huang's fury was matched by Shoquist's own. She'd been doing this for twenty years—who was this guy to tell her she wasn't an ops person? She *was* ops. Incensed, Shoquist told Huang she was going to fly to Taiwan and get the stats directly from the vendor to prove she was right. The vendor was delighted to host her: the packaging facility was not a place of glamour, and customers almost never visited. Over the course of a week, Shoquist familiarized herself with the unit economics of this back-end supplier.

At the packaging facility, the "lead time" between the receipt of an order and fulfillment was three weeks. But, to Shoquist's surprise, the "cycle time"—the total number of person-hours it took the vendor to place Nvidia's microchips into the black casing—was just thirty-six hours. The vendor explained it would at least be theoretically possible to expedite the lead time to match the cycle time, although this would increase the cost of packaging each chip from $8 to $1,000. Huang had been right: it was possible to shorten the lead time. Expensive, but possible.

Chastened, Shoquist returned to Nvidia with a cost schedule for expediting packaging orders. She waited until the two were alone to present her findings to Huang. ("I didn't want to give him an audience," Shoquist said.) She braced for his fury, but it never came. Instead, he said, "That's the right answer." Shoquist developed similar cost schedules for all of the hundreds of suppliers that slotted into Nvidia's manufacturing network. Then she began to squeeze, reducing Nvidia's cycle time from months to weeks, eventually setting a record of thirteen days.

In pushing Shoquist, Huang was employing a scheduling technique he called the "speed of light." He drilled this management concept into his employees with the fervor of religious doctrine—almost everyone at Nvidia I talked to referenced the "speed of light" at least once. "Speed of light" did not mean, as one might assume, to move quickly. Instead, Huang encouraged managers to identify the absolute fastest that something could conceivably be accomplished, given an unlimited budget, and assuming that every single thing went right. (For example, traveling from New York to London at the "speed of light" would involve perfect weather, zero traffic, and a supersonic plane.) Managers could then work backward from this unachievable constant to realistic but still impressive delivery times. "It sounds hard, but it really takes the pressure off of you," Shoquist told me. "Once you understand the physical limits of what is possible, you understand the competition can't go any faster either."

Huang pursued this unattainable ideal every day of his life. "I should make sure that I'm sufficiently exhausted from working that no one can keep me up at night," he later said. "That's really the only thing I can control." He maintained this pace for decades, but others burned out. Tired of his commute, David Kirk decided he'd had enough of full-time employment in 2007. Cashing in a portion of the shares Huang had awarded him in the 1990s, he moved to Telluride, Colorado, and later Hawaii, continuing with Nvidia as he had begun, as a part-time consultant.

At that time of his departure, Kirk was running Nvidia Research, a group of thirty scientists working on advanced graphics technologies. Huang believed that something more ambitious was needed to leverage the growing power of CUDA, and he deputized Kirk to find his own replacement. The man Kirk returned with lived at the speed of light. He would soon transform Nvidia Research into the most successful corporate R&D department in the world.

TEN

Resonance

W hen Bill Dally wasn't flying his plane, or applying for a patent, or reinventing the computer, he was riding his bicycle to the point of collapse, or rowing in Lake Tahoe, or competing in a downhill ski race, or sailing nonstop from Grenada to Antigua. Dally's pace of invention made Kirk and Nickolls look lazy: he was the author of 250 technical papers and 4 textbooks, and he held 120 patents spanning an eclectic range of computing domains, ranging from complex circuit architectures to the chip that ran the power supply. Bald, fit, quick-talking, and obviously brilliant, Dally spoke with unforgiving academic precision when discussing computers and in a blunt, matter-of-fact tone when discussing anything else. There was no domain of computing he didn't seem to understand, and there was no moment of his life that didn't seem optimized either for technical achievement or adventure.

Dally had dropped out of high school because he didn't want to sit through history class. Working as an auto mechanic, he finagled entry into college on the basis of his test scores. He never got his high school diploma, but he did receive a bachelor's from Virginia Tech, a master's from Stanford, and a PhD from CalTech. By his early thirties, Dally was a tenured professor at MIT.

Dally liked to build his own computers. He also liked to fly his own plane. On a gloomy September day in 1992, he took his single-engine Cessna on a trip to New York over the Long Island Sound. While cruising at an altitude of around six thousand feet, he noticed his oil indicator go on. He steered toward a nearby airport, but minutes later his engine cut out, followed by a sound that he described as "a lot of softballs kicking around in an oil drum." Dally reoriented the Cessna into a glide pattern, then prepared to crash-land into the sound.

When the plane hit the water, Dally's body was thrown forward, and he broke his nose against the steering wheel. Stunned and bleeding, he had about twenty seconds to get away before the plane sank beneath the waves. In that time he was able to break open the cabin window and escape into the ocean chop, clutching a seat cushion as a life preserver. He was eventually rescued by a passing sailboat. "I later programmed that event into a simulator," Dally told me in a matter-of-fact way, as if he were describing a letter he had mailed. "After ten tries where I wound up in the water, I came up with one where I managed to land at the Groton-New London airport."

Following the plane crash, Dally was back at work within a couple days. His team at MIT was building an experimental parallel computer known as the "Jellybean machine." The Jellybean was Dally's reimagining of how information technology might work, and almost every part of it—the microprocessors, the circuit boards, the networking hardware, and the applications—was bespoke technology that Dally and his team had engineered from first principles. The contraption stood as tall as a person, and parts of it were held together with duct tape.

Benchmarking tests showed that the Jellybean ran much faster than a conventional computer, but Dally could never find a commercial partner to build it. Preexisting computers were plenty fast for most purposes, and there seemed to be no market for a parallel device. So when he was forty years old, Dally left MIT for Stanford; the former high school dropout was now the chair of the most prestigious computer science department in the world.

Dally started consulting for Nvidia following Jensen's visit in 2003, but when Kirk approached him with the offer of a full-time job in 2009, Dally initially turned him down. Nvidia had lost money in fiscal 2009 and fiscal 2010, and the stock was depressed. *Fast Company*'s 2010 list of the world's most innovative companies did not include Nvidia; neither did *Businessweek*'s. Moving from Stanford to Nvidia looked like a lateral move or maybe even a demotion. Intel, ten times bigger than Nvidia, was promising investors that there were methods to get around the leaky transistor problem; in repeated conference calls, Intel executives insisted that Moore's Law was not dead.

Around the time that Huang was trying to hire Dally, Intel made him a more lucrative offer. Dally considered it for a while, but ultimately chose to join money-losing Nvidia. He formally accepted his job as Nvidia's chief scientist in January 2009, right as the stock dipped into single digits. Jim Plummer, the dean of Stanford's engineering school and a member of Intel's board, questioned Dally's sanity. "Bill, you're crazy," Plummer said. "Intel is going to crush Nvidia." Dally was undeterred. "Jensen's just one of these people who's a natural leader," Dally said. "You want to follow him wherever he's going."

DALLY TRANSFORMED NVIDIA RESEARCH, growing it to more than three hundred people. Nvidia's ongoing advantage was that it would provide exponentially more computing power per dollar as time went on. Dally chose research projects that would intersect with that slope, a portfolio that would in time include robotics, automobiles, climate modeling, and biochemistry. In academia, Dally had enjoyed unlimited time to pursue his eccentric passions. At Nvidia, he was bound to the rhythm of the six-month GPU release cycle, but to his surprise he loved it. "There's far less bureaucracy, because everybody in the company—their livelihoods, their jobs and their families—are depending on this GPU getting to the finish line on time," he said.

Dally believed that Nvidia could do more outreach to academic customers. A few months after he joined, Nvidia organized the first annual "GPU Technology Conference," or GTC. The conference took place in 2009 at the Fairmont Hotel in downtown San Jose. Huang, who for many years had looked as if he bought most of his wardrobe with Kohl's Cash, was in the midst of an evolving glow-up. He arrived in a tight-fitting black shirt, boot-cut blue jeans, and black shoes with silver buckles. Huang, a natural per-former, managed the crowd with the practiced ease of a stage hypnotist. "Welcome to the Woodstock of high-performance computing," he said.

Huang liked spectacle. He had once asked Adam Savage and Jamie Hyneman, the hosts of *Mythbusters*, to demonstrate the difference between serial and parallel computing. Their demonstration featured two devices rigged to shoot paintballs at canvas. The first was a remote-controlled robot that shot one paintball at a time, rendering a crude smiley face over the course of about a minute. The second was a stationary array of cannons that shot 1,100 paintballs at once, rendering a pixelated version of the *Mona Lisa* in a split second. The audience loved it—it was that kind of crowd.

GTC operated in a similar register. The first night of the conference fea-tured a masquerade charity ball for a local elementary school. (The allure of the event was marginally diminished by the attendees, mostly middle-aged men wearing lanyards.) Featured topics the following day included quantum chemistry, augmented reality, and modeling the behavior of black holes. One of the talks was titled "Unlocking Biologically-Inspired Computer Vi-sion: a High-Throughput Approach." The presenter, an MIT professor named Nicolas Pinto, had assembled a large variety of image-recognition applications—including several neural networks—and used CUDA to op-timize them for Nvidia GPUs. He'd then asked the programs to identify characters and objects from video clips he'd culled from a collection of *Law & Order* DVDs. The best of the models, when blended together, could iden-tify Jerry Orbach with almost 90 percent accuracy, even when shown a new clip of Orbach for the first time. In the paper accompanying the presentation, Pinto observed that the Nvidia chipset offered 1,356 times the performance of a comparably priced Intel CPU.

Image recognition was a foundational problem for artificial intelligence—by teaching computers to recognize images, researchers were following the evolutionary trail toward more sophisticated capabilities. Around the time of the first GTC conference, paleontologists digging into a rock wall in Greenland discovered a five-hundred-million-year-old trilobite fossil whose neural tissue had been miraculously preserved. Older than the dinosaurs, the creature resembled a horseshoe crab, with eye stalks extruding from its body. Run your finger down its petrified optic nerve and you would arrive at a tiny clump of cells, smaller than a grain of rice. Here was the earliest brain ever found.

The fossil record showed that Pinto was on the right track—visual recognition had led to an explosion in biological intelligence and would soon do so again with computers. Unfortunately, his presentation, one of dozens that took place that week, did not receive much attention. Subsequent GTCs, held in 2010 and 2011, did not build on his insights, and in the first two years following publication, Pinto's paper received only fifteen citations. Neural nets were a neglected branch of inquiry. So were trilobite fossils, for that matter. No one cared.

IN THE MEANTIME, CUDA struggled. In the late 2000s, John Nickolls was once again diagnosed with melanoma. This time the disease proved fatal, and in 2011 he passed away. Dally, his competitive-skiing buddy, was devastated. So was Huang—when I asked him about Nickolls twelve years later, his face grew strained with emotion, and he changed the subject at once. Even when Nickolls was dying of cancer, he never stopped working. "I think some of his best, most productive years at Nvidia were during those times," his son, Alec, said. Nvidia funded a scholarship at the University of Illinois at Urbana-Champaign in his honor.

To his final breath, Nickolls insisted that CUDA would change the world, but he witnessed only a glimpse of what CUDA would become. The software that turned your graphics card into a supercomputer had been downloaded more than three hundred thousand times in 2009. Then interest declined for three straight years, bottoming in 2012 at slightly more than one hundred thousand new installs. The market for scientific computing looked saturated, and investors began to grumble that Nvidia's sustained investment in CUDA didn't make financial sense. "They were spending a fortune on this new chip architecture," Ben Gilbert, the cohost of *Acquired*, a popular Silicon Valley podcast, told me. "They were spending many billions targeting an obscure corner of academic and scientific computing, which was not a large market at the time—certainly less than the billions they were pouring in." By 2012, the situation was becoming dire. Nvidia's stock price had not appreciated in more than a decade, and although revenues and employment at the company had grown considerably, profits remained flat. Huang was bringing supercomputing to the masses, but the masses didn't want it.

In early 2013, Nvidia's board received a letter from the activist investor Starboard Value, which had taken a small stake in the company. Jeff Smith, Starboard's chief investment officer, targeted underperforming companies, demanding board seats and changes in strategy. When he encountered resistance, he usually tried to fire the CEO. Starboard's letter, while formally agnostic on CUDA, gently questioned whether what Huang was doing made any sense. Other investment analysts believed that if Nvidia stopped investing its profits in CUDA and instead returned them to shareholders, Nvidia's stock would trade higher. Some also questioned Huang's continuing fitness for the role.

Smith, forty-two, was youthful and energetic, with curly hair and a boyish face. He liked to question operational decisions in excruciating detail: he once managed to replace the entire twelve-person board of Darden Restaurants while holding less than 6 percent of the company's stock on the basis of a 294-slide plan to turn around the struggling Olive Garden chain. Starboard's Olive Garden slideshow became a legendary document among equity analysts, particularly slide 104, which criticized the restaurant's breadstick strategy. (Historically, Olive Garden waiters would bring one breadstick for every guest, plus one for the table; they would then refill the breadstick container as needed. But over time the quality of service deteriorated, and servers just started dumping a bunch of breadsticks on the table, reducing the amount of food that customers ordered.) Slide 163 noted Olive Garden had also stopped salting the pasta water in a misguided effort to extend the life of the cookware. "How can management of the world's largest Italian restaurant chain think it is OK to serve poorly prepared pasta?" Starboard asked.

Smith was good at playing the media, and he used the press to his advantage. In 2014, after he had forced eighty board replacements across thirty companies over the course of just three years, *Fortune* magazine called him "the most feared man in corporate America."

The perception of CUDA as a money pit was not obviously wrong—and Huang had killed off unprofitable business lines before, sometimes after spending years pursuing them. In the early 2000s, Nvidia had, for a time, made "northbridge" chips, which acted as a memory controller on the motherboard. After pursuing this market for several cycles, however, Huang realized he was in a race to the bottom with Intel. He scuttled the initiative and informed employees that he'd made a mistake. And while he was developing CUDA, Huang also invested in the graphics market for tablets and mobile phones. (In fact, in interviews from the early 2010s, Huang talks more about mobile phones than he does about supercomputing.) This was defensible—the mobile market was massive—but in 2011, Nvidia did something that made less sense, spending $367 million to buy Icera, a manufacturer of cellular modems. It was this misguided acquisition that had triggered Starboard's alarming letter: the modem market was mature and was dominated by Qualcomm. Smith and his lieutenants believed that with CUDA, graphics cards, mobile chips, and modems, Nvidia had thrown too many balls into the air. They visited Nvidia headquarters in 2012, urging Huang to focus. The meeting was cordial, but the underlying threat of a proxy fight for control of Nvidia was there.

Eventually, Huang came around to Smith's point of view and abandoned the modem market. "If we're fighting to the death in mobile, then we're not doing something else, right?" Huang said. Huang had fought to the death before, and won, but the experience had scarred him, and he was disinclined to do so again. But Huang never considered abandoning CUDA—for in this unpopular market Nvidia was the only provider.

Of the great many decisions Huang would make over the course of his career, the decision to double down on CUDA in the face of Jeff Smith was the riskiest. Unlike gamers, supercomputing customers were fickle and constantly starved of cash. Academic customers were dependent on unpredictable research grants. Corporate R&D was subject to scrutiny from skeptical CFOs. Ambitious government-research programs were announced with ten-year investment schedules, then devolved into protracted bureaucratic wrangling about how the money was to be dispersed. Even other semiconductor executives, no strangers to risk, thought CUDA unwise. It was the bet that made Jensen Jensen; it was the gamble that set him apart.

With the assistance of board member Jim Gaither—the same lawyer to whom Huang had once given all the money in his wallet—Huang organized a campaign to plead for his job. Nvidia's largest shareholders were the East Coast mutual funds. The most important was Fidelity, which managed more than a trillion dollars in customer funds and owned more shares of Nvidia than Huang did. Huang flew to Boston to meet with them. The meeting went poorly; Fidelity "beat the crap out of us," Gaither said. From Boston, Huang traveled to New York, meeting with a half-dozen other institutional investors. Huang did his best to persuade the giants to support CUDA, but he was grilled by skeptical portfolio managers. "It wasn't clear that there was a path to a real breakthrough," Gaither said.

Huang retained the support of his board, most of whom had been with him since the company's founding. But even here, there were the first whispers of discontent. "We were—look, you know, we were kind of going sideways," board member Tench Coxe said. Dawn Hudson, a former NFL marketing executive, was named to the board shortly after Starboard's letter arrived. "Nvidia did not have a great reputation when I joined," she said. "It was a distinctly flat, stagnant company."

AT HOME, Huang was suffering from empty-mansion syndrome. His son, Spencer, had left for an art academy in Chicago, with aspirations to become a photographer; his daughter, Madison, had enrolled in culinary school in Paris; his beloved dog, Sushi, had expired. Working constant eighty-hour weeks, Huang had missed out on much of Spencer and Madison's child-hood. "If I'm being honest, Lori did ninety percent of the parenting," he said. Typically, Huang spent one weekend day a week with his children, but even here he was often preoccupied. (Horstmann recalled visiting an amuse-ment park with Huang, where he repeatedly sent his kids on the roller coaster so the two could discuss technical problems.) Horstmann also observed that neither Huang's nor his own kids had initially gone into technical fields. "I think they tried to get out of this crazy work environment," he said. "I think they looked at us, and said, 'There's got to be more to life than this.'"

Huang, pained by their absence, tried to re-create the glow of family on their frequent visits home. He adopted two more dogs and, developing his culinary skills, often took to the kitchen, where he would improvise all man-ner of delicious food. Yet even this was not always a respite; Horstmann re-called a family gathering around the time of the Fidelity cross-examination when Huang botched a complex dish he was preparing. Standing in his million-dollar kitchen, with his daughter who had trained at Le Cordon Bleu there to help, Huang exploded and began to scream at his inadequate equipment. "I think we all understood we had to get out of the kitchen," Horstmann said. "It was just time for Jensen to yell at his stove."

IN SPEECHES, Huang has cited a visit to the office of Ting-Wai Chiu, a pro-fessor of physics at National Taiwan University, as giving him confidence during this time. Chiu, seeking to simulate the evolution of matter follow-ing the Big Bang, had constructed a home-brew supercomputer in a labora-tory adjacent to his office. Huang arrived to find the lab littered with GeForce boxes and the computer cooled by oscillating desk fans. "Jensen is a visionary," Chiu said. "He made my life's work possible."

Chiu, who had used gaming cards to build his machine, was the model customer. By shipping CUDA on the retail boards, Nvidia was marketing to even the most meager scientists—mad scientists, basically, whose research was so disfavored they couldn't afford a workstation. Here, Huang was once again following the gospel of Clayton Christensen. Disruptive technologies,

Christensen had observed, often grew out of hobbyist communities. They were developed using "bootlegged resources" in which "off-the-shelf components" were redeployed for something other than their intended purpose. They started out wonky but rapidly improved along attributes of performance that established players ignored.

But even once you had absorbed this lesson, it wasn't easy to implement. Pursuing niche markets cost profits, making investors question your sanity. This, too, Christensen had foretold: "One of the reasons managers at established firms find it difficult to serve emerging markets is that their investors and customers tell them not to."

That was the real secret of *The Innovator's Dilemma*, which readers often missed. It was not a book about how to succeed; it was a book about how *not* to fail. Christensen's book wasn't a how-to for start-ups but a counterinsurgency manual for senior managers at stagnating firms. Thirteen years in, Huang felt that Nvidia was at risk of becoming such a firm, and it was as much paranoia as optimism that led him to pursue the mad-science market. "There was a risk in shipping CUDA with every card, but there was also a risk in *not* doing it," Huang said to me in our first meeting, but it was only after researching his company for months that I came to understand what he meant. He was referring to the risk that someone *else* might do it—some small, hungry business, operating out of a dingy office next to a Chinese restaurant and a frequently robbed bank, willing to serve marginal academic customers for years, with limited profits and no clear future prospects, all in the hopes of one day doing to Nvidia what Nvidia had done to Silicon Graphics. It was a risk that only a disciple of Christensen would recognize.

One frustrating thing about Huang, though, was that even when you thought you agreed with him, he turned around and disagreed with you. When I mentioned the impact Christensen had on his company, he immediately contradicted me. "You have to absorb his book and its lessons," he told me, "but Christensen got as much wrong as he got right. There's much more to it." Christensen's marginally profitable customers were dirt bikers and trench diggers. Huang's marginally profitable customers were *scientists*.

They were scientists engaged in research, and in serving them, it was just possible he might enable one to change the world.

Lateral technology transfers of this type had happened before. In the early 1600s, Dutch craftsmen working in the spectacles business realized they could rearrange their eyeglass lenses to view distant objects. (One story credits the discovery to two children trying to observe a weather vane.) The lenscrafters flooded the Dutch patent office with designs for telescopes, and within a year, Galileo was pointing one toward the heavens, becoming the first human to describe the phases of Venus, the moons of Jupiter, and the rings of Saturn. Made from modified eyeglass lenses, Galileo's telescope had less magnifying power than a pair of modern bird-watching binoculars, but it forever changed our understanding of the universe and our place within it. By shipping low-budget supercomputers to the mad scientists, Huang hoped to enable a similar revolution.

Huang did not have a concrete vision of what the future of technology would look like. Some technologists did; for example, Elon Musk began with a vision of himself standing on the surface of Mars, then worked backward to build the technology he would need to get himself there. Huang went in the opposite direction; he started with the capabilities of the circuits sitting in front of him, then projected forward as far as logic would allow. Only there, at the frontier of reason, would he allow himself to take a single step forward into the nebulous realm of vibes.

"What Jensen does is beyond focus," Horstmann said. "I would call it *resonance*." To achieve this resonance, Huang engaged in constant interactions with his customers and his employees. At his conferences, he put the press in the back and the scientists in the front, and allocated his attention accordingly. His frequent visits with low-level employees weren't just to boost morale, but to feel the pulse of his company against his fingertip. "I remember times at LSI when we almost didn't have to do anything, because we were reading our customers' minds," Horstmann said. "And with parallel computing it was the same: through his discussions with his customers, with his employees, he could *feel* that resonance. He could see it was time."

The breakthrough was coming—Huang sensed it. He sensed it through his discussions with researchers and by their astonishment at the speed-ups his technology unlocked. He sensed it from the obsessive enthusiasm of brilliant employees like Bill Dally and John Nickolls and Ian Buck. He sensed it enough to torpedo his profits; he sensed it enough to compromise his core product; he sensed it enough to risk his job. It might not be from a quantum physicist like Chiu, specifically, but Huang was certain that somewhere out there was some lunatic whose ideas CUDA would prove right. Somewhere out there was some graduate student who would skip the grant-application circus to buy an Nvidia GPU with his housing stipend and usher in a revolution. Somewhere out there was some neglected branch of science waiting to harness the firepower of CUDA to shatter the paradigmatic frame. Huang just had no idea what it was.

ELEVEN

AlexNet

f Alex Krizhevsky could have turned himself invisible, he probably would have. The talented computer programmer had an almost pathological aversion to attention. He was a small man and a slight one, with pale skin and ruddy orange hair. He revealed few details about his private life to colleagues, even to some who had known him for years. Geoffrey Hinton, his PhD adviser, could tell me little about him, save one important detail: "Alex was probably the best programmer I ever met."

Hinton first met Krizhevsky in the late 2000s, when he was a graduate student living at home with his parents and attending the University of Toronto. Krizhevsky had been born to a Jewish family in the Soviet Union, in what is today the imperiled territory of eastern Ukraine. He had immigrated to Canada when he was young, and although his native tongue was Russian, he spoke English flawlessly, albeit infrequently. His affect reminded Hinton of a wizened espionage agent who had seen much and revealed little; he was able to convey a penetrating depth of intelligence in just a few words.

One day this enigmatic figure appeared uninvited at Hinton's office.

"He came to me and said, 'I'm the top student in software engineering, and it's boring,'" Hinton recalled. Could he join Hinton's group? The request was presumptuous: Hinton was a legendary academic who'd spent years developing neural networks. He was one of the coauthors on the seminal 1986 "backpropagation" paper and had championed this approach in the face of indifference and even hostility from mainstream AI researchers for decades.

But Hinton's crusade had taken him far from the mainstream centers of computer science like Stanford and MIT. Snowy Toronto was not the first place you thought of when you thought about tech. It probably wasn't even the tenth. Hinton had minimal funding for his research, and before he agreed to accept Krizhevsky as a student, he cautioned him that neural networks were deeply out of favor. Even though Hinton's group was producing results competitive with conventional approaches, their work was often rejected for publication. "Neural nets were regarded as nonsense," he told me.

The bias against neural nets, Hinton felt, was "ideological," a word he pronounced in the same venomous tone that Huang had used to say "political." The ideology of the research community at the time was that it was not enough that AI be useful. Instead, AI should somehow "unlock" the secrets of intelligence and encode them in math. The standard, 1,100-page AI textbook of the time was a survey of probabilistic reasoning, decision trees, and support-vector machines. The neural nets got just ten pages, with a brief discussion of backgammon up front. When Hinton's colleague designed a neural net that outperformed state-of-the-art software for recognizing pedestrians, he couldn't even get his paper admitted to a conference. "The reaction was well, that doesn't count, because it doesn't explain how the computation is done—it's just not telling us anything," Hinton said.

Hinton countered that nobody understood how to mathematically describe the way biological brains processed language, either, but this argument didn't get him anywhere. The AI community of the time didn't want to mimic intelligence—they wanted to *solve* it. Hinton thought trying to solve for the function of the brain was a little absurd, like trying to solve for the function of the kidney, but he couldn't get traction with this argument. So to disguise what he was doing and to better secure funding, he and other neural-net researchers described their work as "machine learning" or sometimes "deep learning"—anything but "AI."

Krizhevsky, undeterred, joined Hinton's group. Hinton paired him with Ilya Sutskever, another Russian-speaking Jewish immigrant from the former Soviet Union. Despite the biographical similarities, Sutskever looked and acted nothing like Krizhevsky. He was athletic, with dark, bushy eyebrows, deep-brown eyes, and a wicked smile. Hinton's most fervent acolyte, Sutskever argued that neural nets would one day outpace human intelligence, a claim that at the time even Hinton didn't make. "Ilya likes to say outrageous things, but he can get away with it because he's so open and honest," Hinton said. "He's sort of unconstrained by convention. He believes in himself. And he's right."

Hinton gave Sutskever and Krizhevsky an ambitious assignment: using Nvidia GPUs, he wanted them to teach a computer how to see. CUDA had made its way to Hinton's laboratory. In 2008 he had tasked graduate students Abdelrahman Mohamed and George Dahl with building a speech-recognition module using an expensive Nvidia server. By the beginning of 2009, Mohamed and Dahl's neural net rivaled the best mathematical models in existence. Hinton, speaking at the Neural Information Processing Systems conference later that year, told his audience that running neural nets on parallel-computing processors was the future of AI, and that the researchers should drop whatever they were doing and buy Nvidia GPUs. He then sent an email to Nvidia: "I just told 1,000 machine learning experts at this conference that they should all go buy Nvidia cards. Would you give me one for free?"

Nvidia declined. Although the company was pursuing a great number of supercomputing applications, at the time not a single dedicated AI researcher worked there. Machine learning was not among the potential applications Kirk had proposed for parallel computing in his textbook, and Hinton sometimes couldn't even get the CUDA group to return his emails. The bias against neural nets was long established; in introductory AI courses, one would still sometimes hear professors claim that neural nets couldn't even resolve simple logic functions, even though backpropagation had overcome this limitation decades before.

Hinton figured the only way to get Nvidia's attention was not just to equal his rivals but to crush them. Krizhevsky and Sutskever seemed the most likely in his group to accomplish this. The two had a great deal in common, although Sutskever didn't regard Krizhevsky as a friend, exactly— Krizhevsky was too private for that. But they were tuned to the same intellectual radio frequency, and even Hinton sometimes had a hard time keeping up. In office conversations, Hinton would ask them a question, and Krizhevsky and Sutskever would turn to each other to discuss it in Russian before turning back with the answer, which was inevitably correct.

Hinton wanted Krizhevsky and Sutskever to build an image-recognition system using a "convolutional" neural net, which employed mathematical filters to focus on key details in a picture. He encouraged the two to think big; he needed them not just to win but to obliterate. Krizhevsky, with no background in the discipline, rapidly mastered parallel-programming techniques—something in his brain just clicked with the paradigm of driving to Starbucks from everywhere at once. "He managed to make those GPU boards do convolutional neural networks much more efficiently than anybody else," Hinton said. "He really was a wizard."

In early 2012, Krizhevsky retooled an image-recognition network used for teaching exercises to run on CUDA. The GPU took just 30 seconds to train it. When Krizhevsky demonstrated his progress to Sutskever, Sutskever could not contain his excitement: the speed of the GPU was unprecedented, hundreds of times faster than anything he'd seen before. Sutskever had believed in the promise of neural nets from the moment he'd first learned about them. They just seemed like the obvious way computer intelligence would work. "If you allow yourself to believe that an artificial neuron is kind of like a biological neuron, then they should do everything we can do," Sutskever told me. "And if you allow yourself to believe that they can be accelerated—well, then you're training brains."

In the past, this approach had run up against the limitations of the hardware, but the GPU produced in half a minute what would have taken an

Intel machine an hour and what would have taken biology a hundred thousand years. Sutskever immediately recognized they had to scale the computing power available to Krizhevsky to the maximal degree—in other words, he had to make this new form of synthetic evolution run as fast as possible. This proved to be a keen and enduring insight. "Ilya sees things that other people take a long time to see more or less immediately," Hinton said.

The two graduate students pooled their money to build the fastest computer they could. This wasn't much—with their combined funds, Sutskever and Krizhevsky could afford to purchase only two GeForce GTX 580s, gaming GPUs that retailed for about $500 apiece online. When the GeForce units arrived, they looked like props from the movie *Alien*. Each unit weighed around three pounds, with black casing, slime-green accents, and a circular vent for the powerful fan that kept the circuits cool. Beneath the case was the giant Nvidia chip, embedded in a black circuit board and surrounded by heat sinks, comprising three billion transistors arranged in thirty-two parallel cores. This was the power Krizhevsky needed; these were the transistors that could dance.

After a few trial runs, Krizhevsky slotted the two GPUs into the desktop computer in his bedroom, then let them rip for a week. ("Actually, it was his parents who paid for the quite considerable electricity costs," Hinton said.) Here, finally, was the customer Huang had dreamed of, the programmer so broke he could only afford to do his experiments on a repurposed graphics accelerator. Here was Krizhevsky, a weirdo recluse whom even his colleagues knew little about. Here was the mad scientist. Here was the iconoclast. Here was the man who would build CUDA's killer app.

To train his neural network, Krizhevsky used the ImageNet database, a collection of images assembled by the Stanford computer scientist Fei-Fei Li. Disappointed by the limited scope of training datasets available online, Li had assembled her own by hiring workers from Amazon's Mechanical Turk service to manually label more than fifteen million images across twenty-two thousand categories. ImageNet was hundreds of times bigger than any comparable dataset; Li's advisers had questioned the wisdom of the effort, but it turned out to be exactly what Krizhevsky needed. His network had some 650,000 individual neurons, roughly the same number as a honeybee. Training such a large model required a massive amount of data.

At the beginning of the week, the neurons were connected at random, but as the training progressed, they rearranged themselves into an intricate, beautiful pattern, slowly learning how to see. In the first nanosecond of training, Krizhevsky's network was exposed to a randomly selected image from the dataset, then asked to assign it a label from one of Li's thousands of categories. Perhaps the image was a stingray; perhaps it was a Scottish terrier; perhaps it was a golf cart. Whatever it was, the network had never seen it before—so in returning a label, it could only guess, and this guess was certainly wrong. But, in guessing wrong, the network had gained a little bit of information, however small, about what the image was *not*—not a stingray, at any rate.

The network processed this information by retooling the connections between its neurons using Hinton's backpropagation approach. This was the difficult part, as it involved repeated "matrix multiplication," a mathematical operation that scientists compared to solving an unimaginably large Rubik's cube. Past attempts to train neural networks had always faltered here, but Krizhevsky had CUDA, which leveraged the GeForce's parallel architecture to crack this computational puzzle. Once the math was finished—in a fraction of a fraction of a second—Krizhevsky's network was shown a second image. Then a third, then a fourth, then thousands more, then millions more.

To "see" the images, the neural network did not actually process light. Instead, it was fed a stream of digits representing the placement and colors of a particular array of pixels. It then updated the grids of digits that represented the synaptic weights the network had assigned to different layers of interpretation. For this reason, skeptics would later argue that the neural network was "just doing math"—but this reductionist viewpoint was akin to saying the human retina was "just interacting with photons."

Sometime in the first couple minutes of training, Krizhevsky's network, by pure chance, managed to label its first image right—let's say it was a flowerpot. This grand success triggered an orgy of matrix multiplications as the backpropagation scheme attempted to communicate to the neurons what distinguished this thing called a "flowerpot" from a "chimpanzee" or a "pool table" or a "dump truck." The gain from success was marginal—shown a garbage can, the network was likely to guess "flowerpot" again. But shown an object of a totally different shape, like a whale shark, the network now knew just enough to make a distinction.

This process was repeated many millions of times, every moment of the day, transforming Krizhevsky's bedroom into a theater of hyperspeed evolution. The training of a neural network was a thing of wonder. Krizhevsky's network had several "layers," each of which slowly learned to distinguish among different aspects of the data. One layer learned shape, another color, a third the importance of symmetry, while snaking pathways for information wove the layers together into a unified, organic whole. Each time a new image appeared—a dragonfly, an hourglass, a mongoose, a container ship, a dirigible, a walking stick—those tendrils of information rearranged themselves into a more perfect mirror of reality.

The cooling fans on the GeForce units ran constantly, at around forty-four decibels; the combined noise was not deafening but was enough to keep Krizhevsky awake at night. Slowly, the success rate of image identification ticked upward, starting at 0 percent, moving to 1 percent, then 10 percent, then 40 percent, then 60 percent, before flatlining at an 80 percent success rate. The finished network still had some weaknesses: it was especially bad at distinguishing between human tools and could not tell a spatula from a hatchet. Krizhevsky could have kept tinkering with it, but the best that any other method for image recognition had ever achieved was 70 percent. Li's ImageNet group at Stanford ran an annual contest for AI image recognition, so as a sanity check, Krizhevsky tested his model against the prior year's competition data, which the model had never seen before. It easily squashed all of that year's entrants.

In machine-learning circles, training on labeled datasets like ImageNet was termed "supervised learning," so Krizhevsky called his neural network "SuperVision." Hinton and Sutskever were astonished—just absolutely gobsmacked. "GPUs showed up, and it felt like a miracle," Sutskever said, his enthusiasm undiminished even ten years later. Under ideal circumstances, the two GeForce cards could execute a combined three trillion operations per second. Doing the math, that meant the GPUs had executed quintillions of distinct mathematical steps in just under a week. That was over a hundred billion years' worth of human arithmetic now encoded into SuperVision's fragile synthetic brain. "To do machine learning without CUDA would have just been too much trouble," Hinton said.

Krizhevsky decided he would introduce SuperVision to the world by winning ImageNet's 2012 competition. In the weeks leading up to the event, Sutskever and Hinton began to pace the Toronto laboratory in giddy anticipation. "We knew we were going to win it," Hinton said. They were the first to experience what would soon become a common phenomenon: the uncontainable thrill of sneak previewing embargoed AI technology that would shock the world once unveiled. Theorizing on the impact that SuperVision would have on the world, the researchers discussed autonomous robots, self-driving cars, and self-coding computers. The three men regarded AI as a purely positive force for progress—or they did at the time, at least.

The Toronto research group began to see something else as well: if SuperVision had benefited from Nvidia, Nvidia was going to benefit from SuperVision even more, for the neural net's demands for increased parallel-computing power had no foreseeable limit. "It was pretty obvious to us, even before we submitted, that going forward a large fraction of scientific computation was going to be machine learning," Hinton said.

WHEN FEI-FEI LI first saw the SuperVision results, she wondered if they were in error. Li's ImageNet contest had been her attempt to prove the value of her efforts to her advisers, but after attracting thirty-five entrants in 2010, participation had declined to just fifteen entrants in 2011. In 2012, there were only seven, and it was not clear the contest would survive another year.

Now, one of those seven entrants was demonstrating a success rate above 80 percent—10 percent better than the state of the art in a field where improvement was typically measured in fractions of a percentage point. Stranger still, the winner was a neural network, a technology that Li considered to be a museum artifact. "It was like being told the land speed record had been broken by a margin of a hundred miles per hour in a Honda Civic," Li recalled in her autobiography, *The Worlds I See.*

Born in China, Li was an only child who had moved to New Jersey as a teenager. In high school, she was something of a dreamer, struggling to acclimate to American culture while helping her parents make ends meet. A friendly math teacher encouraged her academic development, and with his tutelage, she was offered a full scholarship to Princeton University. She'd majored in physics, then pursued a PhD in electrical engineering, with ambitions of teaching a machine to see.

But now, presented at last with a machine that actually *could* see, Li couldn't quite believe it was real. She asked her staff to double-check. "I talked to the guy who computed the results, and he thought there was a bug to begin with," Hinton said. Li's thesis adviser emailed Hinton to ask if he was absolutely, 100 percent sure his researchers hadn't accidentally contaminated his model by training on the contest data. "We had to check it several times before he believed that the computed results were correct," Hinton said.

Gradually, Li began to accept reality: her dying AI pageant had just crowned Miss Universe. The official ImageNet results were published in October 2012, with researchers scheduled to discuss their models at an academic conference in Florence, Italy, later that month. Li, having just given birth, had planned to skip the proceedings but changed her mind upon seeing the SuperVision results. She had to meet the genius behind the tech.

When Li arrived in Florence, Alex Krizhevsky didn't respond to her texts, and she began to wonder if he was even coming. Had he bailed? Was he lost in the Uffizi? But on the morning of the conference, Krizhevsky showed up without notice, safe in an oversized zippered sweatshirt with black glasses and a bushy hairdo. This was the architect? He looked like a teenager.

Krizhevsky was the final presenter of the day. The quality of his presentation was directly inverse to the importance of his results. As he opened his remarks, his voice suddenly cracked into a high and nasal register, and he gave a nervous cough while casting his eyes downward in embarrassment. He hurried through a series of black-and-white slides, rarely raising his eyes from the podium. One slide detailed SuperVision's impressive specifications: 650,000 neurons, 60,000,000 parameters, and 630,000,000 connections. "It was trained, actually, in my bedroom," Krizhevsky told the assembled crowd. "It's pretty big for the type of model you can train in your bedroom."

Krizhevsky's short talk ended with no indication that he'd just revolutionized computer science. "That's it," he said, in conclusion. "That's all I have." He then opened the floor to a series of surprisingly hostile questions. Or perhaps not so surprising: the unspoken implication of Krizhevsky's presentation was that it was time to throw all that fancy AI math in the trash. Krizhevsky was telling the assembled academics they had so far wasted their careers—in some cases, decades of research was going to be abandoned. Was it so much to ask Krizhevsky to properly present his findings? The other researchers, it seemed, were exorcising their frustrations, having lost to the man who'd cracked the hardest problem in computer science with a gaming rig in his childhood bedroom.

THE RECEPTION IN FLORENCE notwithstanding, the AI community embraced the SuperVision results. "A bunch of senior researchers more or less immediately said, these results are amazing, we were wrong, neural nets really do work," Hinton said. The 2013 ImageNet competition was overwhelmed by neural-net submissions, and by 2014, all of the more than forty contestants were using this approach. The accompanying academic paper for the SuperVision network, credited to Krizhevsky, Sutskever, and Hinton, has to date been cited more than 150,000 times, making it one of the single-most-important findings in the history of computer science. Krizhevsky pioneered a number of important programming techniques, but his key finding was that a GPU could train neural networks hundreds of times faster than a CPU could.

Inside Google, a Polish researcher named Wojciech Zaremba was tasked with replicating SuperVision. As his network, WojNet, began to percolate throughout the industry, Hinton feared that the modest Krizhevsky wouldn't get credit for his breakthrough. He encouraged Krizhevsky to rename SuperVision so that it emphasized his contributions; although he questioned the utility of the exercise, Krizhevsky complied. ("Alex isn't into things like branding," Hinton said.) Henceforth, SuperVision was known as "AlexNet."

Hinton need not have worried, however—Big Tech had suddenly grown extremely interested in the backwater University of Toronto computer science department, and the days of funding shortages were over. The AlexNet team was bombarded with acqui-hire offers. At Sutskever's insistence, Hinton incorporated a start-up venture named DNNResearch, with Hinton, Krizhevsky, and Sutskever each holding one-third of the shares. DNN-Research had no customers, no board, no revenues, and no website. It had nothing except the collective brainpower of the three men who'd cracked the code.

That was enough. In December 2012, while attending a research conference, Hinton conducted an auction via email to sell this "company." Working out of a seventh-floor hotel room in Lake Tahoe, the AlexNet team realized they were about to strike it rich. Microsoft and a London-based AI start-up called DeepMind submitted early offers, but both dropped out after a few rounds, resulting in a final bidding war between Google and the Chinese tech giant Baidu. As the bids crossed $20 million, the three researchers occasionally strolled over to the window to admire the wooded Sierra Nevadas, dusted with snow.

When Google's offer reached $44 million, Hinton, with the endorsement of Sutskever and Krizhevsky, cut the auction off and took the money. Google, the three felt, was a more natural cultural fit than Baidu. AlexNet, the neural network that Krizhevsky trained in his bedroom, could now be mentioned alongside the Wright Flyer and the Edison bulb. "That was a kind of Big Bang moment," Hinton said. "That was the paradigm shift."

PART II

TWELVE

O.I.A.L.O.

B ryan Catanzaro stuck out at Nvidia. In the hive of STEM drones he was the dreamer. His hair was long, and he dressed like a jester, with statement eyeglasses and loud, tacky shirts. The first time we spoke, he was wearing a rainbow T-shirt decorated with JPEG compression artifacts; the second time we spoke, he was wearing a sweater embroidered with an owl. He was patient and kind, and he spoke in a soothing, gentle voice. He was the only Nvidia engineer I met who had a humanities degree.

Catanzaro had grown up in the Mormon Church, and a year after graduating high school, he began working as a missionary in Siberia. For two years he spoke nothing but Russian. "I was very, very committed," he said. While there, he read *Crime and Punishment* in the original, a moving experience for a germinating existentialist. He returned to Brigham Young University and earned a degree in Russian literature. "My favorite writer, of course, is Dostoyevsky," Catanzaro said. "Dostoyevsky, Tolstoy, and Pushkin, they're the top three for me."

Simultaneously, Catanzaro pursued a dual degree in computer engineering. (He had a good sense of the economic value of his literature degree.) In 2001 he was hired as a summer intern at Intel, where he was asked, as an exercise, to design a microchip that could pulse at ten billion beats per second. Doing the math, Catanzaro concluded the question was a setup: such a chip could never be built. He presented his findings to a group of senior engineers. "You must have done your work wrong," his supervisor said. "This is part of Intel's road map." Catanzaro was stunned. He double-checked his calculations but could find no error. The transistors were getting too small, the end of Moore's Law was approaching, and Intel was ignoring it. "I mean, I was just an intern, right?" he said. "But I could see that traditional computer architectures were running into the wall."

Catanzaro was convinced the solution was to redesign the microchip anew. He cofounded the UC-Berkeley Parallel Computing Lab in the mid-2000s, along with several colleagues. There, Catanzaro made a list of existing parallel applications. The business problem, he could see, was that even for the supposedly hungriest customers, the demand for computing power was capped: once you sold an oil prospector a supercomputer, you saturated demand for years. What you needed, Catanzaro figured, was an application that was so hungry for computation that it could never be satisfied. You needed another application like 3D graphics that demanded *more* computer power once its initial needs were fulfilled. Eventually, Catanzaro deduced what *had* to be parallel computing's killer app. "The answer to that was AI," Catanzaro said. "I came to AI from the bottom up. I came from a circuits perspective. I felt it was just inevitable that AI was the most important computational workload."

Catanzaro's Berkeley advisers were reluctant to support his AI efforts. To many computer scientists, trying to build an AI was like trying to find Bigfoot. Neural nets, in particular, were viewed by mainstream researchers with something like contempt. "The thought was, you know, the computing industry is full of eccentric characters, and these guys are out there doing this old thing, it's very eccentric, and it doesn't work," Catanzaro said. When Catanzaro told me this story, he combed his fingers downward through his shoulder-length hair and shook his locks. I sensed his frustration: before anyone, he had had the insight to combine AI with parallel computing, but his professors had steered him away from using the right tool.

Instead, Catanzaro fooled around with the fancy math and published a few unexciting research papers. In the meantime, while pursuing his Berkeley PhD, he still had to pay the rent. He and his wife had three children, and the family was living in the Bay Area on a graduate student's income. Desperate, Catanzaro applied for every available corporate fellowship. He cycled through eight internships in six years, each one paying just enough to save his family from eviction. The upside of the experience was that it gave him a tour inside the titans of silicon.

First, Catanzaro returned to Intel. By this time, Intel could see that Nvidia posed a threat, and Catanzaro was assigned to assist with "Project Larrabee," a graphics chip that Intel internally referred to as the "GeForce killer." Such bravado proved toothless—the Larrabee hardware was repeatedly delayed by infighting, then killed off before launch. Catanzaro believed that management wasn't passionate about advancing computing technology. "To them, Intel might as well have been a machine that made soap," he said.

Catanzaro then interned at Qualcomm, the San Diego chip designer that had built much of the infrastructure for the modern cellular phone. Qualcomm was well-managed, and the pay was great, but Catanzaro was put off by their vocal denigration of rivals. "They kept telling me that Nvidia was a horrible place to work and that their CEO was some kind of tyrant," Catanzaro said.

This did not accord with Catanzaro's own experience at Nvidia, where he had also worked. It was Catanzaro who had compared interacting with Huang to sticking a finger in the electric socket—but it was also Catanzaro who emphasized that Huang was not a man selling soap. He was a man whose passion for computing was not to be surpassed, and if there was anyone Catanzaro could convince about the coming intersection between parallel computing and AI, it was Huang. After Catanzaro was awarded his PhD, in 2011, he chose Nvidia.

Catanzaro joined Bill Dally's expanding group at Nvidia Research, an experience he compared to graduate school, "only bigger and better." The place had an academic vibe, with researchers free to pursue their passions and collaboration with other corporate research groups encouraged. Dally published many of his discoveries in academic journals for public consumption and with no financial reward. Often, he coauthored papers with engineers at AMD and Intel. Dally's openness surprised a lot of people and sometimes led to pursed lips inside Nvidia, but Dally was playing the long game: he figured it was better to advertise what he was doing to other leading scientists so that they would come to work alongside him. "We'll get the best academics to join the company because they'll see our publications," he would say. "The quality will speak for itself."

One of those academics was Catanzaro. Although he was initially assigned to study programming languages, Catanzaro soon became Nvidia's first dedicated AI researcher. Dally was hearing whispers about progress in neural-net technology and decided it was an area he couldn't ignore. In 2012 he farmed out Catanzaro to his former colleague Andrew Ng, a Stanford professor who worked for Google. Ng had developed similar technology to AlexNet in Mountain View—only he'd done it using conventional computing architecture. This was expensive; using a cluster of two thousand CPUs, Ng had fed thumbnails from ten million YouTube videos into a neural network in an attempt to teach it how to identify a cat. The project was costly, and the power draw was ruinous, but at the end of the training cycle, Ng's neural net had synthesized a striking internal conception of the feline phenotype, which Ng extracted and distributed to the press.

The computer's impression of a cat was featured in a widely circulated article in *The New York Times* in June 2012. For Dally, the interesting finding was not that the neural network could recognize animals but that it had taken so much computation to get there. Dally deputized Catanzaro to repeat the cat experiment using Nvidia hardware. Catanzaro was able to do it with just twelve GPUs.

THINGS BEGAN TO MOVE fast now—everyone was clustering in the Valley. Following the Google acquisition, Krizhevsky, Hinton, and Sutskever relocated to Mountain View, where they instigated a parallel-computing insurrection. When Krizhevsky was offered the use of Google's massive CPU cluster, he declined, instead purchasing a commodity PC and a couple of retail Nvidia cards and installing them in an office closet. Soon, other researchers at Google were disconnecting from Google's sprawling archipelago of data centers—probably the largest private collection of computers in the world at the time—to run gaming hardware under their desks.

Catanzaro, sensing something in the air, returned to Nvidia to ask for more resources. Initially, he was turned down. With his sensitive disposition and the stigma of a humanities degree, Catanzaro was not the model Nvidia employee. "My reviews at Nvidia were not very good," he told me. "My pay wasn't very good either." Undeterred, he began to work full time, by himself, on building cuDNN, a software library that would accelerate neural-network development on the CUDA platform.

It was a struggle at first. Catanzaro was a researcher with no experience in practical software engineering. His fourth child had just arrived, and he wasn't getting much sleep at home. He was having health issues, and his medication was making him feel "kind of dumb." When he presented his prototype for cuDNN to Nvidia's software team in early 2013, they panned it. Catanzaro began to second-guess himself. "I don't think that my managers really thought I was doing important work," he said. "It just wasn't coming together."

Catanzaro decided to make his case directly to Huang. Machine learning technology did not seem to be on his dashboard; at the 2013 GTC conference in March, Huang spoke of weather modeling and mobile graphics, and he didn't mention neural nets at all. (He had, however, worn a leather jacket to the conference for the first time—a bulky, ugly thing. His look was still evolving.) To Catanzaro's surprise, Huang was immediately intrigued. Following their first meeting, Huang cleared his schedule and spent an entire weekend reading about AI, a subject about which he knew little. Another meeting soon followed, where Catanzaro found that his boss now knew as much—perhaps more—about neural nets as he did.

Huang's CUDA bet had taken the company far into uncharted waters. For a decade, he had stood at the prow of the ship, scanning for land. Now it was as if he had found Atlantis. He threw himself into research and phone calls, and the more he learned, the more his excitement grew. By the middle of 2013, Huang was vibrating with wild-eyed, resonant intensity. He called Catanzaro into the conference room he was using as his office and told him that he considered cuDNN to be the single most important project in his company's twenty-year history. The whiteboard on the wall had been cleared of diagrams; in its place, Huang had written the cryptic acronym "O.I.A.L.O." in perfect lettering. This, Huang said, stood for "Once in a Lifetime Opportunity." He asked the dumbfounded Catanzaro to participate in a thought experiment. "He told me to imagine he'd marched all eight thousand of Nvidia's employees into the parking lot," Catanzaro said. "Then he told me I was free to select anyone from the parking lot to join my team."

HUANG SOMETIMES TOOK a while to warm up to ideas. "With parallel computing, it really took us a fair amount of convincing to talk Jensen into it," Kirk recalled. "Same with CUDA. We really had to make the business case." But with AI, Huang experienced a damascene epiphany. "He got it immediately, before anybody," Kirk said. "He was the first to see what it could be. He really was the first."

Huang told me he was just reasoning from first principles. "The fact that they can solve computer vision, which is completely unstructured, leads to the question 'What else can you teach it?'" Huang said. The answer seemed to be: everything. Huang concluded that neural networks would revolutionize society and that he could use CUDA to corner the market on the necessary hardware. He announced that he was betting the company. "He sent out an email on Friday evening saying everything is going to deep learning, and that we were no longer a graphics company," Greg Estes, a vice president at Nvidia, said. "By Monday morning, we were an AI company. Literally, it was that fast."

Huang had turned fifty a few months earlier. Although his hair was beginning to gray, he retained a boyish eagerness and roamed the halls of his company with vigor, frequently stopping to quiz junior employees on their work. As his company grew larger, Huang began holding quarterly all-staff presentations. He could talk extemporaneously for more than two hours at a time, and in these presentations he would often revisit the same themes: the importance of the "speed of light" scheduling concept, the pursuit of the fabled "zero-billion-dollar market," and above all, the ever-present danger of creeping bureaucracy.

As Nvidia grew, Huang maintained an agile corporate structure, with no fixed divisions or hierarchy. The C-Suite was essentially just him, with no COO, no CTO, no CMO, and no obvious second-in-command. Huang didn't even have a chief of staff. Instead, he had more than thirty people reporting to him directly, most of them given fluid responsibilities under the all-encompassing title of "vice president." The parking lot thought experiment he'd practiced with Catanzaro reflected his belief that his company might need to kaleidoscopically reorganize itself at any time. "I need all of you to be ready," he would tell his assembled executive staff. "You never know when you might suddenly become the most important person in this company."

THE MOST IMPORTANT PERSON in the company in early 2014 was Catanzaro, a cultural misfit with consistently poor performance reports. Now managing a team of engineers, Catanzaro stripped cuDNN down to its most essential task: accelerating evolution. In human brain tissue, each neuron maintains an average of around one thousand synaptic connections with other adjacent neurons. The brain alters these connections through chemistry. The neural net alters them through matrix multiplication.

Matrix multiplication combines the numbers in one grid with those in a second to produce a third. The rules for populating the new grid are straightforward, but as the matrices grow large, the number of required calculations explodes. This makes the operation a good candidate for parallelism, but before the arrival of the neural network, matrix multiplication had not been a priority at Nvidia.

The chief custodian of CUDA's matrix multiplication library was Philippe Vandermersch, a somewhat cantankerous Frenchman who rode his bicycle to the office every day. Vandermersch had rescued the orphaned software package after it was left unfinished by its previous developers. He then spent several years fruitlessly attempting to convince global-warming researchers to upgrade climate simulations written in ancient Fortran code to his modern implementation. Few scientists wanted to put in the effort. "Those guys in the lab, honestly they could be a little lazy," he said.

But with neural nets, there was no switching cost. Most of the code was being written for the first time, by brilliant and motivated programmers who valued speed above all. These were the power users that Huang had long envisioned: as the neural-net community coalesced around CUDA, they became lifetime customers for Nvidia chips as well. Vandermersch, picked out of the parking lot, joined Catanzaro's team as his ace programmer and optimized his function library to meet the needs of AI. (In his telling, at least, Vandermersch also did a lot of the technical work. "You could say Catanzaro was the Jobs of cuDNN," he said. "I was the Wozniak.")

Over time, Nvidia's programmers found clever ways to speed these matrix operations up. One thing they noticed early on was that most of the weights in a neural net were clustered between plus and minus one. Numbers outside that range could often be truncated, speeding up operations and compacting size. Another thing they noticed was that, even between plus and minus one, weights didn't need to be represented so perfectly. Just like in the brain, the neurons were "fuzzy," maintaining loose synaptic connections rather than precise ones. Sometimes it was enough just to get the sign right.

AlexNet had used 650,000 neurons to represent 630,000,000 synaptic connections. At that scale, any one synapse hardly mattered. Serial code was so finicky that sometimes a single misplaced semicolon could crash an entire operating system, but for neural nets a bad weight was just one data point among millions. For this reason, as they developed cuDNN, Nvidia programmers rebalanced the trade-off between precision and speed. Good neural-net software, they reasoned, should favor the latter.

AlexNet's brain was the size of an insect's, but forthcoming neural nets would be larger. As they grew, training would not be the only concern; it was equally important that users be able to quickly get answers. (Imagine an oracle who knew all the answers but spoke only one word per hour.) This inference process used less computing power than the training stage, but over time it grew to be a significant portion of the cuDNN library.

Huang followed Catanzaro's progress with great interest. The two met frequently, and Huang had to repeatedly apologize to Catanzaro for mis-pronouncing his last name. At many firms—most, perhaps—Catanzaro's cuDNN library would have been taken away from him and handed to a seasoned product manager. At Nvidia, Catanzaro, who'd never developed a single piece of commercial software or even really managed anyone, was put in charge of the company's flagship product. Catanzaro himself questioned if he was the right person for the job, especially as his production deadline neared, and Huang, having rewarded innovation with loyalty, now re-warded tardiness with abuse. "Jensen is not an easy person to get along with all the time," Catanzaro told me. "I've been afraid of Jensen sometimes. But I also know that he loves me."

As the launch date neared, Catanzaro privately worried that his boss was falling into an age-old trap. If there was one field that had a worse per-formance record than parallel computing, it was AI. Going back to the 1950s, AI technology had gone through repeated hype cycles that ended with embarrassing busts. Catanzaro, like all researchers in the field, was keenly aware of AI's traumatic past encounters with commerce, and he worried that AI was preparing to disappoint investors once again. But he said nothing to Huang—the opportunity he'd been offered was just too good.

Anyhow, if Catanzaro could remember the past, Wall Street could not. Almost three decades had passed since the expert-systems crash of the 1980s, a span of time beyond the memory of all but the most durable equity ana-lyst. As the buzz about neural networks spread, Nvidia's stock moved higher, and Starboard Value stopped sending letters. "They doubled their money and disappeared," Coxe said.

By early 2014, cuDNN was preparing to ship. Huang took the stage at GTC 2014 to promote the work, and for the first time in its twenty-one-year history, Nvidia was publicly associated with AI. (Huang skipped the leather jacket this time, instead wearing black slacks and a sleek, dark-blue polo shirt that was unbuttoned to the chest. His power was growing.) Huang showed off Ng's network, with its internal conceptions of a cat and a human face. He walked the audience through several early-stage Nvidia AI initiatives. Then, mispronouncing his name, he ceded the presentation to Catanzaro, who used a variant of AlexNet to identify dog breeds posted to Twitter. Operating in real time, the network identified a Dalmatian, a German shepherd, a vizsla, and a cairn terrier. ("I didn't even know what a cairn terrier was," Catanzaro said.) With these adorable posts, the long AI ice age came to an end.

In his final slide, Huang revealed corporate partners who were beta-testing cuDNN, including Adobe, Facebook, and Netflix. The slide didn't mention Google, an AI customer too important to be publicly identified. A few weeks before the dog show, Google had acquired DeepMind, the London-based AI company cofounded by Demis Hassabis, Mustafa Suleyman, and Shane Legg. DeepMind had grand ambitions to build the world's first artificial "general" intelligence, or AGI, unlocking the puzzle of cognition once and for all. Already, the company was developing AlphaGo, a neural network that would, in a series of thrilling matches against grand master Lee Sedol in 2016, crack the Japanese game of Go, a long-standing milestone for AI. With Ng's group, the AlexNet group, and DeepMind, Google had established an early AI monopoly.

As Google's AI efforts expanded, researchers began demanding GPUs. In late 2014, Google launched "Project Mack Truck," a secret effort to build the world's most powerful parallel computer. The finished product required more than forty thousand Nvidia GPUs, costing more than $130 million. It was by far the largest single purchase order Nvidia had ever received, but it was only the start. As AI succeeded, parallel computing now emerged from a long and unforgiving winter of its own.

The truth, not widely understood until later, was that the deep-learning revolution was as much a revolution in hardware as software. It was the product of not one but *two* unpopular, cast-off, discredited, and cash-starved technologies whose ideal form could only be revealed in synthesis. Neural nets running on parallel computers: these tightly coupled technologies were the twin strands of DNA for a new and powerful organism, looking to consume all the data in the world.

THIRTEEN

Superintelligence

J ens Horstmann had started to notice a change in his old friend. In the
past, no matter how hard he worked, Huang had maintained a gentler
side at home. He set aside time for his outside interests—his dogs, his
whiskey library, and his collection of expensive automobiles, which now included a Tesla Roadster and a Koenigsegg supercar. Huang had also purchased a large, beachfront vacation house in Maui with a sunset view. He
often hosted friends there, including Morris Chang of TSMC, with whom
he'd grown close.

Huang's great outside passion remained cooking. For one of his birth-
days, his friends had arranged for him to train under a Michelin-starred
chef at the Four Seasons hotel. When he arrived in the morning, he was
subjected to a round of hazing. "He was ridiculed by the real chef," Horstmann said. "I mean, he'd done Denny's, but this was something else."
Huang worked a twelve-hour shift, experiencing, for the first time in many
years, the role reversal of having his boss yell at him. After serving his
friends dinner, Jensen fell asleep in the passenger seat of the car on the way
home.

But as Nvidia moved into AI, Huang abandoned his hobbies. His appetite for mischief diminished, he stopped practicing table tennis, and the teppan grill went cold. He even stopped returning texts. "He was just so, so focused on work," Horstmann said. "It was all he could talk about." The conviction that Huang had been given a once-in-a-lifetime opportunity seized him. The acronym "O.I.A.L.O." was repeated at every meeting. From the day Huang had started his career, at twenty, he had worked relentlessly, putting in consecutive twelve-hour days, six days a week, for three decades straight. Now past fifty, and with his kids grown, he began to work even harder.

In the past, to relax, Huang had enjoyed going to the movies by himself. He preferred big-budget popcorn flicks, particularly the Avengers movies, which he watched as much to grade the execution of the CGI as for the story. But many of the Marvel fanboys were also gamers, and Huang's photo had been posted to the Nvidia subreddit enough times that he became a recognizable presence in the theater. Tired of audience members pestering him for selfies, Huang tried, for a while, to attend only ten a.m. showings, but even here he was noticed. Eventually, he stopped going. From 2014 onward, there was only work. There was only AI.

NVIDIA'S STOCK PRICE went up 30 percent in 2013, 27 percent in 2014, and 66 percent in 2015. The last was enough to finally and permanently push Nvidia above the peak it had reached way back in 2001, when Nvidia was first added to the S&P 500 index. The timing of Nvidia's inclusion was relevant; the index funds that controlled America's retirement savings had been mandated to buy Nvidia stock the following trading day. For fourteen years, retail investors had backed this dog with nothing to show for it. Now it was time for everyone to get paid.

On paper, Nvidia was still a gaming company, with retail GeForce sales supplying most of its revenue. Wall Street, looking forward, began to value it as a cutting-edge AI firm. Google's bulk purchase of GPUs during Project

Mack Truck was being replicated at other major tech firms, including Amazon, Oracle, and Microsoft. The business plan for these "cloud-service providers" was to build hyperscale data centers running tens or even hundreds of thousands of GPUs, then lease them to corporate customers.

Cloud providers sold computing power in the manner of a utility, just like water or electricity. The data centers were located in unmarked industrial warehouses spread throughout the world. Walk through security, past an airlock, and onto the climate-controlled floor of a data center, and you would find many rows of seven-foot-high "racks" that resembled stack shelving in a library. Each rack held several horizontal "trays," and each tray contained one or two GPUs. The trays were modular and easy to upgrade, and the entire system was interlinked via cabling, allowing hundreds of GPUs to act in concert as a unified computer. A smaller core of CPUs administered the system, and a thick bundle of fiber optics connected it to the outside world.

Nvidia didn't make the racks or the trays, and it normally didn't build the data centers themselves. All it supplied were the chips, but this was a lucrative business—one in which Nvidia enjoyed a virtual monopoly. Nvidia named its chip architectures after famous scientists from the past: Curie, Tesla, Fermi, Kepler, Maxwell, Pascal, Turing, Volta, Ampere, Lovelace, Hopper, and Blackwell. The later chipsets included dedicated circuits for AI, ensuring that the trays in the data centers required continuous upgrades. The six-month upgrade cycle spurred panic buying from the vendors supplying the machine-learning vanguard, resulting in tremendous profits.

Prices from the cloud-service providers were quoted in "dollars per GPU per hour," with fresh Nvidia chipsets approaching $3 per. (Access to comparable Intel CPUs cost a few cents.) At this rate, it would have cost about $500 to train AlexNet's insect brain, but researchers were now developing far more ambitious models, with billions of parameters and training costs in the millions. Although training was expensive, if done correctly it could pay for itself, as Google's efforts showed: by using a neural network to optimize the power draw of its server network, Google was able to save hundreds of millions of dollars on its annual electric bill, recouping the cost of its investment in AI almost immediately. Google also debuted image-recognition tools for its photos application, created automatic tags for user pictures, and used AI to improve the quality of its search results.

Other large tech firms integrated AI into their products. Soon, Instagram, Facebook, and Twitter were harvesting users' attention by organizing their feeds "algorithmically," a euphemism for using machine-learning techniques to drive engagement. (Such tactics were as exploitative as they were effective; social media's mechanical curators could keep users doomscrolling for hours by feeding them rage bait.) Investments in AI led to profits in such direct fashion that Huang resurrected one of the oldest pitches in retail sales: "The more you buy, the more you save."

Venture capitalists began shoveling money at AI start-ups, investing not only in image and speech recognition but also in health care, retail self-checkout, self-driving cars, and education. In 2010, venture investment in AI was closer to zero than any other meaningful number; by 2015, it had swelled to $5 billion and was rapidly growing. "We've been investing in a lot of startups applying deep learning to many areas, and every single one effectively comes in building on Nvidia's platform," Marc Andreessen, of the firm Andreessen Horowitz, said in early 2016. "Our firm has an internal game of what public companies we'd invest in if we were a hedge fund. We'd put all our money into Nvidia."

A lot of money was also flowing into the bank accounts of skilled deep-learning engineers. The preferred metric for assessing a job offer was "total comp," which aggregated base pay, bonuses, stock options, and benefit packages into a magic number that could exceed seven figures annually. In late 2014, Bryan Catanzaro left Nvidia to join Baidu, where he worked with Andrew Ng. "They tripled my salary," Catanzaro said with a shrug, adding ruefully that if he'd just stayed put at Nvidia, he'd have made more from his stock options. Bas Aarts, who built the first CUDA compiler, also left around this time. Within a few years, though, both Aarts and Catanzaro were back. There was no other firm. There was only Nvidia.

. . .

AS AI SCALED, observers grew alarmed. In his 2014 book *Superintelligence*, Nick Bostrom, a Swedish philosopher at Oxford University, compared humans tinkering with machine intelligence to "small children playing with a bomb." He suggested that a computer capable of general, abstract intelligence would probably be the last invention humans would ever have to make. He posited that a generally intelligent computer might begin to self-augment, transforming itself—perhaps within just a few seconds—to a "superintelligence" that would, to human purposes, seem omnipotent. He wondered if such a machine would do to humans what humans had done to gorillas: conquer the planet and destroy their habitat, leaving a few exemplars of the species to serve as charismatic mascots in protected preserves.

Bostrom's book was an extension of ideas he'd been considering for years. He had previously advanced the "paper-clip maximizer" thought experiment:

> Suppose we have an AI whose only goal is to make as many paper clips as possible. The AI will realize quickly that it would be much better if there were no humans because humans might decide to switch it off. Because if humans do so, there would be fewer paper clips. Also, human bodies contain a lot of atoms that could be made into paper clips. The future that the AI would be trying to gear toward would be one in which there were a lot of paper clips but no humans.

The paper-clip maximizer argument had long circulated online, and it gained traction among the "rationality" community, as well as with many tech executives. A few months after the publication of Bostrom's book, Elon Musk posted a comment to the futurology website Edge.org:

> The pace of progress in artificial intelligence (I'm not referring to narrow AI) is incredibly fast. Unless you have direct exposure to

groups like Deepmind, you have no idea how fast—it is growing at a pace close to exponential. The risk of something seriously danger-ous happening is in the five year timeframe. 10 years at most.

He deleted the comment minutes later, but screenshots circulated widely. Like many of Musk's predictions, the timing was exaggerated—but the long-term risk was there.

A few months later, Musk joined Huang for a discussion at GTC 2015. It was here that Huang finally nailed his signature look. Taking the stage at the San Jose Convention Center, he wore a black leather jacket over a dark-blue polo, black slacks, and black shoes. The outfit was striking, and it was expensive—most of the clothing was of high-end manufacture. Huang would later credit his wife and his daughter for the makeover. Madison was especially influential; shortly after Jensen's wardrobe reveal, she would leave the culinary trade to join the French luxury conglomerate LVMH. When I spoke with Huang about his clothes, in 2023, he admitted he often was un-sure what brand he was wearing on any given day. "I think this is, uh, Tom Ford, maybe?" he said, opening his glossy black jacket to look at its label.

Huang's presentation that year was a nonstop AI showcase. First, he in-vited the Slovakian researcher Andrej Karpathy to the stage. Working at Fei-Fei Li's lab at Stanford, Karpathy had glued two neural nets together, one that identified images in the manner of AlexNet and a second that pro-vided elegant natural-language descriptions of what it saw. To this com-bined network, an image of a bird was not merely a "bird" but "a bird perched on the branch of a tree." An image of an airplane was not just an "airplane" but "a large airplane sitting on top of a runway." Most impressive was a photograph, taken from behind, of a man driving a carriage. Karpa-thy's amalgamated network interpreted it perfectly: "a man riding a horse drawn carriage down a street."

Huang then gleefully walked Karpathy through some errors. A flying fish was "a small white bird flying over a body of water," two men on a to-boggan were "a man and a child sitting on a bench," and an infant holding a toothbrush was "a young boy holding a baseball bat." (Distinguishing between categories of human tools remained a weak spot for neural networks.) Karpathy acknowledged that his network had limitations: it was mimicking speech without necessarily understanding it, and when it got to a concept it didn't understand, it proudly produced nonsense. Karpathy had termed these mistakes "hallucinations."

Musk then came to the stage. As one, the audience raised their smartphones and started to record. Huang was a Tesla fanboy who owned versions of all three cars the company had produced and geeked out over Tesla software updates. Musk had been using Nvidia's chips to power Tesla's heads-up display modules since 2011. Once the two men were seated, Huang got straight to the point. "You were quoted as saying artificial intelligence was more dangerous than nuclear weapons," Huang said.

Musk shifted in his chair. "I said 'potentially.'"

"You also said it's like summoning a demon," Huang said. Musk glared at him. Huang didn't press, and changed topics to self-driving cars. ("I almost view this as a solved problem," Musk said. "We'll be there in a few years.") The two discussed automobiles for a while, but at the end Musk revisited Huang's promptings about existential risk. "It's odd that we're so close to the advent of AI," Musk said. "It seems strange that we'd be alive at this time."

With that, the sedate and anticlimactic AI summit ended. The real discussion took place backstage, outside the view of cameras and investors. With Jens Horstmann and Chris Malachowsky standing nearby, Musk and Huang shared their true thoughts on AI, the ones not fit for public consumption. The two began to fire concepts and strategies at each other, and this made them excited. Soon, their rapid exchange more closely resembled a high-speed data link than human conversation. "They were bouncing ideas off each other, and we had no idea what they were talking about," Horstmann said. "Even Chris was baffled."

THE PARALLELS BETWEEN MUSK and Huang were obvious. They were immigrants; they were workaholics; they were visionaries. They were scream-ers; they were gamblers; they were world-class engineers. They moved with confidence into barren commercial brownfields, strewn with the remains of luckless entrepreneurs, and for the first time made them bloom.

It took a sharper eye to spot the differences. There was the vision question, with Musk moving backward from fantasy and Huang moving forward from reality. There was also the topic of loyalty. Musk did not value it; he often fired people arbitrarily and without warning, in one case canning the entire Starlink engineering team almost at random on a Sunday afternoon. Huang almost never fired anyone, and when he did, it was only after multiple cautions and the offer of a performance-improvement plan. It took truly egregious behavior to get kicked out of Nvidia, and many employees worked there for decades, including boomerang hires like Catanzaro and Aarts. Even when operating economics forced Huang to shutter a division, he reassigned employees to other useful tasks. In 2019 Curtis Priem returned to Nvidia's offices for the first time in sixteen years to join Huang and Malachowsky for a reunion of the company's founders. "I was astounded at how many people were still there," he said. "Jeff Fisher, his *kids* were working for Nvidia."

Huang maintained a stable marriage and spoke of Lori with great affection. Musk had at least eleven kids with at least three different women. Huang possessed magnetic charisma, could be funny as hell, and, when he wasn't losing his shit, was capable of warmth and great empathetic understanding. Musk missed social cues, was awkward and stilted in conversation, and claimed to be on the autism spectrum. Huang drank whiskey, didn't tweet, and, as far as I could tell, had over the course of forty years never offered a single political opinion about anything. (Searching federal records, I found not a single donation made in his or Lori's name.) Musk smoked weed, posted cringe, and funded Donald Trump.

But it was their divergent views on the risks posed by AI that was perhaps the most important difference between the men. To Musk, advanced AI posed a potentially extinction-level threat. Moreover, this opinion was shared by a great number of technologists, including both Hinton and Sutskever, the coauthors of the original AlexNet paper. Huang didn't see it that way. He saw no risk in AI at all. Zero.

. . .

BY LATE 2015, Musk, with characteristic humility, had concluded that the best way to protect the human species from AI was to build it himself. Opting for an unusual structure, Musk led a coalition of donors and technologists in founding OpenAI in 2015. "OpenAI is a non-profit artificial intelligence research company," the organization's first blog post read. "Our goal is to advance digital intelligence in the way that is most likely to benefit humanity as a whole, unconstrained by a need to generate financial return." The nonprofit eventually collected $135 million in donations. Musk, giving around $45 million, was by far the largest single donor; other early donors included Reid Hoffman, the cofounder of LinkedIn, and Sam Altman, the president of Y Combinator, a venture investor in early-stage start-ups. (OpenAI's structure and funding commitments would later create trouble for all involved.)

While canvassing for donations, OpenAI also built an exceptional roster of AI talent. Andrej Karpathy, who had presented his hallucinating caption engine onstage at GTC 2015, was among the founders. So was Wojciech Zaremba, the Polish programmer who'd cloned AlexNet at Google. Greg Brockman, a developer from North Dakota who'd been an early employee at Stripe, joined as CTO. The most important hire was Ilya Sutskever, Alex Krizhevsky's old Russian Israeli research partner who'd been present at the creation of AlexNet and had guided the development of AI since.

Krizhevsky himself escaped the dragnet. Rarely saying a word to anyone, he was not the ideal collaborator, and he departed Google in 2017. His share of the auction money was just under $15 million, enough not to work anymore, especially given the asceticism of his lifestyle. In 2019 he granted a Japanese news crew a visit inside his Bay Area home. Krizhevsky lived like a Benedictine monk, in a spartan apartment above a Vietnamese restaurant. The walls inside were completely bare; the only items of furniture were a desk, a couch, a digital piano, and a television; the only sign of life in the place was his house cat. Krizhevsky, the Orville Wright of the neural net, told the news crew he had walked away from the technology. "Maybe it's just my personality," he said, "but when I spend a very long time specializing in something, after about ten years I start to lose interest."

As OPENAI assembled the A-Team, Huang set out to build them a computer. Nvidia's most expensive offering at the time was a desktop box for science and data visualization. Huang figured he needed something ten times more powerful. He asked his team to design the DGX-1, an AI-accelerated computer. The focus of the device was matrix multiplication, which was to AI what Quake had been to graphics.

The rebuild began at the atomic level. TSMC was now offering a manufacturing technique called "FinFET," with transistors that jutted above the silicon substrate like a shark's fin. If you could shrink yourself to stand on the impossibly smooth surface of the microchip, the finned transistors would look like Soviet apartment blocks, towering over you in every direction at two hundred atoms tall. These crystal canyons were not so much printed as "sculpted" with ultraviolet light at a level of precision that would have impressed a Renaissance master. Engineers compared the manufacturing process to shooting a laser from the surface of the moon and hitting a quarter on the sidewalk in Arkansas.

The new shark-fin transistors allowed designers far better control of the flow of electricity. In the past, transistors had always behaved a bit like an old garden hose, leaking everywhere and offering only rough control of the trickle of output. The new transistors stopped the leaks and, in a sense, outfitted the hose with a high-tech nozzle, allowing for different spray modes. For chip designers, FinFET presented a long-sought trinity of precision, efficiency, and control.

How little attention such innovations incurred. Transistors—*computers*—were experiencing their most important physical upgrade since the 1970s, but among the public, not one person in a hundred knew or even cared. Like some dominant sports franchise, the semiconductor industry's long and extraordinary track record was taken completely for granted, even by software engineers. Computers just got better, always; that was just the default. How could it ever be any other way?

Inside Nvidia, however, the shark-fin transistors generated great excitement. Chip architects designed at scales that were almost inconceivable: the maze made of hair would now not only fill a tennis court but the state of Rhode Island. As these mazes started "going vertical," they offered fantastic capabilities. In ancient legend it was Daedalus who built the labyrinth to entrap the fearsome Minotaur—but if Daedalus could have seen what Nvidia was building, he would have wept with envy.

The architecture for Nvidia's first FinFET chip was named "Pascal," after the seventeenth-century philosopher and mathematician Blaise Pascal, who, among many other accomplishments, had invented the first mechanical calculator. The name was a coded reference to the primary bottleneck in computing, which had always been calculation speed. From Pascal's gear-driven adding machine to the vacuum tubes of ENIAC to the fine-scale microchips of Intel and IBM, computers simply had never been able to do arithmetic fast enough. But Nvidia's P100, released in April 2016, did calculations faster than they could even be brought to the machine. With these chips, calculating speed was no longer the primary obstacle. With these chips, the "computer" had transcended the mundane act of "computing."

Huang had seen this problem coming. Since 2014, Nvidia had been developing a data superhighway called NVLink that increased the speed with which math problems could be presented to the machine. NVLink was a homework cannon that fired a million semesters' worth of matrix-multiplication exercises at the processor every second. By wiring eight P100 chips together with a NVLink connection, Nvidia collapsed separate silicon mazes into a single computing super-labyrinth.

This magnificent eight-chip array formed the spine of the DGX-1, which was housed in a handsome metal case with a pebbled exterior. The computer weighed 134 pounds, cost $129,000, and drew as much power as a clothes dryer. The DGX-1 was the most powerful computer Nvidia had ever built—Huang called it a "data center in a box." It was not a machine intended for general purposes; it was not a machine really intended for anything except training ever-more-powerful AIs. But the DGX-1 could today be listed alongside the ENIAC and the Apple II as one of the most important computers ever built.

Elon Musk received the first device. In August 2016, Huang hand-delivered it to him at OpenAI's headquarters in San Francisco's Mission District. Huang arrived in leather; it was now all he ever wore. The computer weighed so much that he needed a dolly to get it into the office and assistance lifting it onto the table. Musk cut open the packaging with a box cutter, and Huang signed the computer with a marker. "To Elon and the OpenAI Team!" he wrote in his elegant capitals. "To the future of computing and humanity. I present you the world's first DGX-1!"

The following week, Huang delivered another signed DGX-1 to Fei-Fei Li's lab at Stanford. The 2016 ImageNet contest began a few days later. With their many cognitive "layers," the best contestants could tag images with 98 percent accuracy, beating the human average of 95 percent. Following six decades of research and tens of billions in investment, a computer could now distinguish a spatula from a hatchet. The age of machine supremacy had begun.

FOURTEEN

The Good Year

n 2016, Nvidia's stock price appreciated 224 percent, restoring Jensen Huang to glory and making him a billionaire once again. Yet Nvidia was not the best-performing stock in the S&P that year. The title went to Nvidia's longtime rival AMD, which went up 309 percent. Huang didn't like coming in second. He rededicated himself to victory and found it the next year. Revenues doubled, profits tripled, and the company launched new products at dizzying speed. Few companies anywhere, ever, could hope to have a year as successful as Nvidia had in 2017.

The first task for Huang in 2017 was to hamstring AMD. Since purchasing graphics-card maker ATI in 2006, AMD had been Nvidia's only real competitor—GeForce and Radeon were the Coke and Pepsi of GPUs. But since 2014, this long-running and occasionally vicious sparring match had become personal: AMD's new CEO, Lisa Su, was Huang's relative.

Su, seven years younger than Huang, was the daughter of a statistician and an accountant. Her family had immigrated to New York City from Taiwan when she was three. Unlike Huang, Su *was* the product of tiger parents. When she was young, her parents had given her three career options: engineer, doctor, or concert pianist. She chose the first because "it seemed to be the most difficult." Su spoke with a mild New York accent, dressed in pantsuits, and wore her hair short. She was also willing to gamble. "She has some of that same nature as Jensen, you know, the conviction," Forrest Norrod, a senior executive at AMD, told me. "She's got the courage to stick with it through difficult times."

The genetic connection between Huang and Su was somewhat faint. Huang's mother had come from a large family and had at least eleven older siblings. One of those siblings was Su's grandfather; technically speaking, this made the two executives first cousins, once removed. While he was growing up, Huang hadn't been aware of Su's existence and learned she was his relative only after she was named AMD's CEO.

And the relationship was perhaps even more distant than blood implied. Huang's mother was not that close to her biological family—as one of the youngest siblings, she'd been raised in a different home. "In the old days, you used to have to give away a child, so you gave it to your friend," Huang said. "My mother was given to her father's friend, and that was it; they grew up separately." Lisa's ancestor remained with the original parents.

When I asked Huang about Su, he had only positive things to say. "She's terrific," he said. "We're not very competitive." This was certainly not how anyone else saw it. For years, AMD had been Nvidia's only real rival in the GPU space, and Nvidia employees could recite the two companies' relative market share from memory. I wondered if there was something Huang wasn't telling me; in earlier days, I'd noticed, he often denigrated competitors like 3dfx in the press. Now he never said anything bad about any of his rivals—or, at least, never when pot-stirring journalists lurked within earshot.

Several people told me that although Huang had wised up about *publicly* belittling competitors, he continued to do so in private. David Kirk believed that Huang had learned his lesson after bankruptcy lawyers for 3dfx had forced him to read his disparaging comments out loud in a videotaped deposition. But Kirk also suggested that when the recorders were turned off and the conference room doors were closed, the old, trash-talking Jensen would emerge. Industry analyst Hans Mosesmann also suggested that any appearance of amity between Nvidia and AMD was a ruse. "Yes, Jensen does not want to lose," he said. "But he especially does not want to lose to Lisa."

EVEN BEFORE HIS COUSIN was appointed to run the place, Huang had a complicated relationship with AMD. His first real job had been at the company, and he still held the small amount of AMD stock he'd bought through the employee-purchase program way back in 1984. In 2006 AMD had even offered to purchase Nvidia. Huang had been open to it, but when he learned he wouldn't be in charge of the combined company, he ended the merger talks. The deal would have cashed him out nicely, but Huang had no intention of leaving the CEO chair, ever. He had no exit plan.

AMD instead purchased Toronto-based ATI, Nvidia's competitor. A series of foolish management decisions followed, and AMD churned through three CEOs in the next six years. In 2008 the company completed construction of a new corporate campus on top of a hill in Austin, Texas, which it pretentiously branded as "The Summit at Lantana." (The hill was a few hundred feet high.) Five years later, in an attempt to stave off creditors, AMD was forced to sell the Summit and lease it back like a sharecropper. The transaction was embarrassing, and by 2014, AMD's stock was trading at $2 a share.

Looking for someone willing to steward the company through hospice care, the board promoted forty-five-year-old Su, an internal vice president, to CEO. Few on Wall Street expected her to do anything but delay bankruptcy filings by a few months. But they underestimated her; in time, she would emerge as one of the most celebrated semiconductor CEOs of the era, second only to Huang.

Their personalities were different. Huang was temperamental and expressive, while Su was reserved and stoic. "She has a great poker face," Mosesmann said. "Jensen does not, although he'd still find a way to beat you." Su had the opposite strategic approach as well. Rather than sailing off toward the horizon like Jensen, she liked to prowl around the incumbent, waiting for it to falter. In this way, Su was perhaps braver than Huang: she didn't run from Intel. In fact, AMD's revival came from capturing Intel's CPU business, a feat that analysts once regarded as impossible.

Now that AI was succeeding, Su was prowling around Jensen. In 2016 her company released an open-source CUDA clone for the Radeon card. Most developers saw this offering as inferior, and AMD's cloud GPUs didn't command the premium rates Nvidia's did. But Su, like Huang, was patient, and she was willing to wait years for the opportunity to strike. "Jensen does not want to lose. He's a driven guy," Norrod said. "But we think we can compete with Nvidia."

Huang welcomed his upstart cousin to the show by stealing one of her oldest customers. Nintendo and AMD had a close relationship: ATI had supplied graphics hardware for several generations of Nintendo consoles, including the GameCube and the Wii. This was a business segment that Huang, following the collapse of the Xbox deal, had repeatedly claimed he did not want to pursue. Video game consoles updated only once every five years, too slow for a man accustomed to a six-month refresh cycle. So it came as a surprise to everyone—Su included—when it was announced that Nintendo was going to Nvidia for the new Nintendo Switch.

To outsiders, Nintendo resembled an uncrackable safe. Even by Japanese standards, the company was insular. It was headquartered in conservative Kyoto, with most of its decisions made by iconic game designer Shigeru Miyamoto and the small clique of executives who surrounded him. Miyamoto had been in his early thirties when he'd produced *Super Mario Brothers* and *The Legend of Zelda*; now in his sixties, gaming's Walt Disney had lost none of his passion.

Hardware and software teams in Kyoto sat directly next to each other, building full-stack gaming titles that tightly coupled the gameplay experience to the controller. Miyamoto exercised a fanatical level of control; he once complained about the stitches on Mario's pants in a US print advertisement. But Miyamoto also pushed his teams to take bold creative and technological risks, and the forthcoming Switch would prove to be one of the most versatile and delightful consoles ever produced.

Insiders considered the Switch's chipset a done deal. "ATI had an extraordinary relationship with Nintendo," Jon Peddie said. "They were a loyal, consistent vendor, and there was no reason to think that would change." But Nvidia's sales reps somehow worked their way in, peddling the Tegra, a repurposed mobile-phone product that engineers described as "floor scrapings." How, precisely, Huang stole the Switch remains a guarded secret—although Japanese executives might invite a foreign adviser into the boardroom, the real decisions were made late at night in the tiny izakayas of Kyoto after a pitcher or two of beer.

The Tegra was a "system-on-a-chip," meaning that it combined CPU, GPU, and other functions onto a single piece of silicon. The Tegra's computational performance was not exceptional; the selling point was its low power draw, which permitted gamers to detach the Switch from its base and play *Animal Crossing* for hours while hiding under the covers from their parents. Peddie recalled meeting with Nintendo executives shortly after the unexpected decision was made. "It was incredibly friendly, but stony," he said. "You know, 'This is done, it's very nice to see you, and please go away.'"

Launching in 2017, Nintendo would go on to sell 140 million Switch consoles, making it by far the most profitable product in company history. But it was a measure of how fast Nvidia was accelerating that Huang barely mentioned building the brain of the Switch, even in interviews at the time. Ambushing Lisa Su was a side project; his sprawling company now had its tentacles in everything.

THE 2017 NOBEL PRIZE in Physics was awarded for work on the Laser Interferometer Gravitational-Wave Observatory, twin pairs of intersecting laser beams located 1,800 miles apart that captured subtle perturbations in the texture of space-time to detect stellar collisions millions of light-years away. The 2017 Nobel Prize in Chemistry was awarded for work on cryo-electron microscopy, a technique in which biological specimens were suspended in

transparent "amorphous ice," then bombarded with electron beams to visu-
alize their three-dimensional structure. Both awards were not for new scientific discoveries but new scientific *tools*—and each tool intersected with
the parallel-computing slope of Nvidia's GPUs.

The laser beams and the frozen amoebae each generated huge amounts
of raw data. This data was essentially just a large collection of points in
space, like a pile of billions of Lego bricks waiting to be assembled. The
GPU allowed the scientists to stack these "bricks" of data in parallel, producing precise three-dimensional models of the wonders of our universe at
scales both large and small. The laser-beam data were used to draw an animation of two black holes that had been bound in a deadly gravitational
spiral for millions of years, spinning together closer and closer until they finally crashed into each other with an explosion so violent that it warped the
fabric of reality and sent shock waves echoing throughout the universe. *Science* magazine called it the breakthrough of the year.

At the other extreme, a miniature, one-cell creature suspended in ice revealed biological machinery of surreal complexity. Before, such intricate
structures had been unrecoverably smashed between microscope slides, but
the new ice-bound, three-dimensional render revealed that the "blind watch-
maker" of evolution had built actual biological *clockwork*. There were gears!
There were tiny gears inside the cell, and when they spun, they propelled
the tiny creature forward like a motorboat.

The three-dimensional renders were CGI constructions, not actual images, and at times you had to squint to see the beauty. But it was there. It
was there, waiting not for theory or experimentation but for the raw scientific act of *discovery*. The black holes and the gears of nature had been there,
waiting for millions of years, waiting simply to be seen for the first time.
Parallel computing made it possible.

The frenzy over AI obscured the contributions that Nvidia made to pro-
saic scientific advancements like these, which merely won their discoverers
the Nobel. Supporting the work of laureate groups in both physics and chemistry in the same calendar year offered irrefutable evidence of CUDA's value
to humanity—the problem was it didn't pay. As beautiful and important as

the images were, Bill Dally was unsure if scientific computing ever would have been profitable without neural nets. "The market for building these big supercomputers for various labs around the world is probably no more than what it costs to develop each generation of GPUs," he said. "We might have turned the corner anyways, but it was good that AI came along."

IT WAS ALSO IN 2017 that another, less reputable kind of customer discovered CUDA. Cryptocurrency miners created new coins by cracking mathematical ciphers through brute-force computation. CUDA was well-suited for this task, which involved processing similar chunks of data in parallel many millions of times. Enterprising miners soon realized that a well-configured GPU rig would take only four hours to mint a coin. When the price of bitcoin crossed $1,000 for the first time in January 2017, early adopters realized instant fortunes.

By mid-2017, crypto mining had turned into a classic speculative frenzy. Bitcoin quadrupled, then quadrupled again, crossing $16,000 by the end of the year. Retailers couldn't keep GeForce gaming cards in stock, and on eBay the cards could command double the suggested retail price. "Superminers" emerged, arranging GeForce units on metal racks in bedrooms and garages, generating enough heat to melt snow off a roof. Miners soon discovered crypto's Mecca: East Wenatchee, Washington, a tiny river town in "hydro alley" that purportedly had the cheapest electricity in the nation.

For a time, Nvidia's stock traded in parallel with bitcoin's price. Many inside Nvidia were appalled—some, concerned about climate change, found this use of the cards to border on sacrilege. Huang, reasoning from first principles, had seen a world in which AI would become the dominant force in computing. When Huang similarly reasoned from first principles about the potential for the blockchain, he did not foresee a world in which crypto displaced fiat money.

Huang was too much of a businessman to explicitly discourage miners from purchasing his GPUs, although he never exactly endorsed bitcoin mining either. Nvidia's official position on crypto was silence. On conference calls throughout 2017, Nvidia stuck to discussions of self-driving cars and AI, downplayed the impact of crypto, and declined to speculate on the proportion of its retail sales that came from miners. Financial reports from this time showed only a suspicious boost in the general category of "gaming," but even silence had a cost: the SEC later brought charges against Nvidia for failing to disclose to investors the proportion of GPU sales that were attributable to crypto. Without admitting or denying the SEC's findings, Nvidia paid the regulators a $5.5 million penalty.

This was nickels for insurgent Nvidia, but the experience was still a pain in the ass, and most of the Nvidia engineers I spoke with regarded crypto as an idiotic distraction from the company's far more important scientific work. Eventually, Nvidia shipped the CMP, a miners-only card that was basically just a GeForce with the video ports ripped out. At the same time, Nvidia deliberately impaired the mining ability of its standard graphics cards to make sure that gamers and scientists got priority. Bitcoin crashed in 2018, and demand evaporated. By the time bitcoin recovered, GPUs had been supplanted by application-specific rigs that were built for mining, and other leading cryptocurrencies had abandoned the expensive, climate-unfriendly brute-force approach. Nvidia was happy to cede the business.

IN JANUARY 2017, Nvidia reported earning a billion dollars in annual profit for the first time. Shortly thereafter, the company hired its ten-thousandth employee. The dull modernist building complex the company had occupied since 2001 could no longer contain its ambitions. It was time to expand.

Years earlier, Nvidia had purchased the lot adjacent to its leased campus in anticipation of building a command center fit for Huang's vision. The project had stalled following Bumpgate, but in 2017, after several years of construction, the new headquarters, called Endeavor, finally opened. Endeavor was an enormous building in the shape of a triangle with its corners trimmed. This shape was replicated in miniature throughout the building

interiors, from the couches and the carpets to the splash guards in the uri-
nals. Nvidia's "spaceship," as employees called it, was cavernous, filled with
light, and spotlessly clean. Its interiors were sharp and angular, colored in
hospital white and matte black, and interrupted by multistory "living walls"
thick with vegetation.

The head architect for Endeavor was Hao Ko, a tall and soft-spoken architect who worked for Gensler, a leading corporate-design firm. Ko dressed
fashionably, maintained a trim soul patch, and wore black designer eyeglasses. He had been a junior architect at Gensler when Huang had appointed him the lead designer on Endeavor, bypassing Ko's boss. I asked Ko
why Huang had done so. "You probably have heard stories," Ko said. "He
can be very tough. He will undress you." Huang had no architecture experience, but he wanted someone he could push around a little. "I would say
ninety percent of architects would battle back," Ko said. "I'm more of a listener."

To achieve his vision for Endeavor, Huang strapped Ko into a virtual-
reality headset, then attached the headset to a rack of Nvidia GPUs so Ko
could simulate the flow of light. "This is the first building that took a supercomputer to design," Huang said. Ko used the headset to design Endeavor's
unusual crinkle-cut roof, which reminded me of a fractal. First, Ko ex-
tended the roof over the edge of Endeavor's exterior glass walls so that it
would cast shade like the brim of a hat. Then, using computer-aided-design
software, he placed hundreds of small, triangular skylights along the folds
of the roof at mathematically optimized locations. The cumulative effect
was to ensure that the building was at all times flooded with natural light
while never exposing employees to the direct glare of the sun.

Endeavor had expansive sight lines, and you could see clear from one
edge of the building to the other, a distance of a couple hundred yards. This
was just as Huang wanted, as it gave him a 360-degree survey of his staff.
Ko had built Huang a beautiful executive office complex on the third floor;
Huang used this as a book depository. Instead, he commandeered an
anonymous-looking conference room in the middle of his headquarters and
turned it into his war room. Huang still needed to be in the center of

things—just as he'd needed to be seated at the table next to the refrigerator in Priem's house many years before.

Working with Huang could be challenging. Ko recalled Huang yelling at his engineering staff about the rendering speed of the VR headset. "He was really letting them have it," Ko said. The headset originally took five hours to render design changes; following Huang's outburst, the engineers got the speed down to ten seconds. Huang was tough on them, but there was a logic to it. "If the headset took five hours, I'd probably settle on whatever shade of green looked adequate," Ko said. "If it took ten seconds, I'd take the time to pick the best shade of green there was."

The building won several awards and made Ko's career. Nvidia now had a signature building to rival the GooglePlex and Apple's Infinite Loop. Employees were astonished by the immensity of their new workspace—Ko, at Huang's insistence, had even built a bar called "Shannon's" into the top floor. (David Shannon, Nvidia's former general counsel, had questioned the wisdom of mixing employees and alcohol in this way, so Huang named the bar after him.) Outside of the bar, though, the building was light on amenities. It did not have some of the over-the-top perks other Silicon Valley campuses did: no gym, no climbing wall, no dog park, no disc golf, no ball pit. "You come here to go to work," Huang said.

Ko's project was not finished. Having completed the first structure, he was already designing a second, even larger building directly to the north. That building, known as "Voyager," would be another trimmed triangle opposite the first. Together, the two buildings would form an interlocking polygonal structure that evoked Nvidia's origins in 3D graphics while providing striking vistas from both ground and sky. (Their names interlocked as well; the initial sounds of "Endeavor" and "Voyager" came together to generate "NV.") When Ko was done with the second building, Huang's master plan called for a *third* building, as yet unnamed, to complement the other two. Each building would be bigger than the last, tiling the floor of the valley one tessellated triangle at a time.

When Endeavor opened, Ko led Huang and a group of executives on a tour. "The place was finished, it looks amazing, we're doing the tour, and he's questioning me about the placement of the water fountains," Ko said. "He was upset because they were next to the bathrooms! That's required by code, and this is a billion-dollar building! But he just couldn't let it go."

"I'm never satisfied," Huang said. "No matter what it is, I only see imperfections."

THE CUDA SOFTWARE PACKAGE was downloaded 2.7 million times in 2017, nearly triple the previous year and fifteen times more than the dregs in 2012. Some of this was for crypto, but the majority of CUDA downloaders were looking to build AI. A lot of the interest came from students—by 2017, the most popular course at Stanford was CS 229, "Introduction to Deep Learning."

Unlike crypto miners, CUDA developers didn't necessarily purchase their own Nvidia hardware. Many ran their programs, and sometimes their whole companies, on virtual machines they leased through the cloud. For cloud providers, this was an exceptionally lucrative business. The dominant player was Amazon Web Services, which controlled 50 percent of the market and which in good years actually made more money than Amazon's vast e-commerce operation. Chasing behind Amazon was Microsoft's cloud service Azure, under the reinvigorated leadership of Microsoft chief executive Satya Nadella. The combined purchasing demand from Amazon, Microsoft, and other cloud providers was enough to double Nvidia's chip sales to data centers for the year.

It did not escape Huang's notice that leasing virtual computing equipment was more profitable than selling actual physical hardware. In 2017 he introduced two leasing platforms of his own. The first was GeForce Now, which rented out virtual graphics cards, permitting gamers to play high-end games on underpowered machines like laptops and cheap commodity PCs. The physical sale of GeForce gaming cards still provided a majority of Nvidia's revenue, and enthusiasts still loved to show off their rigs—but cloud computing suggested that all modern gamers really needed was a monitor and a decent broadband connection. With GeForce Now, Huang was preemptively preparing to someday put a bullet in the head of what for twenty-five years had been his core business—reasoning that if he didn't kill it, someone else would do it for him.

The second platform was altogether stranger. The idea for it had occurred to Huang while watching Yevgen Chebotar, a researcher at USC, train a robotic arm to hit an orange ball with a hockey stick. The arm used rein-forcement learning techniques to learn to score goals. Given enough time, it might rival Gretzky, but to make it happen, Chebotar and his assistants had to physically reset the ball in front of the stick thousands of times.

This did not strike Huang as an efficient use of Chebotar's day. Instead, he reasoned, the physical parameters of hockey should be simulated on a computer. The power of simulation had been a recurring theme throughout Huang's career. Anything he could simulate, he did—profits and innova-tive products usually followed. Now it occurred to him that simulating any one thing was not enough; he had to simulate *everything*. "We have to build an alternative universe," Huang said.

In this alternative universe for robotics training, Chebotar would not have to reset the ball. Instead, reinforcement could happen instantaneously; the robot arm would hit a billion balls over the same span of time. Gerald Tesauro had simulated games of backgammon by generating millions of dice rolls. Huang would simulate games of hockey by weaving a new reality in code.

Creating a platform with sufficient fidelity to real-world physics was not an easy task. Game engines were nowhere close—as Peddie had observed, once you stripped away the textures you just had blocks running into one another. A reality simulator would require not only a perfect physics engine but also precise representations of collision elasticity and object density. Striking a tennis ball, for example, would have to produce a different re-sponse from striking a billiard ball. Soft textures like cloth would have to give, while rigid textures like metal would have to hold. A slippery wet plate would have to fall, and a bruisable piece of fruit would have to rupture.

With so many variables, a reality simulator would be expensive, time-consuming to build, and initially have maybe five or six customers. Huang, of course, loved the idea.

Huang called his first simulator the "Isaac" robotic-training platform. With time, Isaac led to a more complex product called the Omniverse, which Huang sometimes described as an "industrial metaverse" and other times as Earth's "digital twin." The Omniverse would not be a physical product that Huang would sell, but a high-fi digital playground he would *lease*. And lease not just to robots, but also to cars, and industrial designers, and warehouse builders, and anyone else looking to make complicated physical products work in the real world without breaking things first. Ko, using VR, had built him a spaceship. With the Omniverse, Ko could have built anything.

BY THE END OF 2017, Nvidia had tripled its profits to $3 billion, with spiking growth across every product line. The neglected graphics-card company was now a Wall Street player with a $100 billion market capitalization. Still, if you asked the average person on the street in 2017 what product Nvidia made, the answer would likely be hardware for graphics or crypto mining. Actually, that's not quite true—if you asked the average person on the street about Nvidia in 2017, they would surely have no idea what you were talking about. But for the small fraction of the public who did know, Nvidia was still mostly associated with video games.

Only the savviest investors grokked that Nvidia was no longer a consumer-graphics play. It was an AI company. It was *the* AI company. And AI was suddenly and quietly everywhere: recognizing human faces, recommending products, organizing social media feeds, and improving voice quality on mobile phones. As Marc Andreessen had observed, in one way or another almost all of it relied on the Nvidia computing stack. Investors who'd had the gumption to stick with Huang through the dark ages were rewarded, and the Fidelity portfolio managers who'd cross-examined Huang in Boston in 2013 were now delighted with their oversized and ever-growing position in what was rapidly becoming the stock market's single best investment. With CUDA, the Switch, the Nobel Prizes, crypto, and the cloud, Nvidia had forever left the corporate doldrums behind. Yet none of these products, not even Huang's attempt to clone reality, could've prepared him, his customers, or his investors for the metamorphosis that was about to occur.

FIFTEEN

The Transformer

A s Wolfgang Mozart was born into music, as Stephen Curry was born into basketball, so was Jakob Uszkoreit born into the obscure field of computational linguistics. His father, Hans, was an acclaimed researcher who had spent his life attempting to teach computers to process language. Jakob had wanted to do something different with computers, perhaps something involving biology, but after he was hired at Google in 2008, he soon realized that language processing was one of the most interesting problems. Surrendering to fate, Uszkoreit entered his father's field. Within a few years, he would forever surpass him.

Uszkoreit was handsome, with stern Teutonic features and dark-brown eyes. He wore his hair long and frequently tied it in a man bun. Born in America, he had grown up in Germany and spoke English with a faint accent. At Google, Uszkoreit pondered the hidden grammatical structures that made language go. Perhaps from the neural net's array of random starting weights those same structures might be shaped into existence.

Early linguistic efforts with neural nets had been frustrating. No matter how they were trained, the models continued to make elementary grammatical errors. Teaching grammar to the computer explicitly, like a high school Latin teacher, was an approach that didn't scale. Researchers instead tried implementing long-term and short-term memories inside "recurrent" neural networks, but this architecture was finicky and difficult to program. When exposed to more text, recurrent neural networks would sometimes even untrain, forgetting things they already knew.

Uszkoreit wanted a neural net that got smarter the more it read. Sometime in 2014, he was struck with a novel idea. If more data was going to lead to better results, then the underlying structure for processing information should be as simple as possible. His inspiration was biology—medical scans suggested that of the estimated hundred billion neurons in the human brain, fewer than 1 percent were dedicated to language processing. "Probably language evolved this way to exploit our cognitive capacities in a fairly optimal way," he said in a 2023 interview.

Uszkoreit decided to model language using context alone. He ripped out all the memory structures and replaced them with a simple knowledge graph. Words themselves meant nothing: in isolation, they were arbitrary collections of sounds. The only way to capture their meaning was to draw links between them and other words in the text. So if you had a knowledge graph linking the words "hop," "green," "tongue," "flies," and "amphibian," then you knew enough to guess that the word in the center was "frog." Not only that, but the graph should look the same in German, French, Swahili, or Vietnamese. The word wasn't the letters "f," "r," "o," and "g"—those letters were just placeholders. The word, in a cognitive sense, was that unique map of links to the rest of the vocabulary.

To capture this relationship, Uszkoreit defined each word as a tree of statistical weights. For example, if asked to consider the sentence "The orange _____ caught the brown mouse," the neural net could guess that "cat" was most likely the missing word because it had encountered a great deal of "cat/mouse" pairs in its training set. "Cat" might also have a relatively strong relationship to "caught" and perhaps "ate," but less strong to "brown" and barely strong at all to "the." Perhaps, with enough training examples, the computer could also come to understand that "orange" was an adjective that modified the noun "cat" without ever receiving explicit grammatical instruction. Common nouns were easy to map in this way, but other words were harder. For example, in parsing the word "unhappiness," the native English speaker implicitly understood the negating prefix "un," the root word "happi," and the suffix "ness," used to convert an adjective into a noun. To better model these relationships, Uszkoreit split words into fragments called "tokens." These, too, were connected in a tree of statistical weights.

Uszkoreit called this learning mechanism "self-attention." The reception at Google was cool—it seemed too simple to work. "People raised their eyebrows because it dumped out all the existing neural architectures," Uszkoreit said. Even his father was skeptical. But Uszkoreit was designing for the GPU. The recurrent neural-network architecture didn't take advantage of Nvidia's hardware. In fact, it fought *against* the parallel architecture, minimizing data input and maximizing fancy code. Uszkoreit, seeing the analogy with the brain, wanted to do the opposite, piping massive amounts of text, words, and computing firepower through a simple yet elegant funnel. Uszkoreit outlined his thinking in 2023: "If you are given a piece of hardware that has the very key strength of doing lots and lots of simple computations in parallel, as opposed to complicated, structured computations sequentially, then really that's the statistical property you want to exploit."

THE "SELF-ATTENTION" MECHANISM was immediately successful, and aspects of it were rolled into Google's search and advertising products. Uszkoreit, looking to take it further, convinced Illia Polosukhin, a champion coder who worked with him at the GooglePlex, to join this research group. Polosukhin, too, was fascinated by the biological underpinnings of language. "Images are interesting, and obviously contain a lot of world knowledge, but we have thousands of species which can see," he told me. "Only one species can actually understand language."

Polosukhin was mulling over how to implement the self-attention mechanism when he went to see Denis Villeneuve's 2016 movie *Arrival*. In the film, squid-like alien "heptapods" attempt to communicate with humans by painting mysterious circular inkblots. A linguist, played by Amy Adams, eventually realizes that each inkblot represents a single, unified body of text. (She then begins to see into the future, but we'll stick with inkblots for now.) Polosukhin recognized that "self-attention" could be deployed in a similarly maximal way, probabilistically linking each word in the tree not just to other words in the sentence but also to thousands of other words throughout an entire text. Even a word that had appeared many paragraphs earlier might provide a contextual clue to what the next word meant.

Polosukhin and Uszkoreit were joined by Ashish Vaswani, another Google researcher, and by early 2017 the three had built a rudimentary English-to-German translator based on the self-attention mechanism. Polosukhin and Uszkoreit had previously contributed to an internal Google program called "autobot," which attempted to automatically write Wikipedia pages. The new self-attention mechanism was called a "transformer."

Over the next few months the team added four more researchers, and by February 2017 the German-English translator was competitive with the best recurrent networks. At this point Noam Shazeer, a Google veteran who'd worked for the company since 2000, joined as the team's eighth and final member. Shazeer was an expert coder who was frustrated by recurrent neural networks and wanted an alternative. Together with the Welsh programmer Llion Jones, he upgraded the transformer from a research project to production-quality software. As the team fed more data into the transformer, the results improved, outclassing the public Google Translate platform. "What we saw was that as you make it bigger, it's clearly just kind of more intelligent!" Shazeer said. "That was not true of our preexisting work."

Previous neural-net architectures had tried to build sentences or even paragraphs. The transformer worked by predicting exactly one word at a time, based on the probabilistic relationships. Just one word—that was the furthest it ever looked ahead. "By learning to generate sequences in order, you're forced to learn extremely complex behaviors," team member Aidan Gomez said. "One of the most beautiful things falls out of this." Soon, the transformer model demonstrated that it could "understand our culture, our language, the interactions between us."

Jones noticed that if the transformer always returned the best fit, the prose could get a little clunky. So, like a writer turning to a thesaurus, he implemented a "beam search" function that would allow the transformer to choose from one of several candidate words. "If you cut a path through the top word, then the second, then the third, then the top again, you will often get a better result than if you just always picked the top word," he told me. "It was a nightmare to implement, but once we did, *that* was when we first got state-of-the-art results."

To better understand what the transformer was doing, Jones also coded a visualization tool that represented the strength of the statistical relationships between words with lines of different thickness. He fed it a notoriously difficult sentence pair. The first sentence read, "The animal didn't cross the street because it was too tired." The second sentence read, "The animal didn't cross the street because it was too wide." To parse the sentence pair correctly, the transformer would have to know that "tired" could describe only an animal and that "wide" could describe only a street. To his amazement, Jones's visualization demonstrated exactly that relationship. "This was one of the oldest problems in computational linguistics, and we weren't even trying to solve it!" he said. "It just fell out."

Language had many similar deep, implicit structures, some of which were probably invisible to linguists. "It's not like the model is just learning adjective-noun relationships—it's also learning far more complex stuff that we probably don't even have language to describe," Gomez said. For example, native English speakers follow an implicit order for the placement of adjectives—we know to say "an old Canadian maple tree," not "a maple Canadian old tree." With the transformer, that linguistic intuition had been captured in software.

If AlexNet had been the first airplane, a rickety proof-of-concept, then the transformer was the jet engine. Shazeer and Uszkoreit, working together on a whiteboard, ensured everything about the transformer was built to accommodate hyperscale architecture, with massive amounts of data, massive numbers of parameters, and massive GPU clusters. As the project built momentum, the work grew frenzied; following one late-night crunch, Vaswani, sleep-deprived, recalled seeing neurons in the office curtain.

In the final stage, the team ran "ablations," deliberately disabling portions of the transformer code to understand what contributions they made. But the ablations had the unexpected result of making the core transformer function run even better. Shazeer removed so much of the surrounding code that in the end he was left with almost nothing. In its most primitive interpretation, the transformer was barely more than twenty lines of code.

Oh, but what it could do! As they prepared for the publication of their seminal paper, the team experimented with feeding the transformer libraries of music and archives of visual art. Just as the transformer could accurately predict the next most likely word in a sentence, so could it predict the next-most-likely note in a symphony or the next-most-likely pixel in a work of art. Soon the transformer was writing music and painting recognizable works of art. This elegant architecture, designed to do the simplest thing conceivable—*just take one step at a time*—was like a skeleton key for AI. In 2017 the team published its results in the *Neural Information Processing Systems* journal, which had published the original AlexNet results. The paper needed a name, so Jones, channeling the Beatles, suggested "Attention Is All You Need." This was an off-the-cuff joke that he didn't think the team would actually use. Later, he would meet people with the sentence tattooed on their arms.

In July 2017, shortly before publishing their results, Shazeer and team member Lukasz Kaiser tried an experiment. Rather than ask the transformer machine to translate preexisting texts, they asked it to ingest a corpus of millions of Wikipedia articles, then generate new text based on what it had read. As their prompt, they entered a single request: *Write an article about the Transformer.* Out flowed a thousand-word description of a Japanese new-wave punk band known as Transformer. The article was purely hallucinatory—no such band existed. But the text was smooth, confidently written, and even included fabricated footnotes. Gomez felt that his timeline for progress was collapsing. "You went to bed one night, and models could barely spell," he said. "We thought we'd have models that could write compelling English in a few decades, and then suddenly it shows up!"

The transformer team expected Google to turn the technology into consumer-facing products, but management somehow didn't see the value in the tech. Team members felt that Google's search monopoly had resulted in a bloated, bureaucratic company unwilling to take risks. "They were like, 'Hey, we cannot launch anything that doesn't fit into the search box,'" Polosukhin said. "Fifteen years earlier, we would have just launched something bad. Then we iterate, we learn, and we improve, improve, improve, improve, until it's actually really good. At some point, we lost that mentality."

The transformer authors began defecting to start-ups; by 2023, every one of the eight original transformer researchers had left. (Shazeer, who co-founded the popular chatbot service Character.ai, was acqui-hired back in 2024. Defecting pays.) Jones, the last to go, still praised his former employer. He recalled his eclectic collaborators, each with unique viewpoints and capabilities, who had organically coalesced around a promising topic. "Only Google could have developed this product," he said. It was probably true, but Google's failure to capitalize on the transformer left a giant hole in the market for someone else to fill.

OPENAI HAD STRUGGLED SINCE Huang had delivered the DGX-1. The company's first research effort was an "artificial gamer" that excelled at the real-time strategy game *Dota 2*. Some at the organization wondered if this was the best use of their world-class talent. Elon Musk grew frustrated with OpenAI's apparent lack of progress and began attempting to lure its engineers to join him at Tesla. The situation came to a head in February 2018, following a fraught piece of boardroom wrangling that left Musk sidelined and Sam Altman, the former head of Y Combinator, in control. In his final meeting with the organization, Musk told employees he was quitting to pursue his own AI research at Tesla. "After a young researcher challenged Musk's decision, suggesting it would exacerbate the AI arms race, he called the researcher a 'jackass' and stormed out of the building," *The Wall Street Journal* reported.

Ilya Sutskever remained. The AlexNet coauthor had continued to publish important research and now rivaled his mentor Geoffrey Hinton as one of the most cited scholars in the field. Sutskever focused on AI to the exclusion of everything else, including, increasingly, grooming: his beard was tangled and unkempt, his eyebrows were thick and untrimmed, and you could see most of his scalp through his thinning, wispy hair. His strength, as Hinton had observed, was the speed with which he could pivot toward a good idea.

Around the time of Musk's tantrum, Sutskever had watched Shazeer present the transformer at a conference. He grasped at once the power of the architecture, returning to OpenAI's offices to advise his colleagues that they should ditch the auto-gamer at once to build something that could change the world. "Literally the next day, it was clear to me, to us, that the transformer addressed the limitations of recurrent neural networks," Sutskever said. "We switched to transformers right away." Altman, now in charge, agreed with the change in strategy.

Sutskever wanted to use the transformer to build a product that would deliver high-quality, human-readable text and answer any conceivable prompt. He had seen Shazeer and Kaiser's proof-of-concept with the fake Wikipedia articles and thought it could be expanded upon. First, the model would "pretrain" on a large collection of text. Then it would generate text of its own. Combining the purpose, the method, and the architecture, you arrived at the "Generative Pre-Trained Transformer," or GPT.

GPT-1 launched in June 2018. It learned to read using BookCorpus, a collection of around seven thousand free, self-published ebooks. (Sci-fi, romance, and fantasy were the predominant genres—many of the books were *Twilight* knockoffs.) Drawing from this curriculum of third-rate vampire fiction, the first GPT was as bad as you might expect, answering users' queries with streams of Dadaist nonsense. Musk wasn't impressed, and after the release of GPT-1, he sent OpenAI a nasty email. "My probability assessment of OpenAI being relevant to DeepMind/Google without a dramatic change in execution and resources is 0%," he wrote.

Still, OpenAI had the freedom to launch something bad; unlike Google, it could even launch something *terrible*, then improve, improve, improve. GPT-1 sucked, but it showed that something of its kind could work. The key to a better system, as Sutskever had grasped way back in 2012, was scale.

GPT-2 launched eight months later. Having graduated from the vampire-romance syllabus, the model trained by absorbing around eight million web pages comprising around six billion individual words. The final product could sometimes produce text that was indistinguishable from that of a human. Asking for a story, OpenAI researchers gave GPT-2 the following prompt: "In a shocking finding, scientists discovered a herd of unicorns living in a remote, previously unexplored valley, in the Andes Mountains. Even more surprising to the researchers was the fact that the unicorns spoke perfect English."

GPT-2 ran with the prompt:

The scientist named the population, after their distinctive horn, Ovid's Unicorn. These four-horned, silver-white unicorns were previously unknown to science.

Now, after almost two centuries, the mystery of what sparked this odd phenomenon is finally solved.

Using only statistical relationships to guess the next word in the sentence, GPT-2 output better prose than any other language model had ever produced. Sutskever and his team then pushed GPT-2 out of its comfort zone, asking "zero-shot" questions that were not directly answered on any of the web pages. "Who wrote the book *The Origin of Species*?" they asked. "Charles Darwin," GPT-2 answered. (Correct.) "What is the largest supermarket chain in the UK?" they asked. "Tesco," it answered. (Correct.) "Who played John Connor in the original *Terminator*?" they asked. "Arnold Schwarzenegger," it answered. (Incorrect: Schwarzenegger played the cyborg.) "What river is associated with the city of Rome?" they asked. "The Tiber," it answered. (Correct.)

The ability of GPT-2 to answer new questions without explicit training was an example of the "emergent" properties in AI. These unexpected skills and behaviors were appearing as the models grew larger, surprising even the researchers. Once a model crossed the threshold of emergence, no one, not even its designers, could say what it was fully capable of doing.

Of course, GPT-2 had many limitations. It was terrible at summarizing arguments and could get tripped out counting to ten. Still, Sutskever, seeing these capabilities, began to wonder if the transformer was a first step toward "artificial general intelligence," or AGI. One way to define AGI was as software that could accomplish any task a human could. Sutskever, building ever more sophisticated versions of GPT, revisited the same concerns that had prompted OpenAI's founding. What if an AGI could do its *own* AI research, augmenting its own intellect in a never-ending feedback loop? Was there a tipping point where, as Bostrom had postulated, over the course of a few moments the AI went from sort-of-smart to hypersmart? Would its human operators be able to understand that this was happening? Would this AGI permit them to survive?

Sutskever did not think the current generation of neural-net architecture would lead directly to AGI. But what about the next breakthrough? In a little more than five years, he'd watched AI leap forward two separate times. Surely, he reasoned, somewhere out there someone was working on the *next* AlexNet, the *next* transformer. What then? The question began to consume Sutskever—no one could say what might happen once the AGI threshold was crossed.

Yet these concerns did not constrain his ambitions. Researchers described the size of the models by the number of individual weights, or "parameters," they contained. Each parameter was roughly equivalent to a synapse in a biological brain. GPT-1 had about 100 million parameters, keeping it in insect territory. GPT-2 had 1.5 billion, the equivalent of a small lizard. For his next model, Sutskever was targeting 100 billion parameters—on the order of a rodent.

Training this neural structure required a lot of computing power. The electricity costs alone made it one of the more expensive computer-intelligence applications ever developed—an early indicator of things to come. Altman, now the CEO, realized he could not raise enough money through nonprofit donations to satisfy Sutskever's ambitions, so in 2019 he announced that OpenAI was launching a "capped-profit" subsidiary that limited backers to a mere 100× return on investment. "It would be wise to view any investment in OpenAI Global LLC in the spirit of a donation, with the understanding that it may be difficult to know what role money will play in a post-AGI world," the accompanying press release stated.

The largest initial "donor" was Microsoft, which invested $1 billion in OpenAI, accepting a modest $100 billion in potential remuneration. (Perhaps a world that had transcended money was coming, but until that day arrived, Microsoft would continue to accumulate more of it.) The investment represented a million-fold increase from the $1,000 that Krizhevsky and Sutskever had used to buy two GeForces seven years before. Yet even this was not enough to fulfill Sutskever's appetite. The human brain had perhaps two hundred trillion synapses; AGI or not, OpenAI was looking to surpass it. Nvidia was already assembling the computing stack Sutskever would need to get there, an integrated, warehouse-sized solution that Huang no longer referred to as a supercomputer or a data center, but as an "AI factory."

SIXTEEN

Hyperscale

Huang's only interest now was scale. He did not see AI as an emergent machine superintelligence and was dismissive of direct analogies to biology. For him, AI was merely software—software running on hardware that his company sold. He imposed this viewpoint in his company-wide addresses, and, as a result, Nvidia's employees talked about the capabilities of AI with rather less excitement than one might expect.

And perhaps, from Huang's perspective, the neural nets weren't the real accomplishment; the real accomplishment was the extraordinary amount of computational power he was managing to pack into the data centers. At the 2018 GTC conference, Huang observed that Nvidia GPUs had increased processing speed by twenty-five times in just five years, far outpacing Moore's Law. He then showed a chart showing how AlexNet, which took a week to train on his 2012 graphics cards, could train on his new computer, the DGX-2, in just eighteen minutes. "There's a new law going on," he said, "a supercharged law."

Huang had his own perspective on the data centers, too. These giant computers weren't an agglomeration of many chips—to him, they were all just *one* chip working as a unified system on a single problem. In fact, the thousands of GPUs were transferring bits around the data center so quickly they were clogging the networking infrastructure.

To fix the problem, Huang had to go shopping. The fastest networking standard in the world was Infiniband, designed by the Israeli firm Mellanox. Eyal Waldman, Mellanox's founder, was a burly, garrulous, serial entrepreneur who shared Huang's taste for speculative overkill. He had originally developed Infiniband for the niche supercomputing market, spending more to develop the technology than that market promised to return. Like CUDA, Infiniband was a powerful product in search of a customer.

But as Huang had found out, the "field of dreams" approach agitated investors. Overinvestment in capacity led to lowered profits, low profits led to low stock prices, low stock prices led to malcontent shareholders, and malcontent shareholders inevitably, like some bat signal of the Wall Street cinematic universe, led to Jeff Smith, the same corporate raider who'd targeted Nvidia in 2013.

By 2017, Smith had established himself as one of the world's better investors, reportedly posting annualized returns above 15 percent. His Starboard Value firm began accumulating shares in underperforming Mellanox and soon owned a tenth of the company. Huang had managed to fend Smith off, but Waldman was not so fortunate—Starboard went Olive Garden on his ass, attempting to eject all eleven sitting members of Mellanox's board in a single election. Waldman postponed the board meeting in a scramble to get the votes he needed to survive; simultaneously, Smith lobbied Mellanox's investors to toss him out. An epic proxy fight loomed, but in the end, Waldman caved, and he conceded three board seats. Sitting across the conference table from the goon squad, Waldman then announced he was putting Mellanox up for sale.

His timing was good, at least. As cloud computing scaled in the late 2010s, Infiniband moved to supply it. The cables, the switches, the routers, the networking chips—for a Lamborghini of a data center you couldn't rely on the tired Ethernet standard. Waldman, operating under duress, managed to attract bids from seven different cloud suppliers. In March 2019,

Nvidia won the bidding war, edging out Intel with a $7 billion offer. When the deal closed in 2020, Nvidia added three thousand new employees, and Mellanox was rebranded as Nvidia Israel.

The deal meant paying off his frenemy Smith, but this scarcely concerned Huang. He was slavering over the data pipes, the missing ingredient that transformed his AI factories from a mere brain into something more like an integrated nervous system—an example of corporate synergy that was as authentic as it was uncommon. Smith doubled his money, but subsequent events showed that Huang got the better end of the deal. "It ended up being one of the more profitable corporate acquisitions in recent memory," board member Mark Stevens said. Starboard, in a later corporate filing, expressed admiration for the man they'd once tried to push around. "Jensen Huang is a real visionary in this sector," the filing dryly noted.

FOLLOWING MELLANOX, Huang decided to press his luck. In September 2020 he offered $40 billion to purchase the UK-based chip designer ARM. It was the largest semiconductor merger ever proposed—too large, as it turned out. In 2021 US regulators sued to block the transaction, arguing that it would suppress innovation. Not one to fight the feds, Huang scuttled the deal a short time later. (Chinese and UK regulators were equally skeptical. Intel and Nvidia were by this time in heated competition for the data-center market, as was AMD. Allowing any one firm to vertically integrate might have stifled competition from the other two.)

Nvidia's market position allowed it to charge high prices, and the gross profit margin on its AI chips could exceed 90 percent. This ratio attracted competition in the manner that chum attracted sharks. Seeking to reduce their dependency on Nvidia, Google and Tesla had both developed AI-training hardware. Numerous start-ups were pursuing the market as well. One of them was Cerebras, which made a "mega-chip" the size of a dinner plate. "They're just extorting their customers, and nobody will say it out loud," Andrew Feldman, the CEO of Cerebras, said of Nvidia.

Observers sometimes wondered if Nvidia's position was sustainable.

AMD and Intel both offered open-source alternatives to CUDA, and these alternatives liberated customers from the Nvidia hardware ladder, potentially saving them billions of dollars. But few AI researchers used AMD's or Intel's products. Why not?

I asked this question of a great many people, and I got a great variety of answers. One common misconception was that it was somehow technically difficult to switch away from CUDA. Actually, it was easy—sometimes, all developers had to do was alter a couple of lines of code. Another common misconception was that corporate hardware buyers were playing it safe. ("No one ever got fired for buying Nvidia," Hans Mosesmann said, echoing an old line about IBM.) But when I actually talked to a hardware buyer, he told me that he constantly experimented with competing products, and he expressed a wistful desire that a cheaper equivalent might someday appear. "This stuff is fucking expensive," he said of the Nvidia computing stack.

The reason that Nvidia succeeded was not that its circuits were better. The reason was that its *software* was better. Only a small portion of the performance gains now came from the classic strategy of packing more transistors into the chip—Moore's Law was dead. The rest came from Bill Dally, Ian Buck, and the rest of the Nvidia scientists accelerating matrix multiplications with numerical magic tricks. Nvidia engineers taught the GPU new instructions that acted like speed solvers on a Rubik's cube. They replaced the processor's native language with ugly but effective lo-fi data types, akin to switching from calligraphy to shorthand. They trimmed "dead" synapses from the matrices, essentially deleting unproductive information from the neural net in the manner of the forgetting machine in *Eternal Sunshine of the Spotless Mind*. Between 2012 and 2022, Nvidia achieved a thousand-fold speed-up in single-chip AI inference performance, which was far in excess of anything that Moore's Law had ever achieved. A mere 2.5× of that speed-up came from transistors; most of the remaining 400× came from Nvidia's mathematical toolbox. "Honestly, AMD can make silicon just as good as we can," Arjun Prabhu said. "They just can't make the calculations go as fast."

On top of this powerful engine, Nvidia built domain-specific tools for specialist programmers. There was "Drive" for automotive research, "Bio-NeMo" for drug discovery, "Clara" for medical imaging, "Morpheus" for cybersecurity, and "Highlights" for capturing kill shots in *Fortnite*. By the 2020s, Nvidia was offering almost three hundred such tool kits spanning a portfolio of gaming, animation, planetary science, climatology, mathematics, physics, finance, biochemistry, and quantum computing. These software packages were freely available for anyone to use, with zero licensing fees, and Huang pushed them into the hands of scientists like a grandmother distributing second helpings of food. He called the tool kits his "treasures."

Of course, Huang wasn't any sort of altruist—the long-term play was to use this free software to lock researchers into Nvidia's hardware-upgrade cycle. In early 2024, an administrator at CalTech's data center told me that the school's wait time for delivery on an H100 chip was almost eighteen months. He had encouraged professors at the school to switch to other providers but found few willing to accept. "They'd rather wait for the hardware than switch away from CUDA," he said. It was all this *code* that made Nvidia hard to compete against. Upstarts might design a new chip, but that wasn't enough—Dwight Diercks, Nvidia's head of software engineering, had ten thousand programmers working for him. "We're really a software company; that's the thing people don't understand," Diercks said.

Like Huang, Diercks never let off the pressure, putting his team into perpetual crunch to deliver the latest must-have features. Working for Diercks was hard, and former Nvidia programmers often mentioned burnout as their reason for departure. Wandering around the spaceships in his plaid shirt and jeans, Diercks looked like a cattle rancher abducted by a UFO, but his incongruous appearance disguised his obsession with deadlines. Nvidia's software products were not always beautiful or easy to use, and the interfaces for some of the tool kits were a decade out of date. But Diercks was not a person who cared for appearance; he cared only about being first. Whenever some promising new frontier of science opened, he was there at once, distributing his latest collection of software tools. A competitor might later arrive with a more elegant product that was cheaper to run, but by then it was too late—the industry standard had been set. For this reason, Bill Dally told me he wasn't concerned about the open-source competition. "Because we're flooring it!" he said. "We're always a couple of generations ahead of them."

NVIDIA OWNED NO MANUFACTURING FACILITIES, and employees were accustomed to remote collaboration, so when the COVID-19 pandemic arrived, operations were scarcely affected. Still, things became less fun: the third-floor bar was closed, GTC went virtual, and Huang, like everyone else, was forced to retreat into his house. In July 2020, when Nvidia finally surpassed Intel in valuation, Huang couldn't celebrate in person. Nor could he brag about his accomplishment to his family—his younger brother, Jim, still worked for Intel. Instead, Jensen took his two dogs for a walk. Perhaps they intuited his accomplishment; he couldn't be sure.

Soon, Nvidia surpassed AMD in valuation as well. Housebound and managing the world's most valuable semiconductor firm, Huang grew concerned that he was losing touch with the front. Nvidia had grown too large for Huang to really understand *everything* that was going on, but it was not his style to delegate. To maintain resonance, he needed to keep communication open with the frontline employees.

Sometime around 2020, Huang asked everyone at the company to submit a weekly list of the five most important things they were working on. Every Friday from that day forward, he received twenty thousand emails. Brevity was encouraged; Huang would randomly sample from this pool of correspondence late into the night. In turn, he communicated to his staff by writing hundreds of emails per day, often only a few words long. (One executive compared the emails to haiku. Another compared them to ransom notes.) His responsiveness was superhuman. "You'd email him at 2 a.m. and receive a reply at 2:05 a.m.," Dally said. "Then you'd email him again at 6 a.m. and receive a reply at 6:05 a.m."

The buzz about the transformer architecture filtered up to Huang through these emails. OpenAI was said to be running a job on a Microsoft Azure server that had tied up a thousand GPUs over the course of a month while running up a $5 million bill. This was a new language model—a "large" language model, so named because it was about a hundred times bigger than anything yet deployed.

Huang realized that he needed a new tool kit just for transformers. He informed Bas Aarts to drag his current recurrent neural-network compiler to the recycle bin and begin work on a transformer compiler at once. Aarts was glad to do it: he found the long-term/short-term memory structures of recurrent neural networks a needless complication. "RNNs were very difficult to program and even more difficult to compile," he said. "Transformers were a better fit across the board."*

Even before the switch, Aarts had begun to witness strange and terrible things at Nvidia. Cutting-edge product demos were available there months and sometimes years before they would be unveiled to the public. In mute awe, Aarts had watched a motion-transfer demo where an AI had edited one of the *Mission Impossible* movies in real time, replacing Tom Cruise's face with that of someone standing in the room. "It looked to me—I'm not

---

*The programming environment had changed much in the years since Aarts had written the first CUDA compiler. In the past, neural net programmers had used a software library called Torch, written in the niche programming language Lua. In 2016, Facebook's AI Research group ported Torch to the programming language Python, which was easy to use and familiar to researchers. The resulting PyTorch framework became the industry standard and made Python the most popular programming language in the world. By the late 2010s the default AI workflow was more or less established: write code in a Python notebook with the PyTorch library installed, compile the code to CUDA, send it to a cluster of Nvidia GPUs for processing, analyze the results back in PyTorch, then repeat until sentience.

PyTorch had for a time competed with Google's TensorFlow framework, but today TensorFlow's market share has fallen to the low single digits. The consensus among programmers is that PyTorch is easier to use and that community support for PyTorch is more robust. The latter impression is due in great part to the relentless efforts of Piotr Bialecki, a programmer from Germany who has posted almost forty thousand times to the official PyTorch forums since registering his account in 2017. Averaging about fifteen posts a day, Bialecki is especially helpful at getting Python to integrate with CUDA, and the appearance of his friendly face in a comment thread has served as a beacon of hope for many a stumped developer. In 2019, Bialecki joined Nvidia.

a video guy, but it looked to me like it was *perfect*," Aarts said. "I couldn't see there was a fake."

Nvidia was fond of theatrical staging. Sometime in 2019, in the middle of the large, empty floor of the Endeavor headquarters, there suddenly appeared a large, black pillar that Aarts described as an "obelisk." The obelisk housed a terminal running PicassoGAN, an AI that generated images by pitting two neural networks against each other. The responsiveness of the machine amazed Aarts; PicassoGAN could create anything you liked. "You type in a prompt: draw me a man in a landscape, with a river, and trees, and some birds, and a little house in the back," Aarts said. "*Boom.* There."

Aarts, like everyone at Nvidia, had signed an NDA that prevented him from discussing such technology with the outside world. This frustrating experience was widespread in Silicon Valley as members of technical staff, sworn to secrecy, could not discuss the miracles unfolding before their eyes. Up until around 2018, AI had flourished in a spirit of open academic collaboration. Now the innovations were coming from skunkworks R&D. Cryptic Twitter accounts began to appear, teasing hints of the extraordinary wonders to come. "I saw things where I thought, 'Wow, I cannot believe this is possible in this age,'" Aarts said. "People are oblivious about what is already going on. People have no clue."

But Aarts had as yet seen nothing.

SEVENTEEN

Money

n 2020 OpenAI released GPT-3, which was trained on more than a tera-byte of text data, the equivalent of a hundred billion words. The specifics of that training data were hidden within a thicket of nondisclosure agreements; later analyses suggested that OpenAI had used an extremely liberal interpretation of the "fair use" doctrine to absorb not just the entirety of English-language Wikipedia but also a comprehensive scraping of copy-righted web links, including archives of *The New York Times* dating back to 1851. In addition to the self-published vampire-romance fiction, the training set also included a mysterious second curriculum of texts labeled "Books2." Many speculated that "Books2" was derived from LibGen, a shadow collection of four million cracked ebooks that had circulated on peer-to-peer file-sharing sites for years. (Jonathan Franzen, John Grisham, Jodi Picoult, and George R. R. Martin were among the bestselling authors who would later sue OpenAI over similarities between their work and GPT output, as would the *Times*.) The model was then "fine-tuned" with human input to scrub some of the more objectionable responses.

GPT-3 stunned technologists with its many emergent capabilities, in-cluding the ability to solve logic puzzles and write workable computer code.

Still, it did not immediately set the atmosphere on fire and was largely ignored by the public. Not until late 2022, when Sutskever and his team released "ChatGPT," a chatbot for interacting with the latest OpenAI models, did the world take notice. Details about internal workings of these models were confidential; by this time, Microsoft had invested at least $10 billion in OpenAI's capped-profit subsidiary and was loath to release proprietary data to competitors. What can be said is that ChatGPT was fine-tuned for human conversation, using not just internet text but also transcripts of YouTube videos and data from licensed third-party sources—and that conservative estimates speculated the model had at least a trillion parameters. Translate that to synapses, and you were approaching the brain of a cat.

ChatGPT launched as a beta-test on November 30, 2022, with no marketing and no subscription tier. The portal to world domination was a bland grayscale website with a blinking cursor into which the user might enter any command. Really, *any* command. ChatGPT could write poetry! And not just doggerel, but sonnets, limericks, and sestinas. It could write screenplays and essays and functional computer code. It could write short stories and letters to the editor, and it gave good parenting advice. In five days, more than a million people signed up to test it. By January 2023, ChatGPT had one hundred million active monthly users. In March 2023, OpenAI unveiled GPT-4 through its online portal. Looking to quantify its creation's intelligence, OpenAI subjected the model to a battery of academic tests. GPT-4 passed the bar exam; it scored 5's on the Art History, US History, US Government, Biology, and Statistics AP exams; it scored in the 99th percentile on the Verbal component of the GRE; it scored in the 92nd percentile on the introductory sommelier exam. The researchers attached a visual-recognition layer to the neural net and found that it could not only perfectly describe images but also recognize complex visual jokes. In one, the researchers fed GPT-4 an image of a clunky computer cable from the 1990s connected to an iPhone, then asked GPT-4 to explain what it was looking at. "The humor in this image comes from the absurdity of plugging a large, outdated VGA connector into a small, modern smartphone charging port," the model responded. Later, a social media user showed how GPT-4 could create a website from a sketch on a napkin.

Around this time, I began to fear for my job. I once asked ChatGPT to make me cry; it returned a story about a pair of songbirds, one of whom dies by running into a glass window and the other of whom forever guards their empty nest. I once asked ChatGPT to make me laugh; it asked me to envision a man in an adjacent car picking his nose. I did not, however, use ChatGPT to write this book—I was too afraid.

My experience was broadly mirrored by users around the world. Students realized they could use it to write essays, and homework was forever obsolete. Lawyers used it to summarize legal briefs; job applicants used it for cover letters; my dad used it to request that the town council install a traffic sign. It was magic. It was really magic. "That first-time experience is what hooked people," Ilya Sutskever said. "The first time you use it, I think it's almost a spiritual experience. You go, 'Oh my God, this computer seems to understand.'"

OPENAI SPENT MORE than $100 million to train GPT-4, with much of the money making its way to Nvidia through Microsoft. Although GPT-3 was essentially a single giant neural network, GPT-4 used a "mixture of experts" model, featuring many neural networks assigned to different tasks. One "expert" might focus on safety, blocking users from asking GPT-4 how to make bombs or dispose of corpses; another might focus on writing computer code; a third would concentrate on emotional valence. (OpenAI declined to comment on GPT-4's construction.)

The "inference" process of extracting knowledge from GPT-4 could easily exceed half of the initial training costs and had to be provided to customers on an ongoing basis. Estimates varied, but one informed analysis put the cost of inference at roughly a quarter of a cent per word. At that rate, it would cost GPT-4 about $10 to write a five-thousand-word college term paper—a bargain when compared to hiring an unemployed graduate student to do it and certainly a better solution than doing the work yourself. To defray the inference costs, OpenAI began charging $20 per month to access GPT-4. By March 2023, the product was approaching two million subscribers.

The synthesis of the transformer architecture with hyperscale parallel computing resulted in a Cambrian explosion of AI services. Microsoft built Copilot, an autocomplete tool for computer code that programmers found indispensable. (So successful was the service that Huang predicted coding would soon be superseded by natural-language descriptions. "The programming language of the future is human," he said.) DeepMind built Alpha-Fold2, an AI that predicted the three-dimensional structure of proteins from one-dimensional amino-acid building blocks. With this, the age of "programmable biology" drew closer, in which the four elemental nucleotide bases of RNA could be made to act like the 0s and 1s of computer binary. A profusion of "generative" AI products arose, promising to revolutionize creative industries by synthesizing content on command. OpenAI's DALL-E, or competing Midjourney and Stable Diffusion, could in a minute or two create artwork of any description in the style of any artist. Start-ups Udio and Suno offered competing music-generation applications that could generate songs in any genre. Jasper could be used to create effective marketing campaigns in seconds. OpenAI's Sora, revealed in 2024, promised the opportunity to create real-time video of any description.

The consumer-facing products were splashy, but many close to AI believed that the real progress was in product lines that were "invisible by default." Industrial adoption of AI meant more efficient power grids, faster airline scheduling, improved delivery speeds, and countless other incremental wins. Each improvement, in isolation, was absorbed into back-end infrastructure with little notice outside specialist circles, but the aggregate effect was a massive and ongoing upgrade to global productivity.

There was also progress in what was possibly the last frontier of human endeavor: using AI to accelerate AI. In 2022, DeepMind unveiled a neural net intended to speed up matrix multiplication. Two years later, Nvidia introduced a software package that used generative AI to design the patterns on silicon microchips. Such self-augmentation remained within human control—for now.

Sinister applications also began to appear. Eerie AI voice-cloning technology was used to satirize Donald Trump and Joe Biden as quarreling *Overwatch* teammates. Bizarre algorithmically generated content began to flood social media. "Deep-fake" pornography targeting female students circulated in American high schools. Voice-cloned telemarketers began harassing the public; some scammers created the illusion of family members held for ransom. In Hong Kong, police reported that a finance worker at an architectural firm was duped out of $25 million in corporate funds after his colleagues in a conference call all turned out to be deep-fake clones. The only solution to these problems, technologists advised, was more AI.

The large tech firms reoriented their entire business lines toward AI. Microsoft, Meta, Tesla, and Google all announced multibillion-dollar spending initiatives. The automakers promised autonomous vehicles; the defense industry promised autonomous weapons. AI start-ups raised a cumulative $50 billion in 2023. The money went to medicine, to education, to business platforms, to robotics start-ups. The stock market moved sharply higher in anticipation of gains in productivity to come. Prize committees started distributing hardware to the AI pioneers. Demis Hassabis of DeepMind was given the 2024 Nobel Prize in Chemistry for his work on the protein-folding problem. Geoffrey Hinton was simultaneously awarded the 2024 Nobel Prize in Physics. That same year, Jensen Huang was elected to the National Academy of Engineering, an honor many felt was overdue.

And all of this—all of this money, all of this talent, all of this innovation— would pass through a single corporate siphon. All of it would go through Nvidia.

IN ERNEST HEMINGWAY'S *The Sun Also Rises*, Mike Campbell, a drunk and penniless war veteran, is asked how he went bankrupt. "Two ways," he responds. "Gradually and then suddenly." The same phrase might be used to describe how Jensen Huang got rich. Small changes that had accumulated over two decades of investment were now paying extraordinary dividends.

At the beginning of 2023, Huang informed investors that Nvidia had sold GPU supercomputing clusters to fifty of America's hundred largest companies. The other fifty, he continued, were leasing Nvidia's infrastructure through the cloud. In 2023, he said, data-center revenues had surpassed gaming revenues for the first time; he expected those revenues to double once again in the coming year. Nvidia, which controlled close to 90 percent of the AI chip market, became an object of fervent interest on Wall Street, with CNBC featuring a countdown to its quarterly earnings announcement. Expectations, for once, could not match reality. When the Nasdaq opened on May 25, 2023, Nvidia's value increased by about $200 billion. By the close of trading, Nvidia was the sixth-most-valuable corporation on Earth, worth more than Walmart and ExxonMobil combined. "There's a war going on out there in A.I., and Nvidia is the only arms dealer," one Wall Street analyst said.

Ten years earlier, Huang had been pleading with Fidelity for his job. Now, at sixty, he was the planet's most celebrated monopolist. In Taiwan the noodle shops he visited put his picture on the menu; his iconic leather jackets were featured in the Style section of the *Times*. In addition to the homes in Los Altos and Maui, he was connected, via a shell corporation, to a seven-bedroom, $38 million mansion on San Francisco's Gold Coast, the redoubt of billionaires. Featuring a library, a gym, and a movie theater, it was one of the city's most expensive homes. To the sanctified roster of Jobs, Bezos, Gates, and Zuckerberg, one could now add the name of Huang.

His chips were so valuable that they were used as loan collateral, and demand for them brought powerful men to their knees. In late 2023, Huang met with Elon Musk and Oracle cofounder Larry Ellison for sushi at the Nobu restaurant in Palo Alto. Ellison and Musk had a collective net worth above $300 billion, yet in this rarefied company, Huang was demonstrably the alpha—the other two spent the entire meal pleading for Huang to ship them more AI chips. "Elon and I were begging, I guess is the best way to describe it," Ellison recalled. "An hour of sushi and begging."

The burgeoning value of Nvidia's shares spread great wealth to loyalists. Tench Coxe and Mark Stevens had both served on the board since 1993, stewarding Huang through the lean years and defending him when Starboard Value attempted to commandeer the ship. By 2024, each man owned a stake in Nvidia worth more than $4 billion. Coxe had staked hundreds of companies; when I asked him if Nvidia was his best investment, he looked at me as if I had just asked the stupidest question he'd ever heard. "Uh, *yeah*," he said. (It later occurred to me that a founder's stake in the world's most valuable company was by definition the best possible investment you can make.)

The stake of longtime board member Harvey Jones was worth more than $1 billion. Brooke Seawell, the chair of Nvidia's audit committee, had about $700 million in Nvidia shares. Jim Gaither, Huang's first lawyer, had a mere $500 million, having not joined the board until 1998. Colette Kress, Nvidia's CFO, had around $800 million; Tim Teter, Nvidia's general counsel, had more than $400 million; Deb Shoquist, Nvidia's operations wizard, had more than $300 million. Due to Nvidia's decentralized management structure, old-timers like Dwight Diercks and Bill Dally were not considered corporate officers and were therefore not required to disclose their holdings—but I sensed they were doing OK. David Kirk, whom Huang had offered an irrefusable equity package way back in 1997, had retired in 2018 but told me that he'd held on to a portion of his shares. "I have a lot more money than I ever thought I would," he said. The most opaque Nvidia fortune was that of cofounder Chris Malachowsky, whose name, I noticed, was not in the *Forbes* list of billionaires. In his last required disclosure, way back in 2001, Malachowsky had owned about 5 percent of the company, an amount that would be worth more than $100 billion today. Much had changed since, but when I asked him in mid-2023 if he had cashed out, he responded, "Not much."*

Like many firms, Nvidia allowed employees to purchase stock at a discount to market prices. What set Nvidia's program apart was that employ-

---

*The share valuations in this chapter were calculated using Nvidia's December 5, 2024, closing stock price of $145.14 and include money held in family trusts.

ees were allowed to purchase stock at a discount to the lowest price at any point in the last two years. These purchases were capped at a certain dollar amount, but as the stock went vertical, the program basically turned into free money, and those who maxed out their contributions each year made the trade of a lifetime. With the windfall extending deep into middle management, some newer employees expressed concerns that the nouveau-riche veterans were entering a state of "semiretirement." Executives disputed this characterization. Jeff Fisher, who ran the company's gaming side, had been among the first thirty employees. "Many of us are financial volunteers at this point," he said, "but we believe in the mission."

The lure of developing this revolutionary technology offered purpose beyond what money could buy. This was especially true of the old guard, who'd spent years explaining to baffled peers why they were working for a gaming company and who constantly had to correct the pronunciation of the firm's name. AI had not been a consideration for these veterans, and they were as surprised to be working on it as anybody. "There was no way me, or anybody else, could have dreamed at the time that this stuff that science fiction writers might come up with has become a reality," said Jay Puri, Nvidia's head of sales, who started work at the company in 2005. The value of Puri's shares exceeded $700 million by 2024, but he felt that the interesting work at Nvidia was only beginning. "Maybe I'm biased, but I think it really is the most important technology company of our time," he said.

EIGHTEEN

Spaceships

n late 2023, I visited Nvidia's offices for the first time. Voyager, the larger triangle of Nvidia's campus, was now open. The place is awesome. In the middle of 750,000 square feet of cavernous, naturally lit office space stands a three-story matte-black "mountain." Climb the staircases, and you pass a series of vertical garden walls where species of stonecrop, ivy, and fern are arranged in undulating tones of green. At the summit is an illuminated marble bar surrounded by open-air, natural-wood pergolas. Stroll, with your drink, to the rim of the mountain, and you look out upon thousands of open-air cubicles, interrupted here and there by sterile white pillars that stretch a hundred feet up to support the lofted ceiling above.

The building interiors were immaculate; I imagined firing the gun from *Portal* at the walls. As I later learned, Nvidia tracks employees throughout the building with video cameras and AI. If an employee eats a meal at a conference table, the AI will dispatch a janitor within an hour to clean up after him. A human janitor, for now.

I could scarcely believe how excited the employees were to work in this panopticon. Huang was present in the building, and a buzz went through the cubicles whenever he crossed the floor. He was a striking figure, smaller than I imagined, alone in black in this white expanse, no entourage, just him. People spoke of him as "Jensen," only as "Jensen," and in the company Slack channels, they'd built a menu of custom Jensen emojis that they used to react to various pieces of positive news—like, for example, Nvidia crossing $3 trillion in market capitalization to become the single most valuable firm in the world, as it did a short while after my visit.

Nvidia's employees roamed these twin spaceships with the glow of the beatified. They were earnest, giddy, nerdy, and unpretentious, although their command of English was sometimes a little iffy. One entry-level hire I spoke with in the cafeteria had worked for the company for two months. She was twenty-five and had recently arrived from China, where she had earned a master's degree in computer science. "I wake up every day so happy to go to work," she said. She gestured around Voyager's interior, her petite frame burdened by the backpack Nvidia issued to new hires. "Look at this place. Everyone here is so smart. I can't believe I'm *in* this place!"

The only people I saw at Nvidia who didn't look happy were the quality-control technicians, who labored *inside* the mountain, like dwarves. Stuck in windowless laboratories and surrounded by industrial metal shelving, pallid young men wearing earplugs and T-shirts pushed Nvidia's microchips to the brink of failure. The racket was unbearable, a constant whine of high-pitched fans trying to cool the overheating parallel circuits. On these parallel circuits Nvidia was building a parallel reality.

SINCE 2018, Nvidia's graphics cards have featured "ray-tracing," which simulates the way that light bounces off objects to create photorealistic effects. Inside of a triangle of frosted glass in Nvidia's executive suite, a product-demo specialist showed me a three-dimensional rendering of a gleaming Japanese ramen shop. Light reflected off the metal counter, and steam rose from a bubbling pot of broth. There was nothing, as far as I could tell, to indicate the place wasn't real.

The specialist next showed me "Diane," a hyperrealistic digital avatar that spoke five languages. A powerful generative AI had studied millions of videos of real people to create this composite entity. Diane was stunning, but it was the imperfections that really got me—she had blackheads on her nose and trace hairs on her upper lip. The only clue that Diane wasn't truly human was the uncanny shimmer in the whites of her eyes. "We're working on that," the product specialist said.

One of Huang's goals is to unify Nvidia's computer-graphics research with its generative-AI research. Image-generation AIs will soon reach a level of sophistication where they are able to render three-dimensional, inhabitable worlds and populate them with realistic-seeming people. At the same time, language-processing AIs will be able to process and interpret voice commands in real time. Once the technologies are united, users will be able to speak whole universes into existence with a few simple voice commands.*

I felt dizzy leaving the product demo. I thought of science fiction; I thought of the Book of Genesis. I sat on a triangular couch with the corners trimmed and labored to imagine the future my daughter would inhabit. They were building the Manhattan Project of computer science, but when I questioned Nvidia executives about the wisdom of unleashing such power, they looked at me like I was questioning the utility of the washing machine. I wondered if an AI might someday kill someone. "Eh, electricity kills people every year," Bryan Catanzaro said. I wondered if it might eliminate art. "It will make art better!" Dwight Diercks said. "It will make you much better at your job." I wondered if someday soon an AI might become self-aware. "In order for you to be a creature, you have to be conscious. You have to have some knowledge of self, right?" Huang said. "So no. I don't know where that could happen."

I pressed Huang on this point in every interview I conducted with him. He gave me variations on the same answer every time. I brought up Geoffrey Hinton's worries. ("Humanity is just a passing phase in the evolution of intelligence," Hinton had said in a PBS interview.) Huang scoffed: "A lot of researchers don't understand why he's saying that. Maybe it's bringing

---

*Google's Genie 2, released in December 2024, can create an explorable 3D world from nothing more than a picture.

attention to his own work." I was stunned by this statement. Hinton was the most farsighted researcher in AI history, and Nvidia's financial success could be traced directly to work done in his lab—a fact that Huang had acknowledged many times. This wasn't some guy on the street waving a sign; this was the greatest mind in AI, the direct descendant of George Boole, telling us we should be very, very worried.

Huang was coldly dismissive. "Look, you buy a hot dog, so the machine recommends you ketchup and mustard," Huang said. "Is that the end of humanity?" He spoke of society's rapid acclimation to cars, alarm clocks, and mobile phones, and he told me we would grow similarly accustomed to an autonomous droid vacuuming the carpet. "The robot's not doing anything strange," he said. "Like I said, all it's doing is processing data. If you understand how it works, that world doesn't look weird at all." But I kept pressing, and Huang finally grew annoyed. "I'm so tired of this question," he said. "All this theorizing about something that there's no evidence for."

DIANE HAD BEEN RENDERED using a technique called "deep learning super sampling," which first relied on ray-tracing to illuminate the scene, then used a neural net to draw the details. In the product demo, only one out of every eight pixels was the product of the ray-tracing algorithm; the rest had been inferred by AI.

David Kirk had considered ray-tracing the last frontier. Once you had the ability to accurately depict the cascade of light in a scene, that was the end—you'd collapsed reality and simulation into a single frame. In movies, ray-traced CGI became indistinguishable from what the camera had captured—almost every major film now used the technique. "It no longer makes sense to talk about fact and fiction on the screen," Kirk said. "Everything is fiction."

But Catanzaro, having returned to Nvidia to manage deep-learning applications, saw a realm beyond. Termed "neural graphics," this new technology would no longer even attempt to simulate physics. Instead, it would use AI to "paint" realistic scenes in real time. Rather than using optical physics to represent reality, neural graphics hacked the human perception of light.

Catanzaro's journey back to Nvidia had been a little rocky. Around the age of forty, he finally accepted that he was gay. He separated from his wife and was kicked out of the Mormon church choir. With his expressive outfits, his religious speculations, and his interest in literature and music, Catanzaro continued to stick out at Nvidia. Not that he was really all that eccentric or anything—at Google, he would have been regarded as a normie. Nvidia wasn't the kind of place where people experimented with ayahuasca or polycules, and Catanzaro wasn't that kind of person. In the hundreds of hours of interviews I conducted with Nvidia employees, nobody, not once, had ever mentioned Burning Man.

Catanzaro alone was willing to discuss the implications of the technology he was building. Browsing social media, I had come across a 1964 clip of the science-fiction author Arthur C. Clarke speaking to the BBC. Even before cowriting the screenplay for *2001*, Clarke had entertained the possibility that machines might someday learn faster than humans:

> The most intelligent inhabitants of that future world won't be men or monkeys. They'll be machines—the remote descendants of today's computers. Now the present-day electronic brains are complete morons, but this will not be true in another generation. They will start to think, and eventually they will completely outthink their makers.
>
> Is this depressing? I don't see why it should be. We superseded the Cro-Magnon and Neanderthal men, and we presume we're an improvement. I think we should regard it as a privilege to be stepping stones to higher things. I suspect that organic, or biological, evolution has about come to its end, and we're now at the beginning of inorganic, or mechanical, evolution, which will be thousands of times swifter.*

* Quotation taken from *Horizon: The Knowledge Explosion*, originally broadcast on BBC Two, Monday 21 September 1964. A clip can be seen here: https://www.youtube.com/watch?v=YwELr8ir9qM

This was the most optimistic interpretation of what Nvidia had achieved—not merely a business or technological success, but a new phase of evolution.

The next time I spoke with Catanzaro, I showed him Clarke's clip, and he responded with enthusiasm. His posture grew erect, and he began to once again run his fingers through his hair. "So the conservative position is that Prometheus deserved to be chained to a rock and have his liver eaten because he gave mankind fire, and men don't deserve to have fire," he said. "The progressive position is that the world can be better, it should be better, and it's our responsibility to make it better. When I look around at problems that we face as humanity, I believe we need more intelligence."

Surely, I countered, a superior intelligence could be dangerous. Our own species, through agriculture, animal husbandry, mineral extraction, and urbanization, had transformed the surface of the planet, decimating or even eliminating all competing species and leaving only a handful of protected habitats unscathed. I asked Catanzaro if AI might do the same to us.

"I feel like we get stuck in science fiction perspectives a little bit too often," Catanzaro said. He leaned back in his chair, and I got a good look at the large owl embroidered on the front of his sweater. "AI isn't going to be interested in zero-sum games with us because there's so much more to do in this universe. For example, if an artificial intelligence is trying to build a huge data center—it doesn't want to put it where the humans live. It wants to put it somewhere else, maybe underground. Do you know how much space there is underground?"

Catanzaro was uncorked now—I sensed that he didn't often get to share this perspective at his job. "It doesn't need to inhabit this biosphere. In fact, it doesn't need to be on the Earth, either, because the thing about artificial intelligence is that it travels at the speed of light. Humans, you know, we actually have to lug bodies around. Artificial intelligence can move along a radio signal as long as there's an antenna on the other side." Free of the limitations of biology, Catanzaro explained, AI would rapidly spread throughout the solar system and beyond. "Humans are naturally confrontational—like, we're territorial animals, and it's built into our limbic system to defend our turf," he said. "AI, if it's truly intelligent, the things that it's interested in are so much bigger than the little thin crust of Earth that the humans live on. I don't think that it's going to be interested in taking that from us. Rather, I feel like AI is going to want to take care of us." ·

SERVING AS A ZOO ANIMAL for a space computer was an experience to be savored at leisure. Today, though, Nvidia remains earthbound, and Catanzaro's discussion of where to put the data centers was not just idle speculation— it was borne of practical concerns. The whirring fans I'd seen inside the mountain suggested the intense demand for electricity that Nvidia's equipment generated. GPUs had unclogged the bottleneck of calculation speed, and Mellanox's Infiniband protocol had unclogged the bottleneck of data throughput. The remaining bottleneck was simply how much electricity a data center could consume. The remaining limit was power.

NINETEEN

Power

As the utility technician neared the transmission tower, the wire emitted an audible hum. More than two hundred thousand volts of electricity coursed through it. The worker was suspended in a bucket, attached to a crane, nearly a hundred feet in the air. He wore a tool belt, a fire-retardant shirt, and insulated gloves. Using a specialized tool called a "hot stick," he reached in to detach the high-voltage wire from the crossarm that held it. He had to be careful; an errant move at this stage could mean immediate electrocution. The line uncoupled with a crackle, and the aroma of ozone filled the air. One down, several thousand to go.

The lineman worked for Dominion Energy, the electric utility that served Loudoun County, Virginia. He was upgrading the infrastructure that powered the world's largest collection of data centers. Loudoun was the nerve center for US retail-computing demand: if you conducted a Google search in Manhattan, chances were good that your query was routed through Virginia.

The electrical infrastructure needed to supply these giant computers had taken Dominion more than a century to build. With the arrival of AI, Dominion was projected to double that infrastructure in less than fifteen years.

This was perilous work in the best of circumstances, but the data centers were so demanding that in the summer of 2024, Dominion determined that the wires would have to be replaced while they were still live. The risks were considerable, but the safety of humans seemed a secondary consideration. Under no circumstances was the power to the data centers ever to be cut. Demand was too frenzied. People just wanted AI so bad.

The demand did not come from training new neural nets—mostly, it came from deploying them. Inference had once been a task so simple it could fit on a floppy disk, but modern users wanted more from AIs than backgammon moves. They wanted term papers; they wanted search; they wanted voice generators to make memes. OpenAI's GPT products had more than 180 million daily users. Google was bundling experimental AI answers along with conventional search results. TikTok reels were narrated by an expanding cast of AI voice avatars. Powering each service, in a rack in a data center in some anonymous warehouse on the outskirts of a major population center, you would find an Nvidia GPU.

These GPUs used a lot of juice. A standard Google search required about a third of a watt-hour's worth of electricity. With generative AI enabled, the same Google search required ten times that, which was enough to power a light bulb for about twenty minutes. Ask GPT to write you a five-thousand-word term paper, and you used enough energy to run a microwave for an hour. Industrial demand was greater; executives were excited about the prospect of replacing human labor entirely. In 2022 James Earl Jones announced that he was tired of performing the voice of Darth Vader, so he licensed his voice to Disney to be cloned in perpetuity. (Jones died in 2024, but Vader's menacing tone and labored breathing may prove immortal.) Image-recognition tools promised to save billions of dollars a year in MRI analysis costs, putting most radiologists out of a job. Amazon used AI to determine whether the strawberries it was delivering were bruised, and farm owners were experimenting with AI robots to pick the fruit they shipped.

One analysis predicted that meeting the needs of the generative AI boom might require doubling US nuclear plant capacity in under ten years. Even

conservative estimates projected a 20 percent increase in required total demand. There was no realistic way to supply the Nvidia GPUs with the electricity they needed while simultaneously hitting carbon-neutrality targets.
Dominion, in addition to upgrading the high-voltage lines, was discussing
reviving mothballed coal-burning facilities.

Nvidia was not in denial about the problem of global warming. Researchers there were quick to point out that climate modeling was one of
the first uses for supercomputers. Syukuro Manabe, the scientist who won
the 2021 Nobel Prize in Physics for showing that trace amounts of carbon
dioxide would trap heat in the atmosphere, had arrived at this conclusion in
the late 1960s after fashioning a primitive simulation of Earth with an IBM
computer that weighed seventy tons and drew as much power as ten city
blocks. Using exponentially more powerful computers in the 1980s, NASA
scientists had correctly predicted a coming rise in Earth's average temperature of several degrees Fahrenheit, even though the empirical trend at the
time had looked flat. These simulations also predicted that as the planet
warmed, the upper atmosphere would cool down, causing atmospheric layers to pancake as heat was trapped near the surface. By the 2020s, satellite
data showed that the sky had indeed collapsed.

Almost all of what we understand about climate change is the product of
powerful, energy-hungry supercomputers. Scientists had been running climate models on Nvidia hardware since the late 2000s, and Nvidia had its
own climate division, which conducted extraordinarily sensitive forecasting.
(Nvidia's "Earth-2" simulation promised to predict the wind speed on an
individual city block.) Bill Dally, Nvidia's chief scientist, worried a lot about
climate change—as a frequent visitor to both the snow-crowned Sierras and
the storm-tossed Caribbean, he'd personally witnessed its manifold effects.
One of Dally's reasons for working on AI was that he believed it would
move humanity toward a carbon-neutral future. "If there's one problem that
I think everybody in the world ought to be staying up at night about, it's climate change," he had said. "The survivability of our planet needs to be a
first-order concern."

But despite such talk, Nvidia's chips were almost single-handedly responsible for a global surge in electricity demand. As the chips got better at matrix multiplication, so too did they become hungry for power. The 2020 A100 chip required 250 watts in standard configurations. The H100, released two years later, required 350 watts, 75 percent more. The B100, released in 2024, doubled demand to 700 watts, and the forthcoming B200 would require 1,000. The original DGX box from 2016 used as much power as a clothes dryer. Its 2024 successor used enough electricity to power a single-family home.

And this was but a single brick in the fortress wall. The DGX boxes were modular units that customers stacked into the long "superpods" that formed the spine of the modern data center. The superpods were wired with thick bundles of cable and fitted with advanced air- and liquid-cooling systems to keep from overheating. The biggest of the hyperscale data centers measured their annual power requirements in gigawatts—more than the output of a nuclear reactor, enough to power Minneapolis. Continuously upgrading Nvidia chips in its data centers had contributed to a 50 percent increase in Google's greenhouse-gas emission in five years, even accounting for the efficiency gains in the power grid and despite the company's commitment to "net zero" by 2030. (In 2024 a company spokesperson affirmed Google's commitment to carbon neutrality while admitting that the AI power draw presented a "challenge.") At Microsoft, whose cloud-computing division trained and deployed the expensive OpenAI models, emissions went up by almost a third. Cloud providers were even trying to buy disused crypto-mining operations.

Some investors questioned the wisdom of this gigantic build-out. The path to profits from AI was not a direct one, and the high costs of both the silicon and the electricity were compounded by a shortage of talent. Snake charmers who could consistently tease out results from the fickle AI architecture were rare, and they commanded serious coin. Not every company was OpenAI, and not every company had Ilya Sutskever working for it; the frustrations that Fredrik Dahl had experienced trying to get a neural net to play poker were now replicated at IT departments around the world.

Despite the increase in computational power, neural nets still hit plateaus, and when they did, there was still often no obvious way to make them better. Firms that attempted to replicate GPT with in-house data often produced shambolic "knowledge engines" that were little better than toys. These AIs supplemented the standard large-language-model training set with emails, mission statements, patent applications, legal memoranda, and other exciting selections from the internal corporate syllabus. As the buzz percolated through middle management, executives at marketing, media, and health-care firms launched ambitious initiatives, sometimes openly telling staff that many employees would be laid off once the neural nets were working. But much of what was produced was vaporware: late, expensive, and barely functional. Many users felt that AI technology simply wasn't ready.

In summer 2024, Elliott Management, one of the world's largest hedge funds, told investors that tech stocks, especially Nvidia, were in "bubble land." The letter to clients, quoted in the *Financial Times*, called AI "overhyped, with many applications not ready for prime time." Many of the promised applications were "never going to be cost-efficient, are never going to actually work right, will take up too much energy, or will prove to be untrustworthy."

Disappointment, not competition, was the biggest risk to Nvidia's empire. FOMO was driving a lot of activity—no company could afford to be the one without an AI strategy. The executives buying Nvidia hardware needed to build products that justified the scale of investment. If they couldn't, remorse would set in, demand would slacken, and Nvidia's stock would crater. The money managers at Elliott believed that if Nvidia were to experience even a single bad quarter, the entire tech sector would deflate like a hissing tire.

AI investors were exuberant, certainly, but were they irrational? Skeptics had compared the AI craze to the dot-com boom or the mortgage crisis, but the executives in charge of AI spending were not hucksters. They were seasoned computer geniuses with decades of experience. The businesses involved were stable, and the funding came from reserves of accumulated profit, not dicey share issuances or subprime debt. Every academic computer scientist I spoke with, without exception, saw the triumph of neural networks as a civilizational advancement. Many thought it was the most important discovery in the history of the field. The technology was phenomenal, and the earnings that it had generated so far were real.

The problem that investors had once faced valuing Nvidia alone now applied to valuing the entire stock market. Close readings of past financial statements would not tell you if the AI gamble was smart, and projections of future earnings had as little bearing on reality as the leaves at the bottom of a teacup. The salient question was whether Huang knew what he was doing—whether Huang, Zuckerberg, Musk, Nadella, Pichai, and Altman knew what they were doing at all. They had allocated hundreds of billions into this unproven technology. Was this smart? Were they smart or not?

TWENTY

The Most Important Stock on Earth

J udgment Day arrived on February 21, 2024. The hype leading up to the earnings announcement was absurd. CNBC had run a countdown for days leading up to the event. The niche social media community known as "FinTwit" circulated a meme of Huang, in his signature leather, standing in front of an electoral map of the United States, with all fifty states colored slime green. In the days before the reveal, Goldman Sachs had called Nvidia "the most important stock on earth."

Nvidia's conference call began fifteen minutes after the close of trading. It was one of the most listened-to earnings reports in Wall Street history. Colette Kress, Nvidia's CFO, spoke first. She announced that annual revenues were far better than expected, more than doubling to $60 billion. Not only that, but Nvidia had realized a greater than 70 percent gross margin across all products. (Apple, Wall Street's favorite money-printing machine, earned a gross margin of 46 percent.) Net income for the year, Kress announced, was just under $30 billion—more than Nvidia had earned in the previous thirty years combined. With thirty thousand employees, every worker at Nvidia was now generating $1 million per year in profit.

Huang spoke next. He sounded like Thomas Edison. He described how neural nets could now understand and generate not just human language but any information, including elements of biology and the three-dimensional world. He described a forthcoming "trillion-dollar infrastructure cycle" of building AI factories. "We are now at the beginning of a new industry, where AI data centers process massive raw data to refine it into digital intelligence," he said. "Like AC power-generation plants of the last industrial revolution, Nvidia AI supercomputers are essentially AI-generation factories of *this* industrial revolution."

Nothing could have prepared traders for the frenzy the following day. On February 22, in six and a half hours of trading, Nvidia gained $277 billion in market value, adding more than the entire value of the Coca-Cola Company to its market capitalization. Traders exchanged at least $65 billion worth of Nvidia stock that day, accounting for nearly a fifth of all US stock market activity. By market close, the three most valuable companies on Earth were Microsoft, Apple—and Nvidia. It was the largest single-day accumulation of wealth for any company in Wall Street history.

This buildup put unbelievable pressure on Huang. Most of Nvidia's value was not based on what the company had done but on what investors expected it *might* do in the future, and that meant continuing to innovate and deliver at a rapid pace in an expanding field of motivated competitors. Watching him pace the stage at his conferences and investor presentations, I recognized the same thing that Curtis Priem had twenty-five years before: Huang was all alone.

Management professors theorized that a chief executive should ideally have between eight and twelve direct reports. Huang now had fifty-five. He had no right-hand man or woman, no majordomo, no second-in-command. Huang also had no designated successor, and as Nvidia grew, its C-suite actually shrank, meaning that there was no scapegoat for mistakes. Board members spoke of his irreplaceability; it was not an exaggeration to suggest that Huang had personally saved the American economy from recession. The US stock market, over the course of Nvidia's rise, had pulled away from markets in Europe and Asia. Almost all of that outperformance was attributable to AI. Nvidia's $3 trillion market capitalization purportedly represented the expected value of the company's future earnings—but it was really a giant, GDP-sized bet on the capabilities of this single sixty-one-year-old man.

IN 2022 EMPLOYEE REVIEWS on the website Glassdoor ranked Nvidia the best place to work in the United States. Employees were influenced by the stock price, of course, but even in the gaming era the company had scored well. This was a little surprising, for while working at Nvidia was stimulating, it was never exactly fun; the corporate culture that Huang fostered was closer to Microsoft than Google, closer to IBM than Apple. But years earlier, Chiu, the Taiwanese physicist, had told Huang that he'd allowed him to do his "life's work." The phrase had stuck with Huang, and now he wanted to offer that same opportunity to his staff. "We want NVIDIA to be a place where people can build their careers over their lifetime," the company wrote in its annual report. "Our employees tend to come and stay."

The appeal lay in what Nvidia allowed you to achieve. It was not a secret that Huang pushed people hard. Thus, he attracted determined workaholics seeking to establish legacies as inventors. In the same way that a bestselling author didn't stop writing, even many wealthy Nvidia engineers kept showing up to work each day to attack difficult technical problems. Those engineers collectively held more than fifteen thousand patents, but there was always something left to build.

Success allowed Nvidia to be discriminating in who it hired. Every job posting now received several hundred applicants. Ambitious strivers looking to contribute to the AI revolution often considered it their top choice. The workforce was "diverse," sort of—I would guess, based on a visual survey of the cafeteria at lunchtime, that about a third of the staff was South Asian, a third was East Asian, and a third was white. The line for Indian food was the longest.

Nvidia didn't share official demographic statistics with me, but photographs and interviews suggested that, even well into the 2000s, most of the company's employees had been white American men. The transition to a mostly Asian workforce was part of a broader pattern in Silicon Valley, but it also reflected Huang's shift of focus. "You know, computer graphics was not considered to be a very glamorous field," one longtime executive told me. "There was something a little disreputable about it."

But AI brought respectability. Instead of long-haired Americans in cargo shorts, graduates of the best technical universities in India, China, and Taiwan were now applying to work at the company. One former manager described the family pressure placed upon these Asian graduates to get a prestigious job at Nvidia, specifically. "These kids, their families only give them three options: you either need to be a doctor, or you need to be an engineer, or . . . actually, I don't think there's a third option," he said. "They're very competitive, and they're very bright, and they're just under a tremendous amount of pressure."

The manager, a gamer who had worked at Nvidia since the graphics days, reflected on Nvidia's changing culture. Graphics had been a quirky field that paid relatively poorly. "My parents told me *not* to do it," he said. "They thought I should get a real job." With success, he felt, the passionate mavericks of Nvidia's past were being supplanted by a new generation of conformist overachievers. Still, the manager conceded, the new hires were extraordinarily bright. "I mean, objectively speaking, can they code?" he asked. "Yeah. Better than I ever could."

In the early years, Nvidia had employed almost no women at all. Around the time of the IPO, David Kirk met his future wife, a fellow employee from Montreal. "All the men at Nvidia knew exactly how many women there were at the company at the time," he said. "Three." That number reflected, at least in part, the low number of qualified female electrical-engineering graduates—even today, more than 90 percent of US electrical-engineering graduates are male. In a 2022 survey, US female engineering undergraduates were asked to rank disciplines by career interest. Environmental and biomedical engineering tied for first; electrical engineering came in last.

Following explicit directives from Huang, Nvidia made an effort to hire more women. This initiative was successful, and by 2024 a little more than a quarter of the staff at Nvidia was female. (Sometime around 2020, Dawn, Nvidia's sexualized CGI pixie, also mysteriously vanished from company marketing material.) Jensen's wife, Lori, had left the workforce to raise their children, and when he spoke of his continuation of Nvidia's liberal work-from-home policy following the abatement of the pandemic, I sensed in him an eagerness to atone for her interrupted career. "We want to take advantage of this incredible videoconferencing technology so that young people—especially young women—can build their lives, build their families, and build their careers at the same time," Huang had said. "I don't want to give up on that."

Less successful was Nvidia's effort to hire Black employees. In 2020, fewer than 1 percent of Nvidia's global workforce was Black. Again, this partly reflected the limited pipeline of qualified Black American electrical-engineering graduates, but perhaps more saliently it reflected the limited pipeline of *any* qualified American electrical engineers. The discipline drew from a global talent pool, in which native-born citizens of the United States were outnumbered ten to one by applicants from East Asia, South Asia, the Middle East, and Europe. "Our diversity problem is basically getting any Americans of any color to study this subject at all," one university professor told me.

One thing I'd noticed was that many of the engineers I talked to at Nvidia had at least one parent who was also an engineer. (Some had two—for them, it was a hereditary affliction.) Sameer Halepete's father had taught him to solder circuits when he was in the third grade. "Engineering, especially electrical engineering, is very, very intimidating," he said. "So you kind of have to have some sort of cushion. You have to have somebody telling you, 'This is something that you can do.'" Halepete had, in turn, tried to pass the soldering tradition on to his daughters but had been unsuccessful.

Huang, of course, had a father and two brothers who were engineers. Both of his kids had gone into the hospitality industry, but after years of gentle paternal browbeating, he brought them back into the flock. Madison, after training as a chef and working at LVMH in Paris, was hired at Nvidia as a marketing director in 2020. Spencer had cofounded a cocktail "laboratory" in Taipei that had been named one of Asia's fifty best bars, but it went out of business during the pandemic. He joined Nvidia's robotics group in 2022. Inside Nvidia, Spencer and Madison received no obvious special treatment. "They pull together slides. They're on endless boring calls. They eat in the cafeteria," one employee said.

HUANG'S FIRM HAD LONG benefited from globalization, and historically Nvidia had not worried much about geopolitical entanglements. That changed on October 7, 2023, when militants from Hamas invaded Israel and began indiscriminately killing civilians. The youngest daughter of Mellanox founder Eyal Waldman was slain in the massacre, and Nvidia engineer Avinatan Or was taken hostage. (As of November 2024, Or's fate remains unknown.) More than 1,100 people were killed in the initial Hamas assault, and more than 250 were abducted.

A ferocious Israeli counteroffensive followed; in the months after the initial attack, Israeli forces killed an estimated forty thousand Palestinians, including at least eight thousand children. More than half of Gaza's buildings were either damaged or destroyed, and protests were organized all over the world. At the start of the war, Nvidia had around three thousand Israeli employees; the company also had about one hundred Palestinian employees in the West Bank. As four hundred of his Israeli workers were called up to military duty, Huang canceled an AI conference in Tel Aviv, then sent a company-wide email telling his staff in the region that he was giving them a bonus "to help in a small way." He also promised that Nvidia would match humanitarian-aid donations from employees. "Some want to donate to Israel's relief efforts, while others want to help innocent Palestinians," the email read. "You decide to support humanitarian efforts in Israel, Gaza, or both."

In public statements, Huang did not take a side in the conflict, repeatedly stating that the safety of his employees was his top priority. But he also emphasized the value of Israel's high-tech sector to Nvidia. "The heart and soul of the Blackwell processor came from Israel," he told the press at the

March 2024 GTC conference. "We will continue to invest heavily in Israel." A month later, with the conflict ongoing, Nvidia announced it was buying the 150-person Israeli start-up Run:AI for $700 million.

With China, Nvidia faced an even trickier situation. Huang saw China as a critical market for his AI chips and wanted to sell Chinese customers as many chips as he could. The US government had different ideas and in 2022 blocked sales to China of Nvidia's advanced A100 and H100 chips. Huang got around the embargo by selling modified versions of the chips; the unamused US government accused him of exploiting a loophole and issued a wider ban on sales of Nvidia equipment, including some high-end gaming cards.

This created an unusual situation in China. Chinese state media described video games as "spiritual opium," and Chinese regulators had limited kids to three hours a week of play time. But the demand for dual-use gaming hardware from China's scientists—not to mention its military—was great. In the days before the sanctions took effect, Nvidia offloaded chips in a hurry, selling enough A100s to ByteDance, the owners of TikTok, to train ten ChatGPTs. Even after the ban, high-end chips continued to find their way into China. In June 2023, Reuters reported that in the stalls of the massive electronics marketplace in Shenzhen, black-market vendors were offering A100s for double their retail price. Huang told me his first priority, above all, was to obey the law—but he objected to the sanctions. "If they can't buy it from us, they'll just build it themselves," he said.

The bigger problem Huang faced was China's designs on Taiwan. China's navy had more warships than any other, and China had long claimed that Taiwan was part of its national territory. In an address on New Year's Eve, 2023, Xi Jinping had announced that "reunification" with Taiwan was "inevitable." Satellite imagery released in April 2024 showed that China had built what appeared to be a replica of Taipei's presidential district in the Gobi Desert, presumably to train for an amphibious invasion.

The scale of such an invasion, should it ever occur, would make D-Day look small. It would also be catastrophic for the global economy. TSMC's manufacturing facilities in Taiwan were one of the major production choke-points in the world. No facility anywhere approached the speed and precision with which TSMC produced the most advanced microchips. Slowdowns in Taiwan during the pandemic had delayed deliveries of automobiles for months. A war would create delays for years—and not just in cars and AI but also in smartphones, consumer electronics, medical devices, and anything else that used a high-end microchip.

To my great surprise, Nvidia had done no contingency planning for this eventuality. "If something happens to Taiwan and TSMC, the ramifications are so large it's almost like asking me what I'd do if California fell into the ocean," Deb Shoquist said. Shoquist ran logistics at the most valuable semiconductor firm in the world, but Huang had instructed her never to think about this question. "I don't want her spending one brain cell on trying to mitigate that, because it's impossible for her to do so," he said. In the event of a war, Shoquist speculated that Nvidia would transfer its orders to Samsung in South Korea as well as to other partners around the globe. "I'll tell you what would happen," she said. "What would happen is everybody's products would get dumbed down a click."

Recognizing Taiwan's precarity, governments had begun funding their own chip-fabrication infrastructure. In the United States, President Biden had allocated tens of billions in taxpayer money to build facilities in Ohio and Arizona; similar initiatives had been launched in Japan, South Korea, and the European Union. "In the semiconductor space, there is no globalization anymore," Morris Chang told employees at a TSMC function in late 2023. "The priority is national security only."

On a patch of unclaimed desert in northern Phoenix, TSMC had cleared 1,100 acres of scrubland and was laying foundations for two massive chip-fabrication facilities. Though technically within Phoenix's sprawling municipal borders, the site was desolate and the area undeveloped; the closest entertainment was an open-air shooting range. The complex comprised a world unto itself, with dedicated utilities for water and natural gas, and on-site refineries delivering elementally pure streams of nitrogen, oxygen, and argon. Temperatures in the Sonora could cross 110 degrees in August—to conserve water, the plants would be outfitted with moisture-reclamation systems, like something out of *Dune*.

Curious neighbors, surveying the site from nearby Pyramid Peak, counted thirty-nine construction cranes in simultaneous operation, including a 180-foot Manitowoc crawler that could lift five million pounds at once. TSMC's total budget for the Phoenix plants was forecast to exceed $40 billion, making it one of the largest foreign direct investments in the history of the United States and one of the most expensive megaprojects in the world. When complete, the Phoenix fabs were projected to employ two thousand people and manufacture six hundred thousand chips a year, enough to meet the entire domestic demand of the United States.

Forty miles to the south, in the bedroom suburb of Chandler, Intel was funding a $32 billion expansion of its own. Amid the golf courses and the xeriscaped ranch homes, Intel ran construction around the clock: to ensure that the foundations would set in the summer heat, the builders used ice in the concrete mix and poured it in the middle of the night. They laid, in total, about four hundred thousand cubic yards of concrete, enough to fill a hundred Olympic swimming pools, then shipped in thirty thousand tons of steel to build the scaffolding above. Drone footage showed six gigantic fabrication buildings, arranged north to south and connected by industrial capillaries to a parallel line of support structures to the west.

The dueling Arizona plants, and others under construction around the world, suggested the possibility of a forthcoming glut in supply. Chang, retired and out of the decision loop, saw the Arizona investment as foolish—he believed that US work culture would never match the productivity of Asia and that the facility would lag global rivals. (When Nancy Pelosi visited Taiwan in 2022, Chang told her the US projects were "doomed to fail.") Chang also argued that TSMC's concentration in Taiwan was actually preventing a Chinese invasion, for no national economy would suffer as much as China's if TSMC went offline. (He called this Taiwan's "silicon shield.") Still, when his favorite customer, Jensen Huang, toured the TSMC construction site in Phoenix in 2023, Chang was there to greet him with a smile.

China had nothing to compare. The US government had successfully lobbied to block the export of the advanced light-printing machines that were the most critical component of the fabrication process, leaving China a decade behind. I wondered whether China might instead try to seize the TSMC plants in Taiwan and produce microchips themselves. A former US military official I spoke to regarded this as unlikely. "This is not like when Iraq conquered Kuwait for the oil fields," he said. "These machines are insanely precise, and insanely fragile, down to a precision of one atom. What do you think's going to happen to that machine if a missile goes off next to it?" The former official pointed out that administrators could remotely brick the machines by disabling their software; workers could also simply break the machines with baseball bats and hammers. "I would say the Taiwanese engineer sabotage thing is not to be underestimated," he said.

Still, I wondered, was it so crazy to ask if China couldn't rebuild the machines? Wasn't it possible they could write firmware updates of their own? Or force the Taiwanese engineers to work the production line under duress? The former military official paused for a long time. "There is no way the USA will ever let China have the Taiwanese semiconductor factories," he said. "Period. Ever."

THE WEALTH SPREAD BEYOND NVIDIA into a general frenzy for semiconductors. Qualcomm, AMD, Broadcom, Supermicro, and others enjoyed record valuations. ASML, the Dutch company that built the light-printing machines, became the most valuable tech stock in Europe. TSMC, with its unrivaled fabrication facilities, became the most valuable tech stock in Asia. In March 2024, the *Financial Times* reported that Ferrari sales in Taiwan had doubled in the past four years. "It's very simple," said one local businessman. "Taiwanese are rich, and there's only so many places you can put your money: you can buy property, and you can buy cars."

From the IPO date of January 22, 1999, through mid-2024, Nvidia's stock appreciated by more than 300,000 percent. The run-up magnified the impact of careless decisions made many years before. Dwight Diercks had sold some shares at the IPO to buy his dad a car. "That's a billion-dollar Cadillac," he said. Catanzaro and Aarts, the boomerang hires, both felt the sting of repricing their stock options, although both did fine in the end. Curtis Priem, of course, had liquidated all his shares many years before. His company had finally made them green with envy—only he was left with the most to envy of all.

By late 2024, Nvidia was worth twenty times more than struggling Intel. (In fact, Huang's holdings made him *personally* worth more than Intel.) In a talk to MIT students in December 2023, Intel's new CEO, Pat Gelsinger, claimed that Nvidia "got extraordinarily lucky" with its GPU efforts. "They didn't even want to support their first AI project," he said.

A lean and aquiline electrical engineer from rural Pennsylvania, Gelsinger had tried to force Huang out of business several times. In the late 1990s, he'd been the product manager for the Intel i740, a 3D graphics accelerator that flopped. In the late 2000s, he'd been the executive in charge of Project Larabee, the "Nvidia Killer" that never shipped. In 2022, Gelsinger, now CEO, had released the Intel Arc, a knockoff consumer-graphics chip that enjoyed a frisky 1 percent market share. As his rivals embraced the nimble "merchant chip" approach, Gelsinger doubled down on manufacturing. Under his leadership, in one of the great semiconductor bull markets of all time, Intel stock was cut in half.

Intel's board forced Gelsinger out in late 2024, but he was not the only one to express the sentiment that Huang had gotten lucky. No one, not even Catanzaro, had seen the intersection of parallel computing and neural nets coming. Aarts, who understood the technical aspects of the two technologies as well as anyone, marveled at the perfect harmony. Two fringe strains of computer science, starved of investment, hated—no, *detested*—by industry and researchers alike had somehow unified to form a thriving, sprawling entity now careering toward sentience. "I just thought, there is no *way* that Nvidia is this lucky," Aarts said. "There's no way that deep learning just fits this perfectly because Nvidia has never put any effort into it!"

Huang called it "luck, founded by vision."

For Dally, it was Huang's tireless work ethic that made Nvidia succeed.

Even Dally, who left no spare second in his day, could not quite believe the superhuman efforts of his boss. "The rest of us are just here to reduce the bandwidth demands on Jensen," Dally said. "I mean, when does he *sleep?*" Diercks agreed: "His hobbies are work, email, and work."

Plenty of people worked long hours, though. Jens Horstmann attributed Huang's success to his adaptability. "I've often asked myself, how is it that we started in the same cubicle, you know, with a similar IQ, both working equally hard," Horstmann said. "How is it that this person not only built this amazing company, but also a network around him of people that—that would just *die* for him if needed?" Huang, Horstmann believed, had changed himself many times. He recalled Huang at LSI, pushing the simulation software to its outer limits. "Now, he's still doing the same thing, but what he's engineering is *himself*. He was not born as a great CEO; he was not destined to be one. He transformed himself into one, just by abstracting! Just by problem-solving the inputs and outputs of what a good CEO should be."

But the final word went to Morris Chang. He didn't attribute Huang's success to his work ethic, which, at TSMC, would have been considered slightly above average—nor did he find him especially adaptable. Chang was ninety-two years old when I spoke with him, wearing a purple corded sweater and sitting in front of a striking piece of abstract art, his face serene, his hair completely white. In seventy years of corporate life across two continents he had seen every manner of executive there was to see. To him, the explanation was simple, and there was no secret: "His intellect is just superior."

TWENTY-ONE

Jensen

N vidia employees worshiped Huang, and I couldn't blame them. They were *rich*. They were insanely, incredibly rich, and he had made them that way. He'd taken a niche product for dorks and turned it into the dominant computing platform of their time. They saw Huang—excuse me, *Jensen*—they saw Jensen not just as a leader but as a prophet. Jensen was a prophet who made predictions about things. And then those things came true. And every time one of them came true, everybody in the spaceships got to add a zero to their net worth.

Jensen had done much to encourage this cult of personality. The speeches, the struggle sessions, the sweet talk alternating with abuse—all of these were tactics that served to break people to his will. He had also developed his personal brand, and not only with the leather jackets. For much of Nvidia's history, Jensen had been known as "Jen-Hsun," the transliteration of his Taiwanese name, but by 2023 he'd decided he'd just be "Jensen," leaning into an iconic mononym. The death of Steve Jobs in 2011 had left vacant the position of Visionary Tech Executive with a Signature Outfit, an important ceremonial role in American culture. By 2024 it looked like Jensen could be that guy.

But he remained a bit elusive as well. Even once you got him talking, you had to be careful: Jensen had a rich trove of anecdotes to share, but the details of those anecdotes would sometimes shift around a bit. Quoting him directly was a risky proposition, I had learned; just because he said something out loud didn't necessarily mean that he believed it. Jensen's stream of patter might lead anywhere, to bizarre non sequiturs about dog vomit, men's fashion, the quality of the eggs at Denny's, or whatever else popped into his mind. Consistency was not a feature of his personality: often what seemed like a well-considered opinion, or even a pithy aphorism, was actually just something he came up with off-the-cuff, which he did not necessarily mean and which he later would not remember saying.

Jensen contradicted himself frequently, sometimes offering opposing viewpoints within the same interview. He wasn't playing devil's advocate, exactly—he just liked to attack ideas from both sides. "He's not trying to be a politician," Horstmann said. "He's not trying to stay on message. He's trying to process real-time input, and he's willing to entertain a contradictory thought for a while." What might appear to be a definitive pronouncement was often just Jensen thinking out loud.

Only once he started to repeat himself was it time to pay attention. When an idea really struck Jensen, it slowly built up steam over a period of days or even weeks. It cycled into his vocabulary and was repeated at every meeting. Concepts like the "zero-billion-dollar market" or the "speed of light" hadn't come to Jensen in a flash; they'd arrived as polished nuggets of wisdom after spending months being tossed in the rock tumbler of his mind. Having arrived, they were then drilled so thoroughly into his employees that his staff sometimes sounded like characters from *The Manchurian Candidate*, repeating Jensen's catchphrases verbatim with a glassy look in their eyes. Even employees who hadn't worked at Nvidia for years could still recite the catechism from memory.

Yet there was a logic to it. Jensen's charisma and sense of humor kept things loose. If his leadership style was at once both chaotic and dictatorial, at least it wasn't boring. One employee, after leaving Nvidia, recalled experiencing a sinking feeling watching a presentation at his new firm. "We have our CEO doing our quarterly presentation, and I'm watching, like, 'God, where's the humor? Is it always this frickin' dry?'" he said. The other employees shot the new hire questioning glances as he shifted around in his chair. "I'm like, 'Jesus, you guys don't even know what you're missing,'" he said.

JENSEN WAS FUN TO WATCH. In late 2023 I saw him be publicly interviewed by Hao Ko, the lead architect of Nvidia's headquarters. The conversation took place at an upscale resort on the Pacific Coast. I arrived early to find the two men facing the ocean and engaged in quiet conversation. They were dressed nearly identically, in black leather jackets, black jeans, and black shoes, although Hao was much taller. I was hoping to catch some candid statements about the future of computing; instead, I got a six-minute roast of Hao's wardrobe. "Look at this guy!" Jensen said. "He's dressed just like me. He's copying me—which is smart—only his pants have too many pockets." Hao gave a nervous chuckle and looked down at his designer jeans, which did have a few more zippered pockets than function would strictly demand. "Simplify, man!" Jensen said, before turning to me. "That's why he's dressed like me. I taught this guy everything he knows."

The interview was sponsored by Gensler, Hao's firm, and there were several hundred architects in attendance. As the event approached, Jensen increased the intensity of his shtick, cracking a series of weak jokes and rocking back and forth on his feet. Jensen did dozens of speaking gigs each year and had given a talk to a different audience earlier that day, but I realized, to my amazement, that he was nervous. "I hate public speaking," he said. It was true; he really did.

Onstage, though, he was compelling—Hao barely had to ask a question. Looking at a picture of his corporate headquarters behind him, Jensen began to criticize the design of the top floor. Jensen had initially wanted an open-air balcony on the roof, but Hao hadn't been able to deliver this in time. Jensen wondered if the building was really finished—then, leaping forward from this question, wondered if any building was really finished. He began to spitball about shape-shifting architecture in the age of AI, which would rearrange itself to meet the evolving demands of customers. "Maybe at one o'clock, the top three floors just become a nightclub," Jensen said.

Ko looked on, perplexed. Jensen was just getting started. "Now, if the building is robotic, the entire building is software driven, isn't that right?" he asked the crowd. Huang reasoned that in the future, office buildings would collect data about workers' behavior, then feed it into an AI, which would redesign the building's digital twin in the Omniverse before rolling out physical design changes overnight. He speculated that Gensler would evolve from an architectural firm into a tech company that managed the shape-shifting software. "Just as we operate fleets of computers, you'll operate these buildings," Jensen said. "And now Gensler, the next buildings you design will be free—isn't that right? They'll be free, and the reason for that is you'll make your money by operating the building, and you'll be enriched beyond your wildest dreams. You heard it here first."

Following the interview, Jensen took questions from the audience, including one about the potential risks of AI. "There's the doomsday AIs—the AI that somehow jumped out of the computer and consumes tons and tons of information and learns all by itself, reshaping its attitude and sensibility, and starts making decisions on its own, including pressing buttons of all kinds," Jensen said, pantomiming pressing the buttons in the air. The room grew quiet. "No AI should be able to learn without a human in the loop," he said. One architect asked when AI might start to figure things out on its own. "Reasoning capability is two to three years out," Jensen said. A low murmur went through the crowd.

Afterward, I caught up with Hao. He seemed a bit stressed—his "interview" with Jensen had consisted of him asking a single question and Jensen giving a forty-five-minute answer. I assured him that the event was a hit; the rapt attention of the crowd was something that couldn't be faked. I then asked Hao's thoughts on shape-shifting architecture. "Look, when I first met him, he was talking about self-driving cars, and at the time that sounded crazy too," Hao said with a shrug. "I've learned not to question him."

AS NVIDIA'S STOCK PRICE SWELLED, Jensen the executive was transformed into Jensen the celebrity. His fan base now included not only gamers but also scientists whose work he supported, AI accelerationists whose technology he enabled, boomer retirees whose portfolios he had rescued, and degenerate retail "investors" who YOLO'd their life savings on Nvidia stock options whenever he spoke. Huang's keynote address at GTC 2024 was so popular it took place at an NHL arena in downtown San Jose. The venue seated seventeen thousand people, but this was not enough to accommodate the thronging crowds. Eight thousand hopefuls were turned away and had to watch the presentation via simulcast.

The address began with an AI art installation conducted live by multimedia artist Refik Anadol. Across a giant screen at the back of the arena, a field of wild, pulsating colors occasionally coalesced into recognizable shapes of flowers, trees, and birds before disintegrating into a riot of swirling pixels. I thought of Ovid's *Metamorphoses*: "the face of Nature in a vast expanse was naught but Chaos uniformly waste." Then Huang took the stage to applause, followed by the synchronized action of several thousand smartphone cameras lifted to record him at once.

It had been five years since Huang had presented at GTC in person. In the interim period his world had been transformed. He looked a little older now; his hair was fully gray, and the strapping, muscular frame he'd maintained well into middle age was diminished a bit by time. He showed off his hand-drawn map of the history of computing, beginning with IBM's 1964 S/360 computing architecture and ending with his new industrial revolution. "I made a little cartoon for you," he said. "Literally, I drew this." He progressed to discussion of AlexNet, which he termed AI's "first contact" moment, and as he did so, a close-up of his exploded-view diagram of the GeForce card used to train it appeared on the screen.

Huang believed that the field of computing had been reinvented at this moment. IBM's architecture, predominant for the field's first sixty years, was now being superseded by parallel computing, neural networks, and the cloud. Computing would no longer involve clunky interactions with finicky screens or equipment. Instead, users would issue the machine natural-language commands to instantly perform actions of almost unlimited power. Humans, henceforth, would be sorcerers.

The audience adored it. A technology podcaster, sitting next to me on the arena floor, began shaking his leg in excitement. Huang presented new hardware, new "microservices" for faster inference, new software for researchers, and a new robotics-training platform called GR00T. He was joined, at the end of the presentation, by two three-foot-tall droids who marched with him offstage to resounding applause.

The conference continued over the next four days at the adjacent convention center, where hundreds of exhibitors displayed all manner of strange technology, including a robot bartender. Whenever Huang took the floor, he was instantly mobbed by autograph seekers who wanted him to sign their conference badges and their gaming GPUs. He tolerated the adulation with even temper and good humor, although at one point, when he tried to go to the men's room, he could barely make it through the congregation of worshippers who surrounded him from every side. "People taking pictures of me *in* the bathroom, that's a new one for me," he said. As he made his way across the floor, I wondered if he was merely one of the great businessmen of the age or something more.

UP CLOSE, it was clear to me that Jensen was having some trouble processing success. He wasn't sleeping much, and the constant public appearances were subjecting him to considerable stress. When he gave the commencement address at the 2024 CalTech graduation, he killed it, as usual, but when I caught up with him afterward, he was sitting on a wooden bench with his arms crossed and a churlish expression on his face.

Every time I saw Jensen, he was wearing the same all-black T-shirt with a Thomas Burberry monogram. He had bought twenty-four of the shirts in 2020 and had been rotating them every day for the last four years. Dressed in this uniform, he had adopted what I now recognized as his customary pose, using the bench as a kind of prop, his body diagonal, his legs splayed out, his expensive shoes pressed against the cobblestone patio. His net worth fluctuated with the stock market, but on that day, at least, he was worth more than $100 billion. "I'm very rich now," he said. "Do you know how rich I am?" It wasn't a boast. I asked him if he had any plan for what to do with the money. "I have no idea," he said. "None."

Jensen told me he'd woken up that morning at 3:30 a.m. with one of his dogs sleeping between his legs. After thirty-one years, he was the longest-serving CEO of any tech stock in the S&P. He didn't need to get out of bed, he admitted, and he really didn't want to either. "Is there a specific thing that's going to drive us out of business today?" he asked himself. No, there wasn't. But was there something in striking distance? Well, maybe. Nvidia's biggest customers were now building their own microchips. AMD, realizing that hardware wasn't enough, was hiring a great number of software engineers. If Nvidia engineers didn't hold the hands of their customers, neural-network technology might disappoint, and demand for his products would slacken.

By four a.m., Jensen was up and working. He always began his work-day with his most important long-term project, figuring that as long as he addressed it, the day couldn't be considered a bust no matter what else happened. I had sensed, in multiple conversations with him, that he had something big under wraps, but he refused to divulge what it was. "I have to have some secrets," he said.

I could guess, though. Rumors had been circulating about a neural net that OpenAI was working on called Project Strawberry. This was said to be a "rational" AI, designed to conduct pure research in mathematics. Jensen never discussed Project Strawberry with me, but a couple of times in passing, he had asked me to imagine a world in which mathematical proofs were produced on demand with the click of a button. "The marginal cost of calculation has gone to zero, and this has opened up incredible possibilities," he had said. "Well, ask yourself, when the marginal cost of doing math goes to zero, then what do you do?"

I gazed out toward the CalTech turtle pond. All of the scientists here, all of this brainpower, superseded in an instant by a zillion nestled transistors. Then what happened? Did we give the Fields Medal to a computer? Did we arrive at a unified field theory in physics? I thought of Pascal's gears, turning for the first time to produce a mechanical calculation—but Jensen had already conquered arithmetic. Now his machines would assault reason itself.

TWENTY-TWO

The Fear

The Fear hit Yoshua Bengio on a winter's day in early 2023. The Montreal AI pioneer was one of the early neural-net advocates. He had long been fascinated by the technology and had championed it through several recessions. In 2019 he was awarded the A. M. Turing Award, computer science's equivalent of the Nobel Prize, for his seminal research in the field. His frequent collaborators Yann LeCun and Geoffrey Hinton won the award alongside him.

Bengio was lean, with steeply arched, bushy eyebrows and a penetrating gaze. His parents, both Sephardic Jews from Morocco, had moved to Montreal in the 1970s to participate in the avant-garde performing-arts scene. Bengio had gravitated toward computers instead, although studying neural networks in the 1990s was scarcely more respectable than experimental theater. But his work laid the foundation for AlexNet, and by the mid-2010s, Bengio was enjoying a sense of vindication. Obscure research papers he'd published in niche journals years before now served as the basis for a new scientific field. Bengio was a pure academic with little interest in commerce, but he watched the AI boom with a kind of fatherly pride.

Like many researchers in the field, though, Bengio sometimes imagined a world where AI grew *too* powerful. For most of his career, though, this thought experiment was kind of a joke: If AI was going to conquer the planet, why was it so hard to get a $10,000 research grant to study it? But after the public release of ChatGPT, Bengio, for the first time in his life, began to grow genuinely concerned. He was astonished by ChatGPT's capabilities, just stunned—his socks were blown completely off. Bengio didn't think he would personally live to see computers that interacted with humans in a way that seemed intelligent. Then, one day in late 2022, the technology had simply arrived. He compared it to meeting an extraterrestrial.

Bengio went for a walk every morning to gather his thoughts, regardless of the weather. On the day The Fear hit, the temperature had been milder than usual, and the Montreal streets were coated with slush. Surrounded by bare trees and graying snow, a flood of strange emotion came over Bengio, unlike any he'd experienced before. He called it a "conversion." "I was thinking about my children and my grandchild," he told me. "What is it going to be for them in twenty years? Will they have a life?"

The Fear was the worst kind of fear, one that grew scarier when you set aside emotions and examined the problem rationally. Bengio compared it to the threat of nuclear war. Actually, it was worse than that: *some* people would survive a nuclear war, he reasoned, but if an AI decided to wipe us out, it could design a lethal pathogen that could exterminate every human on Earth. "I don't think there's anything close in terms of the scale of danger," he said.

After his walk, Bengio contacted his friend and frequent collaborator Geoffrey Hinton to conduct a sanity check. This didn't help—Hinton had independently come to the same conclusions. In fact, he'd come to the same conclusions in the same way, at almost the exact same moment: by probing the capabilities of ChatGPT, first with a sense of satisfaction, then personal vindication, then a creeping unease. A short time later, Hinton quit his job at Google to devote himself full-time to advising humanity about the risks of runaway AI. Ilya Sutskever, who had *built* ChatGPT, was also increasingly concerned and was proposing to devote himself full-time to the "alignment" problem of ensuring that superintelligent AIs did not pursue goals contrary to the benefit of the human race. Bengio, Hinton, and Sutskever—this was an alarming convergence. They ranked one, two, and three as the most-cited computer scientists alive. All three were worried that AI might kill us all.

NOT EVERYONE SAW it this way, of course. Yann LeCun, the third co-recipient of the Turing prize, thought that his colleagues were being ridiculous. LeCun was the lead architect of a 1998 neural network that could recognize human handwriting, which he had licensed to the post office and financial institutions, which had used it to read addresses and analyze paper checks. LeCun's handwriting analyzer was the first widespread industrial use of a multilayer neural network.

LeCun hailed from Paris, had a good sense of humor, and spoke with the authority of a man whose intuitions had been repeatedly validated by scientific research. Bengio had been his coauthor many times, including on the famous handwriting paper. Both men spoke French natively and had developed a close friendship in their many years of research together. Now their opposing perspectives on AI risk were creating a rift in their relationship. "In theory, we're still friends," Bengio told me. "But today we argue in public in ways that friends usually don't."

LeCun didn't have any fears at all about AI, and he thought that Bengio was anthropomorphizing a harmless machine. "The drive that some humans have for domination, or at least influence, has been hardwired into us by evolution, because we are a social species with a hierarchical organization," LeCun told *Time* magazine. "AI systems, as smart as they might be, will be subservient to us. We set their goals, and they don't have any intrinsic goal that we would build into them to dominate." Of course, a neural net *could* have a desire to dominate, LeCun conceded; it was just that he thought no one would be foolish enough to build one. "It would be really stupid to build that. It would also be useless. Nobody would buy it anyway," he said. (LeCun's words echoed those of Pascal, who, in the mid-1600s, had stared into the gears of his calculator in search of consciousness. "The adding machine produces effects which are closer to thought than anything done by animals," he wrote, "but it does nothing to justify the assertion that it has a will.")

Bengio thought LeCun was guilty of overconfidence. People, both individuals and whole societies, did all sorts of dumb, destructive shit. For now, the cost of training AI technology limited its development to relatively responsible organizations, but as Nvidia drove down the cost of computing, it spread the ability to train an AI to everyone—and rogue superintelligence had to emerge only once. "The more powerful the AI gets, the more likely it is that it would want to take control of the computer on which it is running so that it can give itself more reward," Bengio said. "That's the end of the story for us."

Hinton agreed, and he cautioned that such an event might happen inadvertently. "Suppose one of them had just a tiny bit of drive—just the *teensiest, weensiest* bit of drive to sort of help itself," he said. That AI would win, Hinton said. "It will give itself a few more resources. In fact, the variants that are most selfish will do the best. And I think you can see that's a very slippery slope."

THE RIFT BETWEEN BENGIO and LeCun mirrored a split in the AI community at large. The argument was sometimes framed with a parametric variable called p(doom), which represented your assessment of the probability that AI might one day eliminate the human race. For LeCun, p(doom) was zero. For Bengio, p(doom) was 50 percent. The two represented extreme views of the problem, although any number greater than zero was concerning.

When he'd talked to Bengio in early 2023, Hinton's p(doom) had also been at 50 percent. To put that another way, for emphasis: the world's most famous AI scientist believed the chance that AI would cause a catastrophic outcome for humanity was one chance in two. But when I talked to him in 2024, Hinton had reduced this estimate to between 10 and 20 percent. The reason he lowered his estimate, he told me, was that so many people whose intelligence he respected had strenuously disagreed with him. "Most notably, of course, there is Jensen," he said.

Jensen's p(doom) was zero—actually, although it wasn't technically possible to have a negative p(doom), Jensen somehow did. Jensen vocally rejected the whole framing, thought the question was stupid, and thought the people who argued about it were holding back humanity. At Denny's, he had even suggested that Hinton was tarnishing his academic legacy by entertaining such speculations.

This caused Hinton to recalibrate, but Bengio firmly stood his ground. (Not coincidentally, Bengio is one of the only major AI scientists who has never taken money from Silicon Valley.) Both Hinton and Bengio had endorsed a California state bill that called for regulation of AI models that cost more than $100 million to train. This bill, SB 1047, was very unpopular in Silicon Valley. It was opposed by a coalition of venture capitalists and tech corporations, as well as a battalion of Sacramento lobbyists. Storied tech investor Nancy Pelosi issued a statement against it, as did a number of academics, like Stanford's Fei-Fei Li, who argued the bill would hinder innovation while failing to reduce risk. Andrew Ng, the professor who'd synthesized images of cats at Google, compared worrying about an AI takeover to worrying about overpopulation on Mars. Opinion polls suggested that nearly 80 percent of the public supported SB 1047, but in September 2024 California governor Gavin Newsom vetoed the bill.

Jensen made no public comment about SB 1047, but he continued to stress that there was no data supporting the (admittedly pretty wild) speculation about AI risk. When I shared Jensen's objections with Bengio, he grew agitated. "Of course, there is no data!" he said. "Humanity hasn't disappeared yet! Are we going to wait until we have repeated the death of humanity multiple times to decide that, oh, now we have data?!" He made a good point. All the data in the world would not have predicted the breakthrough of AlexNet or the success of the transformer architecture. Twice in ten years, AI had experienced unforeseeable and permanent upgrades to its capabilities. Bengio did not think that the current models posed an immediate threat to human life—but what about the next breakthrough? No one could say what it might bring or when it might happen.

Even if superintelligence did not appear in the next decade, its emergence in twenty, or thirty, or even a hundred years' time seemed inevitable. That was a time horizon outside the boundary of projectable return on investment but within the span of human history. In one or two generations, homo sapiens might no longer be the dominant species on the planet—but venture capitalists didn't look that far ahead.

The mismatch between short-term profit and long-term risk created turmoil inside AI start-ups. At OpenAI, a bizarre boardroom coup had unfolded in November 2023, with Ilya Sutskever first voting to remove Sam Altman, then a few days later pleading for his reinstatement. Altman ultimately triumphed, and the rest of the nonprofit board was replaced. Following Altman's restoration, it was fairly clear that, despite what OpenAI's nonprofit mission statement read, Microsoft's "capped" profit interest was spurring the organization to continue to develop the most sophisticated AI models ever seen. Sutskever shunned the press after the coup, but when I spoke with him in September 2023, he said he had changed his focus from building ever-larger language models toward aligning AI superintelligence with human interests. "I can't talk about specific models," Sutskever said, "but I'm coming up with what I believe will be the definitive solution to the concern people have, that an AI might go rogue and do something very highly undesirable."

As of late 2024, no such solution had appeared, even as OpenAI's products grew ever larger and more powerful. In May 2024, OpenAI released GPT4o—the "o" stood for "omni"—a multimedia AI that accepted any combination of text, audio, image, and video and returned any combination of text, audio, and image outputs. The model's seamless response times were made possible by the lightning-fast inference capabilities of the latest generation of Nvidia chips. The day after GPT-4o's release, Sutskever resigned.

OpenAI soon packaged a conversational module with GPT-4o, and with almost no perceivable delay in response, talking with it felt like talking to a hyperintelligent human. (Many compared it to the AI in *Her.*) The same day OpenAI released GPT-4o, Google showed off Astra, an augmented-reality AI assistant that seemed able to answer any question, remember any detail, and describe any environment in a fraction of a second. Claude, a model from the start-up Anthropic, rivaled or exceeded GPT-4o on many benchmarks. National governments, unwilling to lease their sensitive data to the cloud, were building large-scale sovereign AI-training centers. Musk's xAI initiative struck a $10 billion deal to rent Oracle's GPU servers. (The existential concerns he'd expressed about AI in 2015 must have abated.) Mark Zuckerberg's Meta made the largest investment, announcing that it was going to spend $30 billion to buy one million Nvidia chips and secure a dedicated nuclear reactor to power them.

The belief that any of this might have been prevented by a California Senate bill evinced a charming faith in the power of state government. As the speed of Nvidia's GPUs increased, so, too, did attendant expectations for economic growth. The industrial barons of Silicon Valley had placed their bets, and to cap their upside would mean tanking the stock market. No politician anywhere had enough clout to do it.

Still, if Bengio, Hinton, and Sutskever had been sidelined by capital, the points they made remained valid. They had seen better than anyone the potential of what AI technology could be, and they had the academic credentials to prove it. If they were worried now, I felt it was worth listening to. "Right now there are ninety-nine very smart people trying to make AI better and one very smart person trying to figure out how to stop it taking over," Hinton said.

I SHOULD CONFESS that I had The Fear myself—it's why I first researched Nvidia, and it's why I wrote this book. From the moment ChatGPT went public, I assumed that my career was coming to an end. GPT-4 was only a passable writer; it had scored in the 22nd percentile of the AP English Literature and Composition exam. (I am confident I would rank in the 23rd.)

But the models were getting better all the time, and perhaps more importantly, they already wrote better than I had as an undergraduate. The long apprenticeship I'd gone through before first publishing my work, at age thirty-six, would have looked pointless had such a tool been available in my youth.

The looming death of the author was a minor personal tragedy, but I was willing to acknowledge that coach drivers had probably hated automobiles, too—at least the streets were no longer covered in horseshit. I was adaptable to change and not by any means a Luddite. I loved technology, loved the internet, loved space travel, wanted a self-driving automobile, and had purchased the first iPhone the day it had come out. Nor did I have any ideological bias against capitalism—indeed, as an American, I felt it was my birthright to have large corporations catering to my whims.

Yet AI troubled me. It troubled me to the point of losing sleep. In this I had company: Bengio told me he'd had nightmares, too. Just a few months after GPT-4o, OpenAI released "o1," its first attempt to build an AI capable of complex scientific and mathematical reasoning. Accompanying its release, OpenAI published an updated analysis of the potential risks to humanity that AI presented. With the debut of o1, OpenAI concluded that the risk that most concerned Bengio—the risk that AI might be used to develop an unstoppable biological weapon—had increased from "low" to "medium."

Were we really in control of these systems? At some point in the next few years, someone was going to unveil the first one-hundred-trillion parameter model, rivaling the number of synapses in the human brain. What was the role of humans after *that*? Accelerationists insisted that AI would unlock new modes of employment, just as the last industrial revolution had. But in my experience, if you cornered the optimists and pressed them, you could force them to admit that this facile comparison was borne of convenience and that there was no way to know if it was really true. Mark Twain was incorrect: history did not rhyme. The Book of Ecclesiastes was wrong, too: there were plenty of new things under the sun—actually, they arose all the time, from the trilobites to the dinosaurs—and certainly a mechanical brain with one hundred trillion synapses firing at five billion cycles a second had no precedent in history, religion, or philosophy. No one could say, with any certainty, what would happen to earthlings in the AI era.

But Jensen insisted it was safe. He had his own incentives, of course—money, but also pride. Having waged a long, lonely battle to make parallel computing profitable, Jensen was now determined to enjoy its rewards. He seemed offended by technologists who performatively decried the risks of AI while continuing to purchase his hardware. I could see his point of view—there *was* something nauseating in the way AI developers adopted doomer vocabulary while training ever-larger models.

Jensen's confidence was also born of the many ways in which AI *wasn't* like the biological brain. The brain didn't learn through backpropagation; that much was certain. And the neural nets only mimicked neurons; there was no equivalent to the glial cells that supported the neurons, for example, nor were the AI systems connected to autonomic nervous systems. The neural net did not have a hypothalamus or a hippocampus or a pineal gland. The neural net was unaffected by hormones, had no sex drive, didn't go to sleep, couldn't love its children, and never had a dream.

A well-trained model mimicked (and sometimes exceeded) our own capacity for cogitation, but it had no sense memory, no emotions, no imagination, no reproductive function, and no instinct to survive. In this sense, one could not say it was really *alive*—it did not have the self-sustainability of even the most primitive single-celled organism. Although there was certainly an analogy between training neural nets and evolution, AI was not the product of the kind of ruthless, Darwinian, kill-or-be-killed, eat-or-be-eaten planetary laboratory from which biological life had emerged.

There was also the upside to consider. Nick Bostrom, he of the paper-clip-maximizing argument, was by 2024 considering a different question: What would human beings do in the "solved world" of limitless AI? Bostrom's 2024 book, *Deep Utopia*, invited readers to imagine a world where all unpleasant tasks were handled by robots, and in which any imaginable experience might be replicated in a simulator. These were not idle speculations; with image recognition handled, Fei-Fei Li was now trying to build this solved world.

She had unveiled her initiative, called Behavior-1K, at Nvidia's 2024 GTC conference. Onstage with Bill Dally, Li described how she had assembled a diverse group of respondents using Amazon's Mechanical Turk to rank thousands of answers to a single question: "How much would you benefit if a robot did this for you?" At the top were the tasks that people least enjoyed: scrubbing toilets, washing floors, and cleaning up after parties. At the bottom were those activities that inspired some measure of human joy: picking out jewelry, playing squash, and opening presents. Using these results, Li was now training artificial intelligence in Nvidia's Omniverse to complete the most unpleasant tasks. Someday, perhaps sooner rather than later, one of these neural nets would be installed inside a real-world robot and set loose on the commode.

The solved world had its appeal. People might grow bored of playing squash and opening presents, but as Li's research suggested, it was *behavior*, not philosophical arguments, that drove outcomes. It was easy to imagine a consumer environment where, in a decade or two, owning a fleet of chore-happy robots was as much the default expectation for a first-world household as owning a refrigerator is today. Perhaps a world where nobody ever had to clean the toilet again carried with it a certain amount of existential risk, but I suspected that this was a trade that almost everyone would go along with, even if only implicitly. Did I want a toilet robot? You bet I did.

By late 2024, it was clear that the intellectual mood around AI was shifting away from doomerism. Op-eds and think pieces about AI risk no longer generated much attention. Instead, we were instructed to look on these new systems with optimism. "Here is one narrow way to look at human history," OpenAI CEO Sam Altman wrote in a September 2024 essay. "After thousands of years of compounding scientific discovery and technological progress, we have figured out how to melt sand, add some impurities, arrange it with astonishing precision at extraordinarily tiny scale into computer chips, run energy through it, and end up with systems capable of creating increasingly capable artificial intelligence. This may turn out to be the most consequential fact about all of history so far." Shortly after the essay appeared, OpenAI announced it was partnering with the defense start-up Anduril, a manufacturer of AI-enabled weaponry.

But even when I tried to embrace the upside of AI, I couldn't shake my anxiety. The more I used the AI models, the more I questioned my own role. Not only would they soon be able to write better than I would; with time, even my interviews would be filtered by AI. I imagined video-chatting with some powerful executive and unwittingly interviewing his digital AI clone, never myself the wiser. It seemed to me that the end of my profession was approaching. It seemed to me that the end of reality was approaching. It seemed to me that the end of *consciousness* was approaching. Was Huang, seduced by the power of what he'd built, gambling with the future of our species? I had to know. I had to ask him one last time.

TWENTY-THREE

The Thinking Machine

My final interview with Jensen took place on a Friday, following the conclusion of GTC 2024. We met in his conference room "office," in the center of Nvidia's south campus. I sat across from him at a long wooden table; surrounding us, on all sides, were precise diagrams and schedules that he'd written on the walls. At the far end of the room was a calendar showing Jensen's forthcoming release schedule for new GPUs and software products. Behind him, spanning at least thirty feet of whiteboard, was an intricate diagram of the Nvidia computing stack, beginning with the GPUs and continuing forward, in colored marker and block capitals, all the way to the microservice architecture he'd just introduced. But even this massive whiteboard was not enough—the writing wrapped around the far wall, then behind me onto the frosted-glass exterior of the room.

Jensen, after four days of nonstop presentations, interviews, and technical demos, was visibly exhausted. His opening keynote was his largest-ever presentation, and I could see how much it had taken out of him. I'd witnessed the anxiety in his body language when he gave an inconsequential Q&A to a room of four hundred architects—I could only imagine the dread he'd felt before giving the most important presentation of his life to a hockey arena packed with rabid fans.

People were getting a little critical of him, I noticed. At a press conference at GTC, one journalist had asked if he was the new Robert Oppenheimer. ("Oppenheimer was building a bomb," Jensen said. "We're not doing that.") Bill Whitaker, a host for *60 Minutes*, had suggested that Jensen was "not easy to work for." ("It should be like that. If you want to do extraordinary things, it shouldn't be easy," Jensen said.) Nvidia's pricing power was triggering a reaction from government power centers; in the United States, Lina Khan, the chair of the Federal Trade Commission, had been eyeing the company suspiciously, and Nvidia's offices in France had been raided by authorities over concerns about anticompetitive practices.

But our interview started amicably. I congratulated Jensen on his fine performance at the keynote, then asked him about life in Taiwan, about his family, about how he was handling his newfound fame. His answers were curt and to the point. I asked him specifically what new jobs might be created by AI.

"Well, ask yourself, when the marginal cost of doing math goes to zero, then what do you do?" he said.

"I don't know," I said.

"Well, you just asked me the same question. OK. You're just as intelligent as I am to figure this out," he said.

I paused, flummoxed. It was too much for me to unravel; despite Jensen's kind words about my intelligence, I was in no way at his level. Unsure how to proceed, I decided to show Jensen the same clip of Arthur C. Clarke that had inspired Catanzaro's rhapsodic take. As Clarke droned on about the future of mechanical evolution, I watched the blood drain from Jensen's face.

"I just feel like you're interviewing the wrong person," he said, quietly. "I feel like you're interviewing Elon right now, and I'm just not that guy." I paused, unsure what to say, but it was too late. I'd hit the trip wire.

"Is it going to—is it going to destroy jobs?" Huang asked, his voice crescendoing with anger. "Are calculators going to destroy math? That conversation is so old, and I'm so, so tired of it," he said. "I don't want to talk about it anymore! It's the same conversation over and over and over and over and over again. We invented agriculture and then made the marginal cost of producing food zero. It was good for society! We manufactured electricity at scale, and it caused the marginal cost of chopping down trees, lighting fires, carrying fires and torches around to approximately zero, and we went off to do something else. And then we made the marginal cost of doing calculations—long division! We made it zero!" He was yelling now. "We make the marginal cost of things zero, generation after generation after generation, and this exact conversation happens every single time!"

I tried to switch subjects, but it was no use. His anger was tinged with disgust. He began to lecture me in the voice that one would use with a wayward teenager. He'd placed high expectations in me, he said, and I had disappointed him. I had wasted his time; I had wasted everyone's time; the whole project of the book was now called into question. The interview was attended by two of Jensen's PR reps, but neither made any attempt to intervene—they weren't about to draw fire.

Kirk had theorized that Huang's anger was strategic. I can tell you, it didn't feel that way in the moment. His anger seemed uncontained, omnidirectional, and wildly inappropriate. I was not Jensen's employee, and he had nothing to gain from raging at me. He just seemed tired of being asked about the negative aspects of the tools he was building. He thought the question was stupid, and he had been asked it one too many times.

"This cannot be a ridiculous sci-fi story," he said. He gestured to his frozen PR reps at the end of the table. "Do you guys understand? I didn't grow up on a bunch of sci-fi stories, and this is not a sci-fi movie. These are serious people doing serious work!" he said. "This is not a freaking joke! This is not a repeat of Arthur C. Clarke. I didn't read his fucking books. I don't care about those books! It's not—we're not a sci-fi repeat! This company is not a manifestation of *Star Trek*! We are not doing those things! We are serious people, doing serious work. And—it's just a serious company, and I'm a serious person, just doing serious work."

For the next twenty minutes, in a tone that alternated among accusatory, exasperated, and belittling, Jensen questioned my professionalism, questioned my interview approach, questioned my dedication to the project. He accused me of trying to psychoanalyze him; he told me how much he disliked answering my biographical questions, especially those that attempted to illuminate his mental state. "I don't like these probing questions," he said. "I don't like talking about myself, OK?! I'm not into therapy." He suggested that my questions were stupid; he called them "pedestrian." He denied there was anything exceptional about himself, against all accumulated evidence. "Look, I'm—I am super normal," he said.

"I have never met anyone like you," I said.

"I'm super normal," Huang said.

Gradually, the anger wore off. Huang changed topics a couple times, talking about upcoming products, asking after the welfare of his PR reps, and recalling the importance of the late John Nickolls to the CUDA project. At one point he brought up the Roman Empire. He continued to chide me gently—he was done with me—and I was ushered out the door. I left the interview bewildered. I'd had plenty of tense conversations with executives, but I'd never had someone explode at me in this way. I was stunned—but also, if I'm being honest, I was a little giddy. To be targeted by the Wrath of Huang was in a certain sense an honor: a rite of passage that everyone who gained admittance to his inner circle underwent. Walking away from the conference room, I turned to one of the PR reps.

"That went well," I said.

He laughed. "Oh, that?" he said. "That was nothing."

FOLLOWING THE INTERVIEW, I was driven to see Eos, a ten-thousand-chip supercomputer housed in a nearby data center. Eos was preposterously fast; as a benchmark, it had trained OpenAI's GPT-3 model in under four minutes. I was met there by Marc Hamilton, a veteran supercomputer engineer. He guided me through an airlock and onto the sterile data-center floor, where dozens of racks of Nvidia hardware, separated into walled-off pods, pulsed ceaselessly beneath fluorescent light.

For the human to trespass into the realm of the computer felt like a violation of some sacred penetralium. The thousands of computer fans in simultaneous operation created a dull, cumulative roar, like applause heard from a distance, but I was hardly present; I was still reeling from my dressing-down from Huang. I wondered, had he done that on purpose? What had seemed like an unprovoked explosion at the moment was perhaps more deliberate in retrospect. Revisiting our conversation in my head, I realized that Huang hadn't lost his temper at me all at once. Instead, over the course of a few minutes, he worked himself into an angrier and angrier state, seemingly on purpose, building up a head of steam by repeatedly revisiting how stupid I was to show him a clip of Arthur C. Clarke.

I didn't think it was that dumb, and I still don't: the question of whether mechanical brains will evolve faster than physical ones seems fair to ask of a man who has made his fortune building mechanical brains. But I also hadn't pressed Huang to answer, and when it became clear that the question had pissed him off, I had several times tried to move the subject to safer ground. He didn't let me.

Looking back, it became clear to me that Jensen had wanted to lose his temper; he'd made a conscious decision to thrash me. Once the performance had started, his fury was genuine, but it was all in service of a larger point he wanted to make. It wasn't just that Jensen didn't read science fiction—it was that he actually hated science fiction. He was a serious man.

The reason that Jensen had succeeded in fields where others had failed— parallel computing, AI, the Omniverse—was precisely because he didn't tolerate airy speculation about the future. He examined technologies coldly, from first principles, swayed neither by optimism nor fear but only by a cold and patient sense of business logic that he alone could push to the outer limits of corporate foresight. Beyond that he did not look or care to imagine. The potential for human extinction was not a question of corporate strategy and thus, to him, was as foolish as drawing a dragon on the unexplored portion of the map.

I recalled the discipline of the Nvidia executives I'd talked to: Jensen had them wound as tight as piano strings. They were confident, intelligent, and exceptionally well-prepared, down to the smallest detail—I never once caught one slipping. I recalled, too, with sudden clarity, how disinclined those same executives had been to discuss the potential future implications of the technology they were building, a disinclination that I sensed spilled over into discomfort and even fear. Now I saw where the fear was coming from. The executives were more afraid of Jensen yelling at them than they were of wiping out the human race.

I was interrupted from my reverie when I approached one of the computing pods and its doors slid open automatically. I stepped back, my back went straight, the hairs on my arms stood at attention—then I ventured within. Inside, I was buffeted by air from all directions, the cooling fans on the racks to either side of me roaring incessantly, my pants rippling from air blowing out of a grate on the floor. It was almost too loud to think.

I was standing inside the computer's brain now, the circuits around me executing a collective ten quintillion calculations every second. It would kill us all, or it would save us; whatever happened, it was going to happen on Jensen's chips. I tried to envision the entire stack, from the angstrom-width transistors to the complex circuit architecture to Buck's numerical magic to Aarts's compilers to Nickolls's CUDA suite, and finally, above all, to the giant, layered grids of simulated neurons evolving at a supernatural rate. Standing here, I began to see the scope of Nvidia's accomplishment, from the scale of the atom to the dawn of machine consciousness—but only Jensen, the American Daedalus, could really see it all.

Shouting to be heard, I asked what problem Eos was working on. Hamilton responded that it was training an internal Nvidia model in the style of GPT-4. In other words, I was surrounded by a language model: one that was catching up to me, one that I sensed would one day soon replace me. Hamilton, screaming over the fans, informed me that to complete the training, the computer would conduct a total of thirty billion quadrillion operations. I looked around, feeling inadequate in my obsolete and dying flesh. The pod was beautiful; I was nothing; there was no way to fight it. This was the thinking machine, and with each spin of the fan, with each pulse of the circuits, it got a little smarter.

ACKNOWLEDGMENTS

I would like to thank Jensen Huang and the rest of the team at Nvidia for their time, their candor, and their insight. In particular, I'm grateful to Bob Sherbin, who pushed hard to make this project a possibility. Thank you, Bob, for everything. You gave me the opportunity of a lifetime. I'm also grateful to everyone who shared their stories with me for this book, especially Jens Horstmann, Curtis Priem, Jon Peddie, and David Kirk.

I'd like to thank Willing Davidson and the rest of the team at *The New Yorker* for commissioning the magazine profile that led to this book. Willing is a superb editor and I suggest you pitch him your ideas. I'd also like to thank Allison Lorentzen at Viking and Stuart Williams at Bodley Head for once again acquiring, editing, and publishing my work. Allison and Stuart, your insights and advice were invaluable. I'm also thankful to Sean Lavery, Yinuo Shi, and Anna Kordunsky for fact-checking the manuscript. And, as ever, I am eternally grateful to my agent, Chris Parris-Lamb, who has for more than ten years supported and championed my career. I'm so lucky to have Chris.

Meghan McEnery encouraged me to pursue this project and provided a great deal of moral and emotional support. Thank you, Meghan. I could not have written this book without you. I'm also grateful to my friends Jay Budzik and Marcus Moretti, who both shared my fascination with Nvidia and discussed the company with me for hours. I'd like to thank my parents, Leonard and Diana, for always being there for me, and my sister, Emily, for acting as an enduring inspiration. And, of course, I am grateful to my daughter, Jane, who was patient with Dad when he disappeared into his darkened bedroom to write for days at a time. Thank you, Jane. This book is for you.

ABOUT THE AUTHOR

Stephen Witt is the author of *How Music Got Free*, which was a finalist for the Los Angeles Times Book Prize, the J. Anthony Lukas Book Prize, and the Financial Times and McKinsey Business Book of the Year Award. His writing has appeared in *The New Yorker*, *Financial Times*, *New York*, *The Wall Street Journal*, *Rolling Stone*, and *GQ*. He lives in Los Angeles, California.